WAR ON WORDS

WAR ON WORDS

Who Should Protect Journalists?

Joanne M. Lisosky and Jennifer R. Henrichsen

Foreword by Chris Cramer

 PRAEGER

AN IMPRINT OF ABC-CLIO, LLC
Santa Barbara, California • Denver, Colorado • Oxford, England

Library of Congress Cataloging-in-Publication Data

Lisosky, Joanne M.

War on words : who should protect journalists? / Joanne M. Lisosky and Jennifer R. Henrichsen; foreword by Chris Cramer.

p. cm.

Includes bibliographical references and index.

ISBN 978-0-313-38557-5 (hard copy : alk. paper) — ISBN 978-0-313-38558-2 (ebook)
1. Journalists—Crimes against. 2. Journalists—Violence against. 3. War correspondents—Crimes against. 4. War correspondents—Violence against. 5. Press and politics. 6. Freedom of the press. I. Henrichsen, Jennifer R. II. Title.
PN4751.L58   2011
323.44'5—dc22   2011009438

ISBN: 978-0-313-38557-5
EISBN: 978-0-313-38558-2

UWE, BRISTOL LIBRARY SERVICES

15 14 13 12 11   1 2 3 4 5

This book is also available on the World Wide Web as an eBook.
Visit www.abc-clio.com for details.

Praeger
An Imprint of ABC-CLIO, LLC

ABC-CLIO, LLC
130 Cremona Drive, P.O. Box 1911
Santa Barbara, California 93116-1911

This book is printed on acid-free paper

Manufactured in the United States of America

We dedicate this book to the courageous journalists around the world who have fought and suffered in the pursuit of freedom of expression and transparent democracy.
And to Michael and Garrett.

A free press can of course be good or bad, but, most certainly, without freedom it will never be anything but bad. . . . Freedom is nothing else but a chance to be better, whereas enslavement is a certainty of the worse.

Albert Camus

Contents

Foreword

I have been in this great profession for more than 45 years. First in newspapers, then at the BBC, at CNN, and now at Thomson Reuters. When I started at the BBC in London the war correspondent was considered the pinnacle of journalism. Each new incumbent carried the company credit cards as medals of honour, demonstrable evidence that he or she had finally arrived at the top.

But times have changed. In the past ten years well over a thousand of my colleagues and those who work with them have died; killed or murdered while trying to do their jobs. Thousands more have been injured, harassed, intimidated, or traumatized by those who see us either as virtual combatants or unwelcome extensions of governments prosecuting war and conflict. Or obstacles. Or simply irritants to be silenced.

This is the price we pay for our work in the twenty-first century.

For the last seven years I have had the privilege of being the honorary President of the International News Safety Institute (INSI) which was established in 2003, shortly after the dreadful execution in Pakistan of the eminent war correspondent Daniel Pearl, while working for the *Wall Street Journal*. INSI's simple mission is to promote the best safety practices in news coverage including journalists' training, operational procedures, equipment provision, and health issues; its formation coincides with the worst period in history for the reporting profession.

Simply put, we are now at war with those in the world who are either trying to stop the work we do or distort the honest and balanced reporting that most of us aspire to.

So what has gone wrong in the past decade?

War reporting has always been inherently unsafe. Journalists have always died in war, usually caught in the crossfire, frequently been in the wrong place at the wrong time, or died in accidents. But the attrition rate has never been higher than now.

War on Words suggests that the reporters' role has evolved from that of an unbiased dispatcher or critical observer to a purveyor of information often designed to generate a positive response to a conflict. Critics of the "cheerleading" by some members of the U.S. media in their reporting of the Iraq and Afghanistan wars would agree with this point. And the same critics would say this has contributed to the dangers facing journalists.

In addition, modern technology like satellites, the Internet, and wireless telephony has drawn more journalists from more organizations to the frontline to report live for television, radio, and online news organizations. And modern day warfare has no frontline. We can as easily be killed by a helicopter gunship from miles away, a pilotless drone operated from a different continent, or targeted by insurgents in the streets.

One UN spokesman has said that war reporting may be one of the most dangerous occupations in the world because of professionals being increasingly targeted by combatants. Not accidentally killed in a firefight but deliberately selected and killed because they are journalists, either to silence their reporting or to send a terrifying message to the rest of the profession.

In some countries the work of the reporter is the most deadly occupation there is with numerous journalists singled out and murdered, often by contract killers. And frequently these are not conventional war zones. Local journalists in Mexico, for example, are being murdered by criminals involved in the drug trade. In Russia, they are being killed for their investigative reporting.

INSI released its own report in 2007 entitled "Killing the Messenger," a report of a global inquiry into the protection of journalists. The work took 18 months and was a painstaking investigation into the legal, professional, and practical issues related to covering the protection of journalists in dangerous situations. The Inquiry's Chair, the former BBC Global News Director, Richard Sambrook, said at the time, "In many countries, murder has become the easiest, cheapest and most effective way of silencing troublesome reporting, and the more the killers get away with it the more the spiral of death is forced upwards. Impunity for killers of journalists . . . shames governments around the world."

One disgusting statistic in that INSI report is that eight out of ten murderers of journalists have never been investigated, let alone prosecuted, convicted, or punished.

This book takes a forensic approach to the new plight of the media professional. It reminds us that those who suggest that the pen is mightier than the sword may live in a truly fanciful world. A world where the assault rifle and the silenced pistol may be fast becoming much mightier—and in real danger of desecrating our profession.

—**Chris Cramer**
Global Editor for Multimedia at Thomson Reuters and Honorary
President of the International News Safety Institute

Acknowledgments

We are grateful to the many people who helped us find and contact interviewees for this project (Gaby Baca, Gay Campbell, Kristin Fraser, Ray Heacox, David Holiday, Sabina Jafarova, Elaine Kramer, Warren Lerude) and those who assisted by translating interviews (Gulnara Akhundova, Gabi Chojkier, Kerley Tolpolar). We also want to thank those who read the early drafts and offered valuable comments (Mikki Altenhofen, Katie Anderson, Michael Bartanen, Jessica Brooks, Chelsea Gorrow, Colin Hartke, Barbara Henrichsen, Chris Henrichsen, and Peter Lisosky). We would also like to thank our favorite librarian, Gail Egbers, for her assistance in finding material.

We are grateful to the Pacific Lutheran University Wang Center for Global Education for providing funding for this project. And we also thank our colleagues and friends in Geneva; Hedayat Abdel Nabi, Françoise Cormon, and Robert James Parsons for their assistance during our visits to Geneva.

Our heartfelt thanks to the more than 60 journalists and media advocates who generously agreed to be interviewed for this text. This book would not have been possible without their passion for the protection of journalists and their keen insights.

Finally, we owe a great deal of gratitude to our supportive partners. Garrett, who kept Jenn fed with late-night dinners and laughter; and Michael who has been Joanne's best friend and keenest editor for a lifetime.

Introduction

Would you be willing to die for your job? Reporters worldwide ask themselves this question every day.

Journalists like Charles Odongtho who reports for Uganda Radio Network struggles with this question during every election period in his country. He has covered two elections where he was struck by rubber bullets, doused with tear gas and trampled by rioters. But, Odongtho still plans to cover Uganda's next election. Another person who has had to ask this question is the Associated Press photographer, Emilio Morenatti, who in 2009 lost his leg in Afghanistan when the vehicle he was riding in ran over a bomb in the desert. Morenatti recovered and has since bravely accepted his new assignment in Haiti. And the Russian journalist, Anna Politkovskaya, asked herself that question for the last time the day she was shot and killed in the elevator of her Moscow apartment building in 2006.

The stories these brave journalists tell are among the most challenging, yet essential news stories of our generation. Timely and accurate information provided by the news media during times of turmoil as well as peace is vital for its political, cultural, and even social value. Journalists who report these stories do so during conflicts in their own countries and around the world. These conflicts do not occur solely in designated war zones. Existing in a conflict situation can mean living under a repressive government or amid the unruly control of warlords and criminal gangs. Information about the conflict situation hopefully serves to mitigate the problem as well as provide global awareness of serious conditions that require action. But correspondents who report about conflict and corruption have more to worry about than where to find their next story. Today's crisis of freedom and democracy is the war on words waged on battlefields in villages across the globe. Those waging this war are not only combatants, but also displeased governments and other belligerents hoping to generate unreasonable fears simply by choosing journalists as their primary targets. Accurate reporting about internal and international conflicts is more than just a job; it is the foundation of democratic governance. Targeting journalists is targeting democracy. Thus, the question arises: whose job should it be to make sure journalists who report about difficult situations have the means and the protection to tell these essential stories and avert this crisis?

Critical information about motivations of military and nonstate actors during conflicts serves all citizens and thus should be diligently protected. Undercover investigations that expose corrupt governments or motivations of menacing warlords allow people to witness these injustices and demand reform. Who will reveal this oppression if not the journalists? In a speech for Press Freedom Day in 2004, Mr. Abdul Waheed Khan, Assistant Director-General for Communication and Information at UNESCO, attempted to respond to the question of journalists' protection when he said that in times of conflict and corruption, providing civilian populations with nonpartisan information can be as vital as supplying food, water, and medical services. He added that assistance to media during times of conflict should be part of any humanitarian intervention.[1]

But Frank Smyth of the Committee to Protect Journalists said this crisis happens closer to home if you happen to be a local journalist.[2] Smyth stated that journalists worldwide face two kinds of potentially fatal threats: being murdered by criminals, or shot, if not targeted, by armed forces. He added that nearly nine out of ten journalists on the job were murdered or otherwise killed within their own country. Statistics provided by the Committee to Protect Journalists showed the percentage of local journalists killed since 1992 outnumbers foreign journalists killed by 87 to 13 percent.[3]

Indigenous journalists suffer the most egregious injury because affronts to local reporters often take place with state government approval and far from the eyes or ears of the larger global community. People living in secure democracies find it unfathomable to learn that the life of a local or indigenous journalist can be threatened not for a hard-hitting investigative report but for a seemingly innocuous story that some more powerful members of the community find unacceptable. These local journalists severely risk their lives whenever they choose to uncover corruption or challenge a government official or a local gang leader. Despite global recognition that democracy and freedom should give voice to the voiceless, some governments still find it acceptable to squash reasonable reporting about suspicious activities. The oppressed journalists often have nowhere to turn for protection from the corrupt forces in their own towns.

The life of the international correspondent has been transformed as well. Conflicts 60 years ago were vastly different. Reporters took great risks but not the same risks as today's frontline journalists. While reporting from the battlefront in the last century, the journalist took the chance of being injured by a stray bullet. They were often seen as heroes risking their lives to tell stories of the atrocities of war. In earlier conflicts, journalists were enlisted by combatants on all sides to proclaim injustices and challenge the motivations of war. But the frontlines of today's conflicts are virtual and viral. Many international and national clashes in today's new wars involve poorly disciplined militias under the control of warlords and ill-trained armed leaders. Combatants have different agendas. Control of territory is not as important as control of information. And the government may not always be the journalists' best friend. As a result, many conflicts exist with fallacious or limited information from battles waged on the ground or, often, in the media.

Insurgents use the Internet to carry their messages beyond their own local battlefields at meager financial costs, while traditional journalists working today must generate stories of enormous complexity with little backup and few funds. When money is tight, foreign media turn to freelancers who often rely only on themselves for initial funding and support. Journalists and media workers are dispatched to invisible frontlines where they are often targets of combatants or government agents who are disguised or not easily identified. The pen may be mightier than the sword, but recent killings of journalists add many complicated points to this adage.

Control of information has become an increasingly powerful weapon in the arsenal of global warfare and local disputes. Groups on all sides have learned the importance of having the media on their side. Journalists not only seek to dispatch unbiased information about the dispute but also have now emerged as central players in justifying the motivations of the players to the public. But the formerly reliable journalists' badge of neutrality has been frayed. Because governments and combatants around the world have found an insatiable hunger to generate positive public opinion, journalists are often used as the catalyst for this project. In addition, the other powerful weapon used in today's conflicts, fear, has found a potent ally in mediated messages. Not only can the content of the message bring terror, but also the terrorizing of journalists has an added benefit to the insurgent or the corrupt official or belligerent. Harassing or killing a journalist has an even greater rhetorical effect because this move can instill fear in other journalists, as well as plant the seed of fear throughout the regional or global audience. As a result, journalists have become an important target in this corrupt arena. More importantly, targeting journalists demonstrates a fundamental threat to freedom of expression, considered by many as one of the most vital human rights—a right that brings all other inhumanities into light. Thus, protecting journalists in difficult situations has materialized in recent years as a serious concern for journalists around the world as well as the international human rights community.

The international community addressed this matter directly in 2006 when the UN Security Council unanimously adopted a resolution that condemned attacks against journalists in conflict situations. More recently, the issue of journalist protection was directly addressed in a panel discussion at the UN Human Rights Council in June 2010. The panel's purpose was to heighten international stakeholders' awareness and understanding of the dangers faced by journalists in dangerous situations. The panel consisted of stakeholders from around the world including specialists on human rights issues and representatives from Reporters sans Frontières, UNESCO, the International Committee of the Red Cross, the Press Emblem Campaign, the Federation of African Journalists, and *Al Ahram* newspaper.

The UN Deputy High Commissioner for Human Rights, Kyung-wha Kang, remarked that reporting from conflict, while inherently dangerous, may indeed be one of the most dangerous occupations in the world because the profession is increasingly being targeted by combatants.[4] Panelist Frank LaRue, Special Rapporteur on the promotion and protection of the right to freedom of opinion and expression, maintained that journalists and media professionals play an essential role in monitoring and exposing human rights violations during war as well as influencing public opinion regarding conflicts.[5] Another contributor to the discussion, George Gordon-Lennox, from Reporters sans Frontières asked pointedly about the United Nations' ability to educate, challenge, and condemn state actors who are often responsible for direct attacks on journalists and the lack of prosecution of those suspected of targeting reporters.[6] This climate of impunity for those who attack journalists suggests another alarming trend for local and international journalists today.

In addition to the United Nations' formal discussion, policymakers from around the world remain concerned about the protection of journalists engaged in stories of conflict and corruption. The primary goal of our study has been to listen to those who report from conflict zones and to inform the international community about ways to develop strategies to mitigate the growing dangers faced by those on the front lines of free expression and democracy. The authors were first drawn to this topic when they met Hedayat Abdel Nabi in Geneva in 2006 as she developed the Press Emblem Campaign. We learned from her about the unacceptable levels of abuse being waged against local and international journalists and the strategies proposed by the international community to combat these abuses. Our research expanded as we uncovered a variety of theoretical, legal, and tactical efforts developed by international, national, and regional organizations to address this affront to journalists. We uncovered, too, disturbing facts about the heinous attacks on local journalists in their own countries. These revelations led to the development of this text.

This book begins with a testament to the vital connection between journalism and democracy and the complex issues surrounding reporting stories of conflict. Chapter 2 offers an introduction to instruments being used today by international policymakers to increase protection for journalists in perilous situations. Chapter 3 discusses various non-state strategies being debated by global stakeholders. In Chapter 4, attention is paid to the disturbing trend toward impunity for those who target journalists. This is followed by honoring a few of those journalists and media workers who have risked their lives in the pursuit of truth by telling their stories. And in Chapter 5, various key stakeholders discuss how to protect journalists who report from today's difficult situations.

The authors have a genuine admiration for the journalists who risk their lives every day to tell vital stories amidst this war on words. The stories that journalists and media workers gather during times of conflict reveal world events that demand interpretation—whether from Uganda, Iraq, Afghanistan, Mexico, or Russia. These correspondents risk their lives to be our eyes and ears on the world. The authors believe these journalists and media workers deserve full and robust protection of international humanitarian law and national jurisprudence.

Journalists' murderers must be thoroughly investigated, and those who abuse and kill journalists must be held accountable in order to decrease the rampant impunity that currently exists and to protect not solely the person, but the social construct of freedom of expression. The authors also believe that serious attention should be paid to efforts to educate all citizens about the vital role of truthful and accurate journalism. The authors contend this comprehensive initiative will serve as a potent deterrent to attacks on journalists around the world. At stake in this discussion is the protection of not only the individual journalists reporting about conflict and corruption around the world, but also the protection of a fundamental component of democracy—a free and unencumbered press.

Chapter 1

Risks and Rewards: Reporting from Armed and Non-Armed Conflict Situations

Journalism has often been described as the first draft of history. If that is true, then reporting about conflict may be considered among the most decisive entries in history books. The intricate relationship between journalism and conflict has been complex yet essential. It is this complexity that makes the question of protection for those who report during open conflict or internal corruption worth exploring.

Conflict is inevitable, but violence is not. In recent years, much of the motivation for wars, interventions, and civil unrest has focused on protecting rights to self-govern and to be free. Of course, many other factors have been involved in wars both hot and cold, but conflicts both within and among nations today can be reduced to the basic motive centered on the protection of fundamental human rights—among them the right of free expression which represents the basic tenet of journalism.

Journalists today face enormous risks when covering conflict and corruption. Different journalists face distinctive risks. Local journalists, often described as journalists with the most to lose, often face reprisals from their own governments and share dangers with their family and friends. What makes them most vulnerable is that they most likely do not have the luxury of leaving the conflict zone. International correspondents have always been viewed as outsiders, and thus suspect. They have been known to descend upon the conflict with limited knowledge of the culture or the controversy which makes them vulnerable to myriad hazards, both physical and journalistic. International journalists now also face the question of whether to be embedded with military forces or to roam the dangerous countryside alone. Freelance journalists face some of the same uncontrollable situations but must rely primarily on their own resources for protection. And women journalists in dangerous situations offer another complex variable that may or may not bring added dangers to these journalists covering conflict. All of these challenging perspectives pose an added burden on those hoping to devise a protection mechanism for journalists on risky assignments.

This chapter begins by explaining why journalism and free expression are vital elements to promote the progress of democracy around the world. The chapter also proffers a brief history of reporting from conflict and the cost—often with their lives—that journalists have paid for this privilege. The issues surrounding the prospect of women reporting from conflict are explored. The chapter also includes a glimpse at how the media and the military have handled their evolving synergistic relationship. The chapter aims to deepen the readers' understanding of how and why journalists have tried to balance the risks and rewards of reporting about and in conflict and how they may have transformed from storytellers to targets.

Journalism and Democracy: The Freedom Alliance

The primary reason to call for a comprehensive international strategy to protect journalists ostensibly stems from the unique symbiotic relationship journalism shares with democracy. In a symbiotic relationship, one element always benefits from the connection. The other element may also benefit or be harmed or unaffected by the relationship—but the two are inexplicably linked.

Journalism in its purest sense is considered a public trust by the people who choose to practice it with integrity. When performed effectively, it demonstrates a responsibility to unbiased truth and accuracy coupled with extremely high ethical standards. Journalism provides citizens with vital information they need to make informed decisions.

Democracy and journalism rely on each other to function effectively. Democracy performs best when the government acquires its ruling powers from the governed, and the governed work better if they are well informed. If interdependence and shared responsibility of citizens is an optimal goal of democracy, then journalism becomes the right tool for the job.

Democracy has been determined to be the world's favorite form of government since the first wave toward democratization in the early 1800s. Democratic nations emerged in the second wave after World War II, and the third wave of democracy began in 1974. This latest wave hit the shore with the liberation of the former communist countries.[1] To substantiate that the democratic form of government was, in fact, the most popular form of government, several research programs monitored the level of affinity the world was feeling toward democracy at the turn of the last century. These empirical research projects included "Barometer" organizations like the New Russian Barometer, the LatinoBarometer, the AfroBarometer, the European Values Survey, and the World Values Survey. Ronald Inglehart was the key researcher who mapped these national inclinations toward democratic governance. The data he gathered from the extensive statistical project that included more than 80 percent of the world's population in 2001, was named the World Values Survey. Inglehart determined empirically from the World Values Survey and European Values Survey that:

> In country after country throughout the world, a clear majority of the population endorses democracy. An overwhelming majority of the population in virtually every society described, "having a democratic political system" as either "good" or "very good." Most of the Islamic countries surveyed rank relatively high: in Albania, Egypt, Bangladesh, Azerbaijan, Indonesia, Morocco, and Turkey from 92 to 99 percent of the public endorses democratic institutions—a higher proportion than in the U.S. Islamic publics may be anti-Western in many respects but, contrary to widespread belief, the democratic ideal has powerful appeal in the Islamic world.[2]

Thus, a nation committed to democracy will be committed to freedom of the press because free expression represents progress towards informed decision making. In a democracy, the majority is charged with making the state's political decisions. In order to make effective decisions and practice good governance, citizens must be able to gather and analyze information and ideas. Thomas I. Emerson in his book, *The System of Freedom of Expression*, posited that suppression of expression denies many opportunities for rational discussion and may leave violence as the only alternative for those wishing to address injustice.[3] The absence of free expression could potentially have a serious and detrimental effect on the political discourse of a country in turmoil.

When journalists are not allowed to practice their trade, local citizens are subjected to limited information about the actions of their government. History has shown that when state officials find journalists' noses too far into the tent and perhaps detrimental to their corrupt causes, the authorities often find unsavory ways to silence them. These serious abuses may pose the most serious threats to free expression. Local and regional altercations represent conflicts where fair and open reporting have the potential to mitigate government corruption. Foreign intervention may be necessary in some cases, but informed local actors calling for the heads of their corrupt officials may offer a more effective and legal way to address internal conflicts. And foreign reporters have the liberty to report what they wish with fewer consequences than the indigenous reporter whose stories are routinely reviewed by criminal operatives.

Journalists practicing in nations that value free expression must serve as the watchdogs and leaders of free expression around the world. They have the responsibility to educate and advocate for global freedom of expression and for their comrades in less free environments. These international watchdogs are essential because some governments and corrupt leaders feel the need to construct fences to keep their local dogs under control. International and national journalism advocacy groups and human rights protectors need to step in to protect the local pur-veyors of truth. Various governments respond to the cry for free expres-sion by saying they need to control journalists in order to maintain order. But state actors striving to construct a more democratic nation must recognize the importance of free expression to the growth of their systems. Media literacy for all people—leaders and citizens—is vital to the growth of democracy around the world.

International media training courses and seminars developed and hosted by organizations like UNESCO and the Institute for War and Peace Reporting routinely educate journalists and citizens about the importance of a free and accurate press for the sustainability of good governance. This kind of public edification should be at the forefront of all educational projects to promote the role of free expression in building and sustaining democracy. These journalism education initia-tives should likewise be part of global development strategies and be tied to international funding operations. Burgeoning nation-states can ben-efit from lessons learned by democratic states about media and their place in building democracy.

The ability to move about freely and uncover the workings of government during conflict situations is the primary element of free expression in a democratic society as this reporting shines a light on all operations. What governments do in the name of their people under the most challenging conditions should be transparent. This openness goes to the heart of a democratic society's ability to make informed decisions about war and conflict. Attacks on journalists either through harassment or murder are fundamental affronts to the transparent actions of government and constitute direct attacks on democracy. Journalists in all societies deserve to not be targeted by their governments or by nonstate actors within a government's jurisdiction. The challenge is to find ways to inform diverse populations of the value of free expression to the greater community, and to hold those accountable who censor or silence it.

Let the Revolution Begin: Freedom of Expression Evolves

Definitions of freedom are dependent on the type of political, economic and cultural climate supported by various nations at different times throughout history. Since the inception of the Magna Carta in 1215, protection of free expression in the West has been debated and its influence on democratic governance appealed. In fact, powerful arguments for freedom of expression were made thousands of years ago in ancient Greece and other places around the world. The history and struggle for a free press includes several important milestones, but the roots of the current notion grew during the European Enlightenment of the seventeenth and eighteenth century. Leading political philosophers of the time wrote eloquent appeals against censorship. In 1644, John Milton penned his famous speech *Areopagitica* and delivered it to Parliament. With his words, Milton created an image of truth and falsehood grappling in an open encounter which demonstrated the ultimate strength of truth. This passage of Milton's doctrine shook the political thinkers of the day, and his "Marketplace of Ideas" notion has endured as a mantra for advocates of free expression worldwide.

The battle for the freedom of the press grew heated during the end of the eighteenth century. The Swedish parliament in 1766 adopted its first law protecting the freedom of the press, a quarter of a century before the proclamation of freedom of the press by French revolutionaries or drafters of the United States Constitution. This act has been considered the world's first freedom of information legislation.[4] The French then demanded freedom for expression and dissemination of "thoughts and opinions" in its Declaration of the Rights of Man in 1789. Another famous and influential milestone of free expression emerged in 1791 from the development and design of the United States Constitution. The First Amendment, which flatly states that the government will not create any laws that might impinge on free speech or free press, has been argued to have fueled the fires of every revolutionary movement for the past two centuries.[5] The freedoms being sought during this period were essentially freedom for ideas, for those who created and propagated them. These freedoms were not being pursued for the elites; instead they were predominantly fought against authoritarian rulers. These rulers were fully aware of the dangers to which they were being exposed by the free dissemination of possibly unfavorable opinions and ideas.

Unfortunately, for much of the rest of the world during this period, freedoms were not being fought for or fully realized. In places like Russia, autocratic rule controlled the flow of information, while in many countries in Africa and Asia under colonial rule, limited freedom of expression was allowed. But gradually, and over periods of many years, these non-Western states began to make progress with regard to press freedom. Journalists in these countries encountered much repression; their papers were often seized or banned during periods of conflict, but they continued to pursue the valuable freedom of ideas and opinions that existed in the West.

These pursuits of free expression led to great strides toward democratic ideas, with the world's largest democracy, India, providing protections for freedom of speech and expression in its Constitution, adopted in 1950. Article 9 of the African Charter on Human and Peoples' Rights adopted in 1981 likewise recognizes every individual's right to receive information and express opinions within the law.[6]

Yet, democracy needs to be practiced in the sunshine in order to survive. It has long been known that democracy's strength is in its transparency. Journalists embody that transparency when they are responsible, free, and accurate. Most reliable governments know that democracy will struggle without independent, reliable sources of information about those in power. They likewise realize that a real need exists to keep voices of free expression strong and alive. A comprehensive review of global constitutions reveals that freedom of expression tends to be balanced against other social values such as the right to privacy, justice, and national security.[7]

Obviously, absolute freedom of expression may be limited by rules of law within a country and this freedom differs vastly among various cultural and political philosophies. The global community has realized that the democratic process may require unabridged dialogue in order to function properly—even though it may be cumbersome and noisy.

Various stakeholders around the world have recognized the need for open and honest journalistic scrutiny as an important component for global political health both within and among nations. Thus efforts toward freedom of information and expression can be found not just in states' documents but in broad international policies as well. In its very first session in 1946, the UN General Assembly adopted Resolution 59(I), stating, "Freedom of information is a fundamental human right and . . . the touchstone of all the freedoms to which the United Nations is consecrated."[8] Abid Hussain, the UN Special Rapporteur on the promotion and protection of the right to freedom of opinion and expression, elaborated on this comment when, in 1995, he reported to the UN Commission on Human Rights: "Freedom will be bereft of all effectiveness if the people have not access to information. Access to information is basic to the democratic way of life."[9]

The Universal Declaration of Human Rights of 1948, often touted as the most translated document in the world, focused on free expression in its Article 19: "Everyone has the right to freedom of opinion and expression; this right includes freedom to hold opinions without interference and to seek, receive and impart information and ideas through any media and regardless of frontiers."[10] Toby Mendel, President of the Centre for Law and Democracy, suggested that the importance of freedom of information rests in its fulfillment of other rights and as an underpinning of democracy, and it is perhaps as an underpinning of democracy that freedom of information is most important.[11] Many foreign policymakers have assigned freedom of expression as the primary human right because when it is diminished, all other injustices tend to become invisible.

U.S. President Barack Obama added his voice to the many people around the world who recognized this primary importance of unfettered information when in May 2010, the president signed legislation to extend the United State's commitment to promote free press around the world. The new law, called the Daniel Pearl Freedom of the Press Act, requires the U.S. State Department to expand scrutiny of news media restriction and intimidation as part of its annual review of human rights in each country. In addition, the U.S. State Department will be required to assess whether foreign governments participate in or condone violations of press freedom. The law was named after Daniel Pearl, a veteran correspondent for the *Wall Street Journal*, who was murdered in Pakistan a few months after the attacks of September 11, 2001.[12]

In recent years, with the help of Western democracies, free expression has made modest progress around the world. Robert L. Stevenson reported that the last years of the twentieth century showed positive trends for market-based Western democracy and likewise for the principles of free press. Technological advancements like the Internet contributed enormously to the ability of the ideas of independence and free expression to spread throughout societies once considered locked tight. Triumphs of independent journalism were witnessed in the fall of the Soviet Union and progress in Latin American and African countries toward multiparty democracy.[13] But with triumphs came serious exceptions and roadblocks. Governments and power brokers in some Asian and Arab countries noticed the emergence of free expression and took great steps to squash this growth.

Unfortunately, the current century has witnessed a number of backlashes against free expression. Freedom House, an independent watchdog organization based in the United States that annually assesses press freedom around the world, reported that in 2010 global media freedom had declined for the eighth year in a row, with significant losses in press freedom outnumbering gains by a two-to-one margin.[14] For the past 30 years, Freedom House has determined its ratings of press freedom by applying its detailed 100-point survey of press freedom in every country and territory and then collapsing this data into three broad categories: free, partly free and not free. In 2009, the data showed only one in six people lived in a country with a free press.[15]

The reasons for the nearly decade-long decline in press freedom, as reported by Karin Deutsch Karlekar of Freedom House, centered on several key points, among them:

- Most governments appear to be unwilling to reform or eliminate laws that punish journalists;
- In countries experiencing conflict, journalists are caught in the crossfire and have become prime targets for threats and restrictions;
- Continuing impunity for past crimes and murder of journalists is encouraging new attacks.[16]

Those who believe free expression is a basic human right and the cornerstone to democracy shudder at these current trends toward diminished press freedom. This decline of the free press may suggest that strides to ensure transparency in governance have decreased around the world.

The fundamental question that requires attention focuses on what and who should protect this vulnerable yet crucial communication vehicle. Worldwide declines in free expression underscore the need for serious discussions about the independence and safety of local and foreign journalists. Experience shows that pluralistic and independent media, by providing a nonviolent forum for debate, not only contribute to peaceful and democratic societies but also are an essential factor in achieving durable economic development. However, this kind of free expression may be difficult to accomplish during times of conflict. Governments want to exert control, while various constituencies want their messages at the forefront—which makes the media a battleground.

At these times of conflict, the journalist is forced to wrestle with allegiances to truth and patriotism. While the role of the foreign correspondent has often been associated with romantic notions, in reality the job brims with ambivalences confounded with allegiances, responsibilities, truth, and accuracy. The local journalist, likewise, must wrestle with personal as well as community or ideological allegiances. While journalists struggle with these dilemmas every day, working under the pressure of conflict adds a unique burden to the journalists' role. Bearing witness to people being killed is a complex business. Add to this the uneasy maxim of conflict itself and the unfortunate realization that you may also be a target and the journalists' pursuit of truth becomes a burdensome goal.

The famous warrior and philosopher Sun Tzu wrote in his sixth century text *The Art of War* that all warfare is based on deception. Truth was originally determined to be the first casualty of war by Aeschylus, the Greek tragic dramatist of the fifth century BC. United States Senator Hiram Warren Johnson revisited this argument when he debated against United States entry into WWI and boldly proclaimed: "The first casualty when war comes is truth."[17]

Today's armed and unarmed conflicts are not restricted to bombs and guns; they are also fought with words and images. Journalists wear many hats into combat besides their protective gear. They are historians, interpreters, and framers of how the war stories are presented. Often they are expected to present the stories in a way that generates positive public opinion about the government and negative energy toward the enemy. The world has come to recognize that the power of media during conflict is formidable—for better or worse. But the question remains, what or who will supply cover for the journalist in this war on words?

The Emergence of the War on Words

The telling of war stories has changed throughout time. The way the stories are told and the impact these stories have on society has transformed the role of the journalist. Today, reporting from a war zone has become an enormously dangerous journalistic pursuit. Wars tend to be the ultimate audit of the state and one of the primary functions of the press since the Enlightenment has been to audit the state. This function becomes increasingly important during times of war. It is not only personally dangerous and professionally demanding, but it can also have a critical impact on the numbers of lives lost or saved. This was not always the case. Since conflicts have existed in human history, there have been those who reported about discord. Early war reports ostensibly counted the war dead and declared which side won or lost the battle. Soldier-correspondents or couriers prepared these war records for a small, elite group of generals or military leaders. These dispatches included details about troop placements, military strategies, and the number of soldiers lost. This information traveled slowly, and it usually took weeks before these reports reached their intended audiences, which often did not include the public.

What evolved from these dispatches were news items that consisted of official reports often written by officers in the field, diplomatic edicts or the occasional traveler's tale of the front. War is horrific, but for centuries its reporting has been considered highly newsworthy. It remarkably has offered journalists the opportunity to be eyewitnesses to the most dramatic points of history and report on anxiety, horror, despair, and triumph all from one location. It has allowed journalists to publish the first draft of history while keeping watch over government actions, both foreign and domestic.

As reporting during conflicts evolved into a journalistic pursuit, correspondents tended to follow the basic tenets of news writing: strive for truth and accuracy while making the stories entertaining and readable. While the content and process of war stories have changed over time, the evolution of these stories has ostensibly revolved around changes in six fundamental elements:

- subject matter
- intended audience
- how stories are told
- transmission of stories

- relationship of media with the military
- impact of war stories on the public

Naturally, reporting about conflict changed with regard to specific subject matter. The actual war stories would change depending on the warring parties, origin of the particular dispute, and the history of relationship between the parties. Disputes that occur within borders have traditionally been covered differently than disputes between different countries. The subject matter of war stories was also altered when reported by foreign correspondents or by local journalists. A vast array of different sources, techniques, and perspectives became enlisted with regard to whether the journalist was from the local community or had foreign ties.

The audience for reports about conflicts changed as the general public developed a taste for the drama of war stories. Initially, the military kept war stories to themselves and reported only the outcome of battles to the public. As war reporting evolved, the primary war story was set in the battlefield. Eyewitness reports from the front became popular news copy. Soldiers and correspondents shared foxholes and often lost their lives while living close to the action. Ernie Pyle and Edward R. Murrow wore army uniforms and brought the war stories home with credibility and honor. The audience for war stories also alters if the stories are reported for local or international audiences. Local journalists have different constituencies and vastly different constraints.

As a result of changes in subject matter and intended audience, journalistic strategies have changed throughout the years in how these stories of conflict are told. As journalists became more familiar with military strategies, they began to seek stories beyond what they were being told to report. Innovative ways of telling stories about conflicts emerged that included narratives about the soldiers and the impact of war on the larger community. Local journalists who observed the freedoms being espoused by foreign correspondents began to learn the value of free expression as well as how this could be practiced in their environs.

The technological advances that altered the way wars were fought also influenced the way war stories were told. Technological improvements in communication have often been at the forefront of experimentation during the world's conflicts. Transmission devices like the telegraph, radio, television, and the Internet have modified the way war stories are disseminated. Radio brought the sounds of war across the ocean. Television brought the moving pictures and the reporters' faces into our living rooms. Masterful dissemination of information continues to be explored on the intricate cables and channels of the Internet.

The complex and changing relationship between the military and the media has had a profound influence on how wars are covered from the journalistic perspective. When journalists are denied access to the main operations of a conflict, it is obvious that war stories are also blocked. When journalists are dependent on the military forces for access to the front, the subject matter of the stories will be affected. This kind of reporting has put enormous pressure on the military and the media alike. Journalists who are embedded with the military often form an inextricable bond with the soldiers yet must resist the temptation to identify too closely with their hosts. The military leaders in this equation must find the will and the flexibility to allow the reporters access to the actual war stories from the troops.

Technological innovations have also had an enormous impact on how local journalists have come to report conflicts. New advances have allowed sources to be heard that were virtually voiceless in the past. Governments choosing to constrain free expression have experienced endless battles to secure the tools necessary to block communication in order to stay one step ahead of those sharing stories of conflict and possible corruption. Recent skirmishes like the post-election riots in Iran were witnessed by the world through citizen journalists willing to document the conflict.

The impact war stories have had on public opinion has evolved from the time of the first war dispatches until today. Reports about conflicts have grown to include not just information but persuasion as well. Governments, militaries, and military actors learned that war stories were more than dispatches; they were and are serious and effective means of contributing to the fundamental battle for the hearts and minds of the public. It may be the result of these fundamental changes that reporters have increasingly found themselves targets of the enemy.

How this evolution has occurred can be viewed best by exploring a brief history of war reporting and the way it has developed into this professional pursuit that was once lauded as patriotic and is now considered increasingly dangerous and deadly.

Journalism Goes to War: The (R)Evolution of War Stories

The birth of modern war reporting began in 1792 when *The Times of London* advertised for a French-speaking gentleman to cover the French Revolution.[18] However, many journalistic historians suggest the first real impact of war stories on conflict occurred during the Crimean War in the 1850s when *Times* reporter William Howard Russell became the first battlefield journalist to expose the chaotic nature of the British military administration, thus altering public opinion at home.[19] Phillip Knightley in his book *The First Casualty* noted that Russell's coverage of the Crimean War "marked the beginning of an organized effort to report a war to the civilian population at home using the services of a civilian reporter."[20] While Russell's voice was the loudest, this kind of war storytelling marked a shift in the subject matter and audience of these stories. Russell's prose about the unpleasantness of war aroused the public. This, in turn, demonstrated an evolution in the rationale for reporting about conflict. Edwin Lawrence Godkin of the *London Daily News* and a contemporary of Russell wrote:

> He (Russell) was a welcome guest at every mess table, from the moment of his arrival in the camp. In his hands correspondence from the field really became a power before which generals began to quail. It brought home to the War Office the fact that the public had something to say about the conduct of wars and that they are not the concern exclusively of sovereigns and statesmen.[21]

In this way, Russell transformed war stories into products of mass education, mass communication and, in turn, mass participation.

Opportunities to tell war stories flourished in the United States during the Civil War, as the public demanded more ways to be shocked, amazed, and horrified by tales from the front. Large staffs of reporters produced newspapers dedicated to the war, often printing daily editions. Newspapers sent staffs to report from both sides of the conflict. For various other social and economic reasons, reading the newspaper also quickly became a daily event for the vast majority of the public, while the newspapers they were reading filled with stories about the Civil War.

The transmission of these stories was being transformed with new technology. For the first time, reporters used the nascent electronic communication, the telegraph, to expedite the delivery of the stories. Reporters sent shorter dispatches straight from the front lines to their newspapers. The railroad also contributed to the speed with which hand-delivered stories were sent to editors. Speed became an increasingly important component in journalistic pursuits. Competition for being the first reporter on the scene and the first to break a story marked a dramatic change in the practice of journalism. Likewise, the technological advancements of photography allowed Matthew Brady and other photographers of the time to produce comprehensive visual accounts of the war to augment the words with pictures. Civil War photographers captured the brutality of the battle with shattering, and sometimes shocking, clarity.

More than 500 war correspondents from around the globe reported the war stories from the North and South during the Civil War. Their stories were often verbally attacked on both sides of the Mason-Dixon Line and around the world. Reporters were arrested for jeopardizing security, and censorship was routinely enforced. Despite this war on words, few reporters were killed during the conflict. While the American Civil War has been considered the deadliest in U.S. history with regard to combat deaths, no data exists regarding the targeting or deaths of journalists during the war.

At the turn of the twentieth century, communication about world affairs was growing, and journalism was playing a part. Audiences from around the world were becoming curious about other nations and other social issues. George Ochs, publisher of the *Philadelphia Public Ledger* said in 1906, "Journalism has become a potential, if not a chief, factor in world affairs."[22] Journalists were contributing to informing the public about injustice and unhealthy working conditions. Journalists were providing the mirror by which the audiences of the world were viewing themselves. Reporting about human suffering beyond the statistics became the role of contemporary journalists. The audiences for stories of conflict were becoming more demanding. This demonstrated a shift in the subject matter of journalistic endeavors as well as the audience for these stories.

Conflicts were also being waged around the world at this time. The British were engaged in the Boer War in South Africa. The French had conquered much of Northern Africa, and the Italian forces had invaded Turkey in the early years of the century to counterbalance the French conquests. Western journalists also flocked to the insurrection in China that occurred in 1900 as Western troops joined the Chinese government to suppress the "Fists of Righteous Harmony" or the Boxers. These conflicts were mainly territorial and were covered primarily by Western journalists with little reflection on what the conflicts meant to the enemy or to the global society. Few at home questioned the need for force to tame unruly masses, while journalists likewise found little use for pangs of conscience on the morality of killing for your country. Foreign correspondents were as limited in their perceptions of the impact of their words on their audiences as the Western armies were of their imperialistic tactics on the world.

Western journalists greatly added to stories about world affairs when they covered World War I. Reporting about war became a formidable profession by this time, and the war was front-page news. A battle cry that the world needed to be made safe for democracy fueled interest in reporting from the front. In addition to alterations in subject matter and means of delivery, an additional aspect of war reporting emerged during this period. Unlike most previous wars, World War I demanded that civilian populations play a role in the efforts against the enemy. American soldiers were enlisted to tell the war stories, and they were transformed into journalists in uniform to contribute to the information being shared with the waiting public at home. Reports from the battlefield, photographs, political cartoons, and editorials were all enlisted to help satisfy the appetite of the American public for news of this war.

Historians contend that World War I demonstrated a unique shift in a rationale to go to war—one based on economic and not just territorial reasons. This new war ostensibly pitted the manufacturing capacity of one nation against that of another, which in turn, required the co-operation and enthusiasm of the people at home. Those in charge of the war effort determined that it was necessary to unite people into solidarity behind their governments. A need arose to forge links between the individual and society and to instill hatred and fear of the enemy. Harold Lasswell, a noted political scientist, wrote, "So great are the psychological resistances to war in modern nations that every war must appear to be a war of defense against a menacing, murderous aggressor. There must be no ambiguity about whom this public is to hate."[23] He added: "A new and subtler instrument must weld thousands and even millions of human beings into one amalgamated mass of hate and will and hope. A new flame must burn out the canker of dissent and temper the steel of bellicose enthusiasm. The name of this new hammer and anvil of social solidarity is propaganda."[24] One of the most effective means of achieving these goals of propaganda often fell on the shoulders of war reporters. Thus the impact on the intended audience was evolving with these stories of war.

Lasswell commented, "There is no doubt about the superlative qualifications of newspapermen for propaganda work. The stars in the propaganda firmament during the World War were mostly journalists."[25] Lasswell researched and wrote a great deal about this phenomenon of propaganda in the aftermath of World War I. His text concluded with the statement: "When all allowances have been made, and all extravagant estimates pared to the bone, the fact remains that propaganda is one of the most powerful instrumentalities in the modern world."[26] Governments found a need to justify their motivations during World War I, and they found a facile mouthpiece to foster these motivations. This changed how war stories were told and the impact these stories had on intended audiences. The frontline correspondent became the initial cog in the giant wheel of perception management aimed at the public. This perception management was recognized as the weapon of the future.

Despite the growth of war stories being used as vehicles to garner support for the war, World War I turned out to be one of the least dangerous conflicts for journalists in the United States, but tragic for journalists in Europe. Although a number of correspondents were wounded, none of the civilian correspondents from the United States were killed during the war. By comparison, Reuters, the British news agency, lost at least 15 out of its 115 correspondents covering the war.[27] While many other wars were occurring around the world, Western journalists parachuting into these areas of discord constituted the majority of those telling the stories of conflict at this time.

By World War II, the means of telling war stories had significantly evolved. Reporting from the front included more than death tolls or calls for support for the troops. War stories included personal narratives about those affected by the conflict on the frontlines and the front porch. Ernest Taylor Pyle (Ernie Pyle), widely regarded as the premiere war correspondent of World War II, told more stories about the people fighting than the fight, more about battle fatigue than the battles. He wrote with great admiration for the soldiers, and the soldiers returned that respect for him. He wrote, "I love the infantry because they are the underdogs. They are the mud-rain-frost-and-wind boys. They have no comforts, and they even learn to live without the necessities. And in the end they are the guys that war can't be won without."[28] Pyle lived with the soldiers and traveled to almost every battle area in North Africa and Europe. His columns appeared in approximately four hundred daily newspapers. Pyle's stories were widely popular with readers at home because he was not telling stories of war but stories about people *in* the war.

Censorship during this period was haphazard. Correspondent Walter Cronkite reported that intelligence officers generally reviewed the

transmissions from the correspondents before they were sent
tors.[29] He explained that censorship rules varied from theater to theater,
from service branch to service branch, from censor to censor. Pyle, for
example, was permitted to publish columns that criticized U.S. officials
for tolerating Vichy French officials in North Africa in 1943. But a year
later, Pyle was prevented from publishing an account of U.S. soldiers
suffering from combat fatigue or "shell shock."[30] But others reported
that Pyle seldom had any difficulty with censors because the military
loved him. The military realized he was good for morale. General Omar
Bradley once said, "Our soldiers always seemed to fight a little better
when Ernie was around."[31]

Pyle was among the 37 American reporters and photojournalists who
would perish during World War II. He was hit by a Japanese sniper in
April 1945.[32] John Hohenberg reported in *Foreign Correspondence: The
Great Reporters and Their Times* that Pyle had been in the Pacific for just
four months when the sniper hit him. "Pyle hit the ditch beside the road
then raised his head to see if everybody else was all right. The bullet hit
him in the right temple."[33]

The audience during these times of conflict had grown to expect news
from the front. Ben Hibbs, editor for the *Saturday Evening Post* had been
concerned that his magazine may be telling too many war stories until
he reviewed the new readership statistics:

> Our surveys showed that every single issue of the *Post* between 1942, when
> I became editor and the dropping of the bomb on Hiroshima, some war
> article was by far the best read feature in the magazine. Moreover, the gen-
> eral level of readership on war articles was substantially above that of
> every other category of material—above fiction, above everything. People
> simply didn't mean what they said in casual conversation; the war was the
> biggest story of all time, it was close to the lives of everyone, and virtually
> everyone read about it avidly, week after week, for three and a half years.
> Our surveys gave us the courage to do what we should do: Cover the war
> thoroughly and conscientiously with the corps of the best correspondents
> we could hire.[34]

War News Takes to the Air

Newspapers' monopoly on war stories was disrupted during World War
II when a new means of transmission sprung from the air: radio. By the
middle of World War II, radio had grown into the main source of

entertainment and information for much of the western world. Mixed in among the music programs were stories from war correspondents who wanted the public to never forget the world was at war. This was radio's first world conflict, and the medium provided the listening public with war stories and information more promptly than ever before. In fact, a British Broadcasting Corporation internal report noted that radio was "the main difference in propaganda between this War and the last."[35] This new vehicle of broadcasting marked not only an evolution in the transmission of war stories, but dramatically altered the impact of the stories on the intended audience.

Known for his opening phrase, "This is London," Edward R. Murrow covered the unfolding dramatic events of World War II on radio. Americans relied on his daily broadcasts from Europe hours before the newspapers hit the stands. Murrow provided the sounds of bombs and anti-aircraft fire that most Americans had previously heard only in the movies.

Allied military authorities regarded war correspondents as vital contributors to the war effort. General Dwight Eisenhower even went as far as to comment publicly that he considered the press as part of the military organization and believed it should be treated as such.[36] Other military leaders of the time recognized the contributions of the new media as a means to encourage civic support of the war. Major General Willis H. Hale praised the press at an event in 1945 that honored the contributions of reporters to the U.S. war effort. He remarked, "To gain the necessary appropriations for the heretofore untried weapon (air power) we needed the support of the entire nation. That we were wholly successful was largely due to the efforts of the press in our behalf."[37] A new medium was being used to transmit the horrors of war, and its effect was profound in securing positive public opinion of the war efforts on both sides of the conflict.

The Axis powers also found radio to be a great weapon in demoralizing citizens in Europe as well as British and U.S. soldiers during World War II. Radio performers Tokyo Rose, Axis Sally, and Lord Haw-Haw broadcasts into the Ally homefront included slanted news stories, prisoner-of-war messages and popular music—sometimes rerecorded with threatening new lyrics.[38] German propaganda minister Joseph Goebbels was proud of the effectiveness of the German broadcasts that he credited with sapping the will of English and the Austrians, Czechs, and French to resist invasion. Goebbels wrote in his diary January 6, 1940, "Our English radio broadcasts are now being taken with deadly seriousness in England."[39] Two years later he boasted, "Our propaganda in England has been more effective than we imagined."[40] This war had demonstrated the birth of a new and powerful medium and honing of unique strategies of words as weapons to weaken the enemy's will. The methods of war as well as the role of the war correspondent were to witness enormous changes following World War II. The conflicts to come would not be world wars but regional conflicts that needed public support to succeed.

Thus, unfortunately, the silent guns after World War II did not signal peace. The bitter division of wartime coalitions caught many wartime storytellers by surprise. The clarity of reporting about conflict had dissolved to an uncertainty about what was or was not a battle but a cold war of words. While the United States possessed sole use of the atomic bomb, the Soviet Union had found solace in developing an effective propaganda strategy aimed at swaying world opinion. Out of the chilling of world relations, the United Nations was born amid a news media that hoped to raise public expectations of this international power. Herbert Bayard Swope, noted war correspondent and Pulitzer Prize winner, was the first to label this period of unease the Cold War.[41] Throughout this period, the United States and the Soviet Union were engaged in many battles of wits and words. One of the primary battles was for "the hearts and minds of the people." During this period, the Soviets, keenly aware of the power of the press, slammed down the Iron Curtain on journalists. Foreign correspondents were generally censored, harassed, and accused of spying.

The cold war was fought at home, too. Americans became terrified of Communist clandestine infiltration. Fear of a Communist takeover of the United States fueled a national audience for Wisconsin Senator Joseph McCarthy's congressional inquisitions. The era of a faceless, yet powerful, enemy had begun. This cold war turned hot in Korea, where fears of Communism became real as Communist North Korea invaded free South Korea.

This conflict was more than just a battle against Communism; it was the first time in history that a worldwide international body had voted for force to be used against aggression. The Security Council of the United Nations had proclaimed two resolutions in 1950, Resolutions 82 and 83 calling upon the United Nations to "furnish such assistance as may be necessary to repel the armed attack and to restore the international peace and security in the area."[42] Despite being a pronounced international incident, coverage of the Korean War was criticized as the worst war reporting of modern times. Miles Hudson and John Stanier in their text, *War and the Media: A Random Searchlight* cited varied reasons for poor reporting in Korea.[43] Difficulties arose in transmitting stories from the front. Korea was considered a far-off country, and journalists were dealing with censorship issues in the country and with the military. During the conflict, journalists were told to be prudent when relaying information that might be of use to the North Koreans, and several were banished because their stories were considered to give aid to the enemy. By January 1951, General Douglas MacArthur imposed formal censorship on reporters.[44] Many stories were being transmitted, however, just as U.S. public support was also waning for American action after the United States hinted at the possibility of using the atomic bomb in the conflict. The media also was the first to report misgivings about the treatment of South Koreans in South Korea. Debate about the war waged at home in the press. Some politicians were reported to say that the United States military should be allowed to use all of the weapons in its arsenal to defeat the Chinese Communists. President Truman and General MacArthur did not agree and were at odds over the means of waging this war; this debate was played out for the public in the press. As a result, the public became polarized but was universally displeased with the way the war was going. Then one of the biggest stories of the war was when the president subsequently fired General MacArthur.

The Korean War was considered one of the most hazardous frontline reporting assignments in modern history because, as one reporter put it, "In other wars you had a pretty good idea of where the enemy was and where you were. In Korea you didn't."[45] As a result, 18 correspondents and photographers lost their lives during the war.[46]

The Television Battle for Hearts and Minds

Another conflict in Asia, in Vietnam this time, brought a new kind of war as well as a new criticism of war reporting. The coverage of the Vietnam War was considerably different from what occurred during the Korean War. During the Korean War, the critics attacked the administration for not being more aggressive and for not using all the weapons available to end the threat of Communist China. In contrast, criticism of the Vietnam War and the reporting of that criticism resulted in a dramatic shift in the way war stories are told, even today.

During the Vietnam War, correspondents were uniquely accredited with the armed forces and granted uniforms, transportation, and protective gear. Hugh Lunn, a renowned Australian Vietnam War correspondent, reported that when he arrived to cover the conflict, he was quickly informed that he needed an American military uniform to wear when in the field, "because it ensured no Americans would accidentally shoot you as a Viet Cong. It also ensured that the soldiers treated you as one of their own because, in the end, you depended upon them for your life."[47]

Many reporters covering the war moved around the country freely. In fact, one particular journalist, Harrison Evans Salisbury, from the *New York Times*, was allowed by the North Vietnamese government to report from Hanoi in 1966. Historian and researcher, Mark Atwood Lawrence suggested that Salisbury found himself in a firestorm of controversy as a result of this assignment largely because his accounts of the war offered a contrast to the reports presented by the Lyndon Johnson administration.[48] Lawrence reported that by validating the North Vietnamese perspective on the war, Salisbury was one of the very few reporters within the mainstream press who stepped beyond the relatively limited range of criticism or what Daniel C. Hallin would call "the sphere of legitimate controversy."[49]

Reporters in Vietnam also found themselves traveling with and becoming part of military units until the journalists moved on to cover another story. Curiously, despite this direct military connection, reporters during this conflict were not subjected to strict censorship, which many critics believe contributed to the unprecedented coverage of the war with stories capturing the conflict from every angle and from all sides.

In another move outside the sphere of legitimate controversy, Eddie Adams captured the horrors of Vietnam in one photo of a Vietnamese soldier being executed on the streets of Saigon during the Tet Offensive in 1968. This photo, which became known as "the shot seen around the world,"[50] provoked a shift in public opinion about the war. Television images corresponded by showing the public moving images of the brutality of the war. Barbara Tuchman in her book, *The March of Folly*, said: "Americans who had never before seen war now saw the wounded and homeless and the melted flesh of burned children afflicted thus by their own countrymen."[51] By 1967, more Americans opposed the decision to send troops to Vietnam than supported it.[52]

Seasoned journalist and television anchor Walter Cronkite, who was a veteran reporter from World War II, explained that when he first went to

Vietnam in the early stages of the conflict, he was in favor of the war.[53] But after the Tet Offensive, Cronkite questioned his support and convinced his supervisors that he should be allowed to offer his opinion on the air. He did that in February 1968 when he proclaimed it seemed "more certain than ever that the bloody experience of Vietnam is to end in a stalemate."[54] Cronkite's role as war correspondent had shifted from objective reporter to critic. The efforts like those of Harrison Evans Salisbury demonstrated the shift in the role of the war correspondent from covering conflict from a patriotic viewpoint to offering different perspectives and at times criticizing the rationale for the conflict that shaped public opinion.

Largely as a result of war stories like this, President Lyndon B. Johnson turned to the television screen to announce he would not seek another term as president. Presidents and scholars have since called this public rejection of the war the "Vietnam Syndrome." Robin Andersen describes this impact of war stories on the public in her book, *A Century of Media, A Century of War*, stating that this syndrome has been viewed by many "as a disease, a set of symptoms, a disorder."[55] Vietnam showed that wars in the current context require symbolic environments that hide human costs and public acceptance of the motivation for the conflict.[56]

Daniel C. Hallin in his book, *The Uncensored War*, reported that the war in Vietnam left the nation deeply divided with no issue more divisive than the role of the media.[57] Hallin concluded that Vietnam was the first sustained war that appeared on television and as a result, significantly affected the transmission of war stories. Images of war were delivered nightly into the living rooms of the intended audience. War became brutal and bloody. Previously, wars had been portrayed in print and radio as just and moral fights. The public had agreed. Reporting on Vietnam offered the public direct contact with the horrors of the front that seemed to change the notion of just war. As a result, television reporting has often been charged with causing that shift in public opinion about the war in Vietnam. More than just affecting public opinion negatively toward the government and military action, television correspondents have been accused of being disloyal and blamed for the loss of the war.

Robin Andersen reported that what ostensibly changed during the Vietnam era was the public's awareness that the government and the military were not telling the truth about the war.[58] Information produced by the media provided the public with more accurate information and ammunition for critical analysis of military tactics. Douglas Kellner argued that extensive media reporting from the Vietnam War challenged military speech.[59] In the end, the Vietnam War was considered the most comprehensively reported war of all time.

Hundreds of war correspondents covered the Vietnam War between 1961 and 1975. At its peak, the press corps consisted of 600 members accredited to armed forces units but not always subject to strict censorship. One of the most significant changes in transmission during this war was the omnipresence of television coverage. Despite technical advances, few of these correspondents had experience reporting on unconventional or guerrilla warfare. Of the 45 correspondents and photographers killed in action in Vietnam, two were women.[60]

As a result of the recognition of the enormous role media reports played in the Vietnam War, strategies of governments and militaries shifted dramatically with regard to how to manage journalists. The battle over who would be granted access to action had begun. Military campaigners had experienced an unprecedented wake-up call and were alerted to the power of the media to wage an effective war of words. The relationship between the military and the media had been transformed forever. Future conflicts would be influenced by the way the Vietnam War was reported and the impact this reporting had on public opinion and the subsequent outcome of the war.

Controlling War Stories

Following the Vietnam War, Western governments struggled to make war once again acceptable to the public. Ministries and governments around the world recognized that techniques needed to be adopted to manage the war stories—but with a delicate hand. When Britain and Argentina went to war over the Falkland Islands in the summer of 1982, the British Ministry of Defense demonstrated it had learned its lesson to control what war stories could reasonably be controlled in a democratic government. As a result, the Ministry of Defense limited access to the battlefield during the Falklands War in an effort to keep the war coverage in line. Correspondents were also vetted to ensure those covering the conflict would be favorable to the British government's position.[61] The news media at the time willingly accepted these conditions because the government's first plan was to not allow access to any journalists to the war zone. This specific media access strategy used by the British government would signal a dramatic shift in the way other governments would try to control the war stories during future conflicts. These strategies still are seen today in the way conflict coverage is controlled in some developing and non-Western nations. The idea of limiting the journalists' access to the battlefield or claiming superior expertise that embarrasses the reporters who depart from the government-established norms is a highly effective way of determining the story.

The U.S. invasion of Grenada in 1983 marked the turning point in modern wartime reporting policies in the United States. The administration of President Ronald Reagan kept the press off the small island and away from the action for the first 48 hours of the operation. It marked the first time in U.S. history that the press had not been at the frontline in the first hours of a conflict.[62] The war stories and pictures were supplied by the Department of Defense and included happy, smiling students being rescued by U.S. forces. The public did not see any of the events that caused 29 soldiers to be killed. As a result, the public remained supportive of the invasion and of the president.[63]

The invasion of Panama in 1989 saw the activation of a new strategy to control the press: the press pool system. The pool system consisted of only a few journalists covering the conflict and sharing that coverage with the others. Here the relationship between the media and the military demonstrated a profound shift in protocol. This project was designed by the military as a creative means to limit media access to a war zone. The military operatives knew enough about democratic principles that they could not completely exclude the press, so the press pool was seen as a way to get journalists to the action without losing complete control of the message. This new strategy became a useful tool to garner a modicum of control over the media and the war stories they told. But reports from Panama were not unlike the stories that were reported during Grenada using only official sources. As a result of this new strategy, the invasion and military actions against General Manuel Noriega drew overwhelming popular and congressional support for President George H.W. Bush. The president's aggressive campaign against Noriega became a means for Bush to rebut the "wimp" allegations and confirm his legitimacy as a forceful, masculine leader.[64]

It was not the control over the press, but the proliferation of new technologies that enabled the news media to provide information and stories as they happened in the 1980s. The symbolic crumbling of Communism was communicated to Western audiences within moments with dramatic pictures. Moving images of brave young people standing in front of tanks near Tiananmen Square, in China, captured the Western television audience while it was happening. War stories had evolved to cover every conflict and transmit the story to every corner of the world in an instant. A new wave of media devices emerged. Small televisions, lightweight camera equipment, and eventually personal computers found their way into the hands of the average citizen. The evolution of war stories was entering a new stage.

The social and political scientists during this time were also keenly aware of the profound effect media consumption was having on the behavior of the powerful and the vast audience of consumers. In *Manufacturing Consent: The Political Economy of the Mass Media* (1988), social critic and political philosopher Noam Chomsky and his colleague Edward S. Herman explored the complex relationships of current-day media and constructed their notion of the propaganda model and how the powerful use media. Chomsky and Herman were greatly influenced by the propaganda research conducted by Walter Lippmann in the 1920s and in fact derived the title of their book from a phrase used by Lippmann. While Chomsky and Herman focused on the economic functions of the media, they were also concerned with the idea of propaganda that was first introduced by Lippmann and how the elites were using the media to control the population. The opening paragraph of their book explains this:

> The mass media serve as a system for communicating messages and symbols to the general populace. It is their function to amuse, entertain, inform and inculcate individuals with the values, beliefs and codes of behavior that will integrate them into the institutional structures of the larger society. In a world of concentrated wealth and major conflicts of class interest, to fulfill this role requires systematic propaganda.[65]

As Chomsky saw it, controlling the domestic population is not just simply a single problem, but the "central one facing any state or other system of power."[66] He added that using the media to control the masses was quickly becoming a vital tool for power. Chomsky and Herman observed media and its effect on the population through detailed empirical analysis of media coverage of U.S. interventions in Central America and Southeast Asia. Their work determined: "To those in power, it seems obvious that the population must be cajoled and manipulated, frightened and kept in ignorance, so that ruling elites can operate without hindrance to the national interest as they choose to define it."[67] For

Chomsky, the rich and powerful seeking this control were those with business interests as well as those in positions of political power.

As the notion grew that population control may be obtained through the words and pictures of the media, those wishing to exercise this control saw journalism in its rawest form as an effective means of doing so. Yet, those wishing to maintain the notion of fairness and accuracy (long held as the original tenets of the discipline) were seen as suspicious in subsequent conflicts.

The factors that have fundamentally affected the role of the war correspondent—the subject matter, the audience, the way stories are told, the means of transmission, the complex relationship between the media and the military, and the impact of war stories on the public—had all swelled during the conflicts of the 1990s. As the conflicts spread, their subject matter enlarged to include critiques of combatants' motives. War correspondents, whose role had once been to dispatch troop movements and report on the dead in battle, now found themselves free to criticize the motivations of friends as well as enemies. Stories that were once written for newsprint to be distributed on the doorstep were now being broadcast instantaneously and into everyone's TV room across the globe. Professionally trained journalists with thousands of dollars of equipment were being outflanked by storytellers with their own means of transmission and little training as to the role or value of journalism. The power of war stories to transform the conflict and not just serve as a report about the conflict was recognized from Baghdad to Berlin to Boston. Social and political scientists were observing this effect as the propaganda model was being applied across media platforms. As a result, journalists' ability to tell war stories was being enhanced, yet compromised in many ways. Journalists who were once considered the providers of information about the conflict were increasingly seen as targets.

Journalists Become the Targets

What followed in the 1990s was a decade replete with examples of conflicts that appeared to burst from nowhere into breaking news. From Somalia to Kosovo, from Bosnia to East Timor and from Rwanda to Haiti, conflicts arose and reporters followed. A total of 115 armed conflicts were recorded during the period of 1989–2001.[68] These armed conflicts also had a greater degree of complexity and uncertainty, with many involving one or more armed nonstate actors fighting government forces or other nonstate actors, as well as an increase in the number of civilians under fire in the conflict environment. Other challenges arose to force those reporting about conflict to adjust to the evolution of war stories. The challenges included:

- Difficulty in labeling the enemy and the emergence of nonstate actors in conflict;
- Rise in conflicts being fought not on frontlines but in populated areas
- Increase in the number of untrained journalists with easy access to the conflicts;
- Rise of 24-hour news coverage and need for more stories of conflict quickly and often without context;
- Unfortunate economic realities of the professional news-gathering business;
- Questions of balance and objectivity in reporting;
- Journalists, both foreign and domestic, becoming targets because combatants recognized the power of words and images to influence public opinion.

The clear, cold enemy of the Cold War melted, and the ideological framework that allowed Western journalists an uncomplicated means of practicing their craft melted with it. The easy dichotomies of previous conflicts were gone. The collapse of the Soviet Union led to various European interstate conflicts that occasionally caught the attention of the entire world—but not for too long. The complicated ethnic and religious conflicts introduced the world to the profound emergence of nonstate actors in warfare. Journalists suddenly became by default the western world's new geography and social studies teacher. Nightly reports came replete with maps to explain where in the world the conflict was occurring. Commentaries in print and broadcast offered explanations about the extensive history of warring parties—not always accurate and at times slanted toward a certain side.

The war in Bosnia-Herzegovina has been described as the archetypal example of the new type of warfare because it mobilized a huge international effort involving all major governments. It represented a significant shift in global political hierarchy represented by the inadequacy of the European Union foreign policy-making capacity, the floundering of the United Nations, and the reemergence of the United States as a world power as well as the redefinition of the Russian role.[69] Journalism emerged from this transformed. In this conflict, it was not just foreign correspondents parachuting in to report on the winners and losers, but local and regional journalists practicing their profession amid unfortunate local consequences. The Committee to Protect Journalists reported that as many as 25 journalists were killed in the region during this conflict.[70]

The editor of the *Sarajevo* daily at the time, Kemal Kurspahić, reported that the first journalist killed in the Bosnian war was a small-town correspondent in Zvornik.[71] Kurspahić added: "I felt that if hundreds of foreign journalists could come and cover the war and the siege of Sarajevo, then we, whose city, whose country, whose families were here, shouldn't just give up and withdraw in the face of the terror."[72]

Tim Lambon, producer and camera person during the Balkans conflict for Channel 4 News in the United Kingdom said that many of the hundreds of foreign journalists who covered the conflict had little experience covering war:

> This was the first European war that anybody could get to—you could take a train from Vienna to Zagreb, or from Italy to Zagreb, and as long as you had a piece of headed notepaper from anything that you could have put together . . . you could get press accreditation from the UN in Zagreb. Then you could jump on a plane into Sarajevo without the slightest clue of what the bloody hell you were letting yourself in for.[73]

In addition to using newspaper, radio and television stories to tell this war, reporters used a state of the art transmission device: the Internet. Stories of the conflict were not limited to foreign war correspondents, but those engaged in the conflict. Public opinion could be affected not only by the military or even the journalist, but by pointed and persuasive communication designed by the combatants to be disseminated directly to the people.

The Iraqi invasion initiated to liberate Kuwait in 1991 and the subsequent launch of Operation Desert Storm or Grandby to the British, constituted the first major global war story following the Cold War. Public support for the "coalition of the willing" was generated by stories that told of Iraqi soldiers who had plucked babies from their Kuwaiti incubators and thrown them on the floor. But this war story about Iraqi soldiers was subsequently found to be the creation of a U.S. public relations firm hired by the Kuwaiti government. This creation signaled the birth of a new twist on an old media strategy during war. Lasswell's propaganda machine had taken a turn toward fabrication.

Those in control of the media fed the propaganda machine as never before. The way Western journalists received information about this conflict was highly choreographed. The military set up a Joint Information Bureau that was run by trained public information officers who set the agenda as they reported the key points of the conflict each day. These reports were presented with regularity on a well-lit stage that was purposely designed for the television audience.[74] ABC News correspondent, John McWethy said of these briefings: "Message control is the way that this administration is trying to communicate what it is trying to do."[75] Thus, the government was providing information to meet the public demand, but not designed to meet the fundamentals of good journalism.

The new concept of a media pool system was fully engaged during the Gulf War. Of the initial 150 journalists chosen for the pool system, only half were allowed to accompany troops and be eyewitnesses to the conflict. Those chosen were then taken under army command to report from the field under strict censorship conditions and required to disseminate their observations to other journalists waiting back at their hotel. What essentially occurred was an overabundance of information about that conflict coming indirectly from the military that resulted in limited diversity in the coverage from the hundreds of reporters attending to the war. Paul L. Moorcraft and Philip M. Taylor reported that one commentator on the BBC quipped, "Never in the field of recent conflict has so little been disclosed to so many by so few."[76]

What made reporting on this conflict unusual was that Western eyewitness-journalists were reporting from behind enemy lines in Baghdad—not unlike how Harrison Evans Salisbury did during the Vietnam War. Moorcraft and Taylor suggested that Saddam Hussein had been following the literature on how previous leaders had used the media to become successful war heroes. Thus, the reason the Western reporters were allowed in Baghdad was Hussein's conviction that the media might be able to help him garner popular support for his side of the conflict.[77] The authors posited, "Desert Storm signaled the start of a process that effectively mobilized the media from enemy countries as an asymmetrical weapon against those countries. They [the media] had become, wittingly or unwittingly, active participants."[78]

The liberation of Kuwait was not an especially dangerous assignment for reporters, despite some of them being behind enemy lines. The Committee to Protect Journalists reported that 13 journalists were killed by U.S. forces firing on Baghdad.[79] Journalists from Al Jazeera, Al Arabiya,

Kurdistan TV, Abu Dhabi TV, Reuters, Telecinco and others were among those killed during the aftermath of this conflict.[80]

The events of September 11 represented another shift in the world of war stories. These attacks were followed by the declaration of the "War on Terror" and the invasions of Afghanistan and Iraq. In October 2001, Special Forces from the United States, United Kingdom, and Australia arrived in Afghanistan, along with nearly 1500 journalists. Yet the conflict in Afghanistan was not a media war in the same way Vietnam was. Journalists were embedded with the military because the conflict, the language, the terrain, and the weather all worked against their ability to tell a complete story. More importantly, the correspondents were increasingly becoming the targets themselves.

Gretchen Peters, author of *Seeds of Terror: How Drugs, Thugs, and Crime Are Reshaping the Afghan War,* covered Pakistan and Afghanistan for more than a decade for The Associated Press, ABC News, The Christian Science Monitor, CNN, BBC, and others. Peters maintained that she remembered when it was safe to proclaim your job in the conflict:

> I can remember in the days when I first started reporting in a war zone in Afghanistan in the early 90s. We would drive around in a little red hatchback with a big sign and a big flag hanging up that said PRESS and AP on it . . . that was about fifteen or sixteen years ago. That was when your identity as a journalist was a form of protection. Now, certainly in some war zones, that can make you a target.[81]

Why Are Journalists Targeted?

The Committee to Protect Journalists (CPJ) confirms that 862 journalists have been killed since 1992.[82] CPJ routinely reports that journalists around the world are being targeted when reporting about conflict. However, the most disturbing aspect of these figures to those concerned with this issue is the numbers showing that of those belligerents who intentionally victimize journalists, virtually all go free of prosecution. The Committee reported on its website, that among those journalists murdered, almost 90 percent of the perpetrators have enjoyed complete impunity.[83] Combatants practice a crude form of censorship by targeting the journalists in the field. Some governments and power brokers find attacking journalists a facile way to control public opinion. There are myriad reasons why journalists have been transformed into targets. State and nonstate actors may be trying to protect their interests from the prying eyes of foreigners or to control the message for their own people. More specifically, the following three factors may contribute to the increased targeting of journalists:

1. **Growth in the power of the media**: Governments and other military operatives have become keenly aware of the power of the media to affect public opinion and subsequently the outcome of conflict. All the stakeholders in the conflict want their stories to be the most persuasive to convince audiences on both sides of the conflict of the merit of their cause. Control of the media has an undeniable effect on the chances of victory.

2. **Perceived or real lack of neutrality of the media:** Ever since war correspondents and the stories they tell have become tools of propaganda and patriotism, journalists have risked being seen as soldiers whose weapons are words. When traditional journalism became a vehicle of opinion along with statistics, the objective role of the media was essentially neutralized. Thus, combatants and those in control have concluded that the best weapon against words is to eliminate the wordsmith. In addition, the current mode of expression in media today fosters sensationalism for the sake of building audiences and often displays a lack of attention to the role of the media to project neutrality and "first do no harm." Ostensibly this form of mediated hate speech was born of the increased attention on the economic benefits of owning media operations and less attention on the social responsibility of the media to society.

3. **Impunity for perpetrators**: Those who target journalists frequently find that their actions do not result in punishment. State and nonstate actors have experienced virtual impunity when directly targeting journalists who are the quintessential guardians of the fundamental human right of free expression.

New wars have resulted in new war stories and have provided added risks for the journalist. In the International News Safety Institute's (INSI) 2007 report entitled, *Killing the Messenger*, INSI found that "the recognition of journalists as neutral observers has largely gone. Increasingly, journalists covering international conflicts are identified with their countries or are seen as either with us or against us."[84] Individual journalists have also experienced this trend, such as CNN reporter Leroy Sievers:

> When I was covering wars in Latin America in the late 1980s, we all put "TV" in big letters on our cars. That was supposed to provide safe passage. It did until the death squads started putting "TV" on their cars too. But I think no-one but us actually believed that we were the neutral observers that we thought we were.[85]

This loss of perceived neutrality has resulted in journalists being seen as spies. Former *Time Magazine* reporter Michael Ware wrote, "In Afghanistan, every Westerner is a spy until proven otherwise ... sensitive questions can provoke accusations of espionage."[86] Journalists may also be perceived as just another representation of occupation, such as the armed forces in Iraq. The former *Washington Post*'s assistant managing editor for foreign news, Philip Bennett, said "(F)oreign journalists are foreigners first, just another element of an occupying force to which (the journalists) don't belong."[87] Awareness of this perception is especially vital for embedded journalists working in situations of international armed conflict, as they are legally part of that military entourage, whether they see themselves that way or not.

The 24-hour news cycle has created a monster with a favorable and unfavorable effect on journalists' craft. This expansion of the news cycle has led to greater opportunities for journalists drawn to covering conflict situations and considerably more global understanding, although at times it may not seem as such. But this hungry news beast has also caught the eye of the financial wizards who initially saw 24-hour news as a cash cow—relatively low cost content that kept the audience riveted as the advertisers sold them soap. But as more and more storytellers found new ways to send out the same information, media corporations consolidated to cut production costs. They found in order to maintain their audiences' attention, they needed to vent more vitriol and spew more sensationalism. This kind of coverage has resulted in a somewhat unsavory media landscape that may have attracted misguided audience members who, when they do not appreciate the content they see, can think of only one way to change the channel—violence.

Frontline journalists have always faced dangerous obstacles that hinder them in practicing their craft, but journalists today must confront the added burden of being a target of military action merely for performing their jobs. Local or domestic journalists who have witnessed the vital role of accurate journalism in the promotion of democracy have likewise watched as their words are subjected to control by those in power. Many argue new ways of waging war have resulted in added pressures for the journalist telling the stories of conflict—at home and abroad. Thus, these journalists may be in need of added protection.

New Wars Foster Unique News Challenges

Recent conflicts have revealed a sustained shift in how combatants wage war. The notion of "New Wars" and its components include the rapid growth of information processing and communications tools with the separate and simultaneous proliferation of regional conflicts and the increased role of guerrilla tactics. These two primary elements have stimulated all sides of a conflict to perceive information as a key military resource and those who collect and generate this information as key players in it. Whether reporting for major traditional news operations or gathering information to tell the story of the conflict to local audiences, journalists are primary operatives in today's new wars.

Mary Kaldor, in *New and Old Wars*, explained that the character of war has changed since the collapse of the Soviet Union. She argued that the nature of war today encompasses political leaders in crumbling states who try to win popular support by mobilizing forms of identity politics through the media which, in turn, lead to civil unrest. She also claimed there exists a blurring of the distinction among war, organized crime and large-scale human rights violations. She added that violence is now decentralized, carried out by militias and directed primarily towards civilians with increased involvement by both nonstate actors (mercenaries and private armies) and by transnational interests (peacekeepers and NGOs).[88]

Howard Tumber and Frank Webster in *Journalists Under Fire: Information War and Journalistic Practices*, explained early in their text the emergence of a new kind of war which they label "Information War."[89] Tumber and Webster see the Information War as one where advances in the technology of war and communication emerge to produce this new kind of combat. In this Information War, positive media presentations are vital to justify involvement in the conflict and to ensure public opinion remains committed to the cause. The authors reported:

> There are so many journalists who congregate in war zones now, often numbering in the thousands, and they come from so many points of origin, that they can be difficult to control from the perspective of perception managers. They also have access to lightweight technologies that enable them to transmit via satellite with immediacy unimaginable even a decade ago. The Internet means that their reports are easily accessed by much bigger audiences than ever before. They can be challenged almost immediately by critics elsewhere and even by the subjects on whom they are reporting.[90]

Closely related to the emergence of the so-called "new wars" and "information war" is the notion of the changing nature of contemporary power.

Political analyst Joseph Nye contended that "soft power" referred to "the power of attraction that is associated with ideas, cultures and policies—and encouraging others to create the coalitions that will eventually limit our hard power."[91] Simply put, this means the ability to get others around the world to do what you want them to do without having to kill them. Nye argued that the effective study of international politics today depends upon our understanding of the relationship between hard (military, economic) and soft (symbolic or media-driven) power.[92] Nye posited that the world might be witnessing the waning of one form of power and the growth of another. He explained, "While hard and soft power are important, in a global information age soft power is becoming even more so than in the past."[93] This could be equated to the waning of the power of territory, money, and guns and the enormous emergence of the power of narrating the world through stories or, ostensibly, journalism. Thus, one of the primary elements of soft power is the information generated by the media and the power that information wields over domestic and international audiences.

Undeniably, telling war stories has become increasingly risky business. The use of words as weapons of war has become normalized in today's conflicts. Unfortunately for those who report about war in these circumstances, the fundamental truths about war continue: those who control the weapons of war control the war.

The western world became acutely aware of direct attacks on journalists when *Wall Street Journal* reporter Daniel Pearl was captured and beheaded in Pakistan in 2002. Pearl was serving as the South Asia Bureau Chief for the *Journal* when he was abducted while covering a story in Karachi. But the data from CPJ suggest that local journalists may experience the greatest risk when their beats include politics, human rights, and corruption.[94] In recent conflicts, from Bosnia to Sierra Leone to Afghanistan, multiple instances of combatants deliberately targeting journalists have been reported, and these attacks have taken place not just on the traditional battlefields. Frank Smyth, of the Committee to Protect Journalists, reported in the *Harvard International Review* that the untold story of risks to journalists focuses not on the foreign journalists who cover conflict but on the dangers faced by local journalists who report from within their own borders.[95] Attacks on local journalists include the deadly Maguindanao massacre which left 32 journalists and media workers dead in the Philippines in 2009, and daily struggle of journalists in Mexico trying to expose the vast underground corruption in that country's drug-related conflict.

This targeting of journalists and media workers stems from the changing landscape of modern warfare and the unbridled corruption found in some developing nations. Wars today contain no frontlines, and some governments and belligerents find unbiased reporting about their activities unacceptable. Journalists are no longer unfortunate casualties but primary targets in a flourishing climate of impunity. According to the International News Safety Institute (INSI), more than 1,000 journalists have been killed in the last 10 years while trying to report the news.[96] This number includes print, photo, and video journalists as well as essential support staff such as drivers and translators. The trend to target media workers increased in 2006 and 2007 with 168 media workers and journalists killed in 2006, and 171 killed in 2007.[97] In 2008, journalist deaths lessened slightly to 109,[98] but in 2009, 133 journalists and media staff members were killed. What makes this information most startling is that only a fraction of these fatalities are under investigation.[99] In 2010, 97 news staff and journalists were killed as reported by INSI.[100] According to INSI's March 2007 report, *Killing the Messenger*, eight out of 10 murderers of journalists have never been investigated, let alone their perpetrators prosecuted, convicted or punished.[101]

Local journalists may be assuming added risk in this modern information war because more foreign bureaus have left countries where these conflicts have been occurring because of budget constraints. These domestic, indigenous, or local reporters become the only journalists telling some of the most difficult stories of our time. The Committee to Protect Journalists reports that in increasingly-violent Pakistan, local reporters regularly face threats from the Taliban and other militants while local journalists in Somalia, the Philippines, and Mexico have likewise suffered devastating losses.[102] In fact, INSI reported in October 2010 that more local journalists and media workers were killed in their own countries during what was considered "peace time" than during war.[103] These attacks have resulted in a chilling effect on journalists' ability to disseminate information not only about conflict but also about other issues like politics, human rights, and regional community affairs. While these journalists are more familiar with the local actors and stakeholders, they are often not trained in hostile environments. They often work for the international news agencies as freelance journalists, but they are not fully under the protection of international media institutions. More importantly, these freelancers often receive little attention when they become targets of unsavory forces—sometimes including government officials. Repressive regimes like China, Iran, and Burma (Myanmar) often find the fundamental job of the journalists contrary to the government's agenda. Thus, the war on words can be extraordinarily difficult on these reporters who are especially vulnerable to harassment, imprisonment, or targeted attacks.

While these attacks on journalists, both foreign and domestic, have been occurring for many years, reportage about journalists as targets has improved in the past 20 years. Organizations such as the Committee to Protect Journalists, Reporters sans Frontières, and the International News Safety Institute provide vociferous advocacy for journalists around the world. These organizations have been instrumental in shining a spotlight on this concern. Their successes have demonstrated that prolonged advocacy may be an effective tool to generate international concern about the protection of those who gather information about the world's problems and conflicts. These groups have been unforgiving in their proclamation that attacks against journalists should never go without investigation and should engender a high level of national and international scrutiny.

CPJ claimed in its most recent book that the "name and shame" approach that worked exceptionally well from the 1970s through the 1990s has held up as an effective tactic in demanding justification for repressive actions against journalists. The Committee stated that in the diffused Internet landscape new opportunities for advocacy campaigns have opened up. CPJ has imposed a great deal of international "name and shame" pressure on repressive governments from Iran to Gambia to the Philippines in recent years. "There is no doubt that international pressure played a role in the release of high-profile journalists such as *Newsweek* correspondent Maziar Bahari (Iranian-Canadian journalist, playwright, and filmmaker) and freelancer Roxana Saberi (Iranian-American)."[104] All told, CPJ said its advocacy efforts contributed to the release of 45 imprisoned journalists in 2009.[105]

The global media market's demand for news in real time has also been blamed for contributing to the growing number of journalists who find themselves targets in the world's battlefields. The advent of the 24-hour news cycle, the proliferation of online current affairs websites and blogs, as well as the rise of the cable news network have enhanced competition among news organizations and led to increasing pressure on journalists to supply stories more quickly. This phenomenon was first considered the "CNN effect" during and after the Gulf War in 1991. CNN, the U.S.

cable news operation, seemed to be everywhere, and wherever CNN went, all the other media outlets followed. This phenomenon relates to the effect of live and continuous television coverage of foreign affairs on the conduct of diplomacy and the waging of war. It is commonly argued that public intervention during the humanitarian crises in the 1990s, including Gulf War I and conflicts in the former Yugoslavia and Somalia, were partially driven by news media coverage of suffering people in these countries.[106]

Madeleine Albright, during her tenure as U.S. Ambassador to the United Nations in the early 1990s, said that CNN should become the 16th member of the UN Security Council. She was only half joking.[107] It was also reported that when Dick Cheney was Secretary of Defense in the first Bush administration, he often acknowledged that he received more timely and relevant information from CNN than from U.S. diplomats.[108] Secretary of State for then President George H.W. Bush, Lawrence S. Eagleburger, said that there was no question that 24-hour news images made a big difference in U.S. foreign policy in places like Somalia and the former Yugoslavia.[109]

In addition, newer communication technology in the battlefield—such as small, inexpensive digital audio and video cameras, satellite telephones, and laptop computers—not only suggested improved ways for the military to conduct its business but also enhanced the ability of journalists to upload feeds directly from a conflict zone. The media in this new information war were easily everywhere the military turned with a camera and a laptop ready to send home images and casualty counts, civilian and military. These advancements have contributed to the notion that the boundaries between the distinct role of the military and the media are blurring, and may contribute to increased danger for the media in the field.

Other challenges coupled with the vexing new wars, domestic politics, technological advancements, and the "CNN effect" have made the issue of protecting journalists during today's conflicts particularly complex.

Obstacles and Obfuscations

The work of telling the stories of war has changed, not only because of the content but also because of the people and relationships involved in reporting these stories. The relationships forged amid the background of conflict reporting demonstrate a dizzying array of complex interactions.

Most profound among these are the relationship between the sexes and the relationship between the media and the military. An examination follows of how women manage the complex obstacles placed upon them in this field and how all journalists engage their military counterparts. A glimpse into these complicated relationships among journalists covering conflict offers a broader understanding of the complex nature of the job and helps to clarify the issue of journalist protection.

War Stories from Women

Conflict is a gendered activity. Warriors traditionally have been men, and women remained home. Women and men have different access to resources, power, and decision-making before, after and during conflicts. This proclamation may be true in the developed world, but even more pronounced in the developing world, and profoundly true in many of parts of the world where overt and subversive conflict occur today. Women in conflict are often caught in a vicious paradox: while they are often the main victims of conflicts, they are often powerless to prevent them because they are being excluded from the negotiations. But this paradox is changing. Many powerful stakeholders in the world today are women. Women hold high offices in foreign ministries, in parliaments, and in village councils. Women, too, in large numbers are covering the world's conflicts.

The induction of woman into the ranks of war correspondents was slow. At the beginning of World War II, only 127 women obtained accreditation from the U.S. War Department, while U.S. military policy forbade women from covering combat until late in the war. U.S. female reporters were barred from press briefings, banned from going nearer to the front than the nurses in the field, and were not provided with transport by the military, unlike their male colleagues. Women reporters had to wait to submit their stories until after the men had submitted theirs. Similarly, when the British government accredited 558 writers, radio journalists, and photographers to cover the D-day landings, not one woman was included.[110]

Before the Vietnam War, only six percent of foreign correspondents were women. However, women correspondents went to Vietnam in unprecedented numbers in the 1970s. While military files are incomplete, available records indicate that more than 300 women were accredited to cover the war between 1965 and 1975.[111] Today, estimates suggest that more than one-third of international correspondents are women, and that same statistic holds true when observing the number of domestic women journalists.[112]

While the women who reported from the early wars of the last century are not as well known as the men, they forged a path for others. Women who are not household names but who risked their lives reporting from conflict include: Margaret Fuller, who reported for the *New York Tribune* from the revolution in Italy in the 1840s; Margaret Bourke-White, hired in 1935 as the first female photojournalist for *Life* magazine; American journalist Dorothy Thompson, who snared a scoop by interviewing an up-and-coming Adolf Hitler in 1931 for *Cosmopolitan* magazine; Oriana Fallaci, who reported from Vietnam; Linda Melvern, who chronicled the genocide in Rwanda; Molly Moore, who wrote about the First Gulf War; and Kate Adie, who reported from many international conflicts from Northern Ireland to Tiananmen Square, in China.[113]

More attention was directed toward women as frontline reporters in the 1990s. Women journalists found themselves covering conflict simply because there were more women in leadership positions in the world's newsrooms. But some women wanted to cover conflict and often found that their sex was an asset that led to greater access to untold stories. Maggie O'Kane, who reported during the Bosnian War for the *Guardian* in London, simply said, "I am a woman. Nobody pays attention to me."[114] former Reuter's photographer agreed, "The men in this region of the world don't take women seriously. And that can be an advantage. It can provide greater access."[115]

Cultural expectations may play a significant role in what many view as this advantage for women covering conflict. Men in the developing world, who tend to be the primary actors in today's conflicts, have been conditioned to view women as nonthreatening and powerless. Christiane Amanpour, perhaps the most recognized woman war reporter of our time, recalls with delight the treatment she and her fellow woman reporters received when on assignment in the Middle East:

> I remember then, as a junior reporter, not getting the plum assignment: Baghdad. I was sent to Saudi Arabia, where there was much commentary in the local press about CNN sending an all-girl team to the famously male-oriented kingdom. For not only was I the reporter, but our camera crew was also all female. It paid off, too. Far from being limited by our gender, we actually got some good scoops—like the first pictures of Saddam's tanks at the border between Saudi Arabia and Kuwait. That

happened because a prince took a shine to us girls and drove us in his personal fleet of cars past all the security and soldiers who had been instructed to send journalists back! The look on our much more experienced male colleagues back at base was a real sight![116]

However, it is not always such a cushy assignment for women. Women are not immune to violence, and they face significant threats that men do not, such as gender-based violence which can often compromise their health in different ways.

But many of the stakeholders in conflict resolution see women's participation as one of the key elements in promoting peace. In 2004, the Council of Europe called on its Parliamentary Assembly to recognize the role women play, in particular women journalists, in conflict prevention and resolution. In its final report, the Council claimed that war coverage by women correspondents "has changed significantly the accent of field reports. While male correspondents tend to focus on conflict and the positions of the parties of it, women look at the impact of the conflict on people's lives."[117] The assertion that women tell war stories differently from men has been a topic of much debate. Sherry Ricchiardi stated that the women she interviewed for an article about women and war reporting, believed that the reporting they were doing about the Balkans war delved more deeply into the human toll of the war than the stories filed by their male counterparts. But Ricchiaridi also found people who disagreed. Don Fry, a former associate at the Poynter Institute for Media Studies, told Ricchiardi that it was sexist to say that women and men write differently. "It's easy to equate men's writing with hard news and women's with features," he claimed.[118]

The report from the Council of Europe in 2004 also stated that "the appearance of women correspondents in the field pushes women to use the mass media to document their human rights violations and to promote peace-building, like in Bosnia, where women are using talk-shows on Resolution Radio to teach conflict-resolution skills." The report also recommended the importance of increasing women's access to media so that women's perspectives and women's voices can be part of the governance process in the world. Regardless of whether the participation of women reporters makes the job of protection more complex and perhaps more expensive, key operatives in world affairs find these contributions valuable and significant.

More recently, the International News Safety Institute conducted a survey of women reporting war.[119] It found that nearly all international war reporters who responded to the survey said they should be treated no differently from their male colleagues when it comes to the issue of safety conflict.[120]

The Military and the Media's Adversarial Relationship

The military and the media bring different values, weapons, and strategies to the battlefield. Reporters and soldiers face many of the same dangers, but they are charged with vastly different obligations. The military are under orders to deal directly with the enemy. The journalists ostensibly make their own decisions to proceed, and while they have a need to write about danger, they have no real duty to engage the enemy. The media want to tell the story, while the military wants to win the war.

Phillip Knightley, in *The First Casualty*, stated that war correspondents face a dilemma from the beginning because the individual reporter will always be challenged with the question: whose side is he or she on? This question has become increasingly relevant since the Vietnam War and in the new information wars of rapid technology and instantaneous information. The military would like to perform their operations as quickly as possible, with little intrusion from outsiders. At the same time, the media would like to observe and report quickly about military actions, bear witness, and record the first draft of history—believing that the pen may indeed be mightier than the sword. But critics often ask when journalists write objective and accurate accounts of the action, are they not hindering the work of the military? Conversely, when the military block the journalists' entry into the fray, are the officials not limiting the freedom for which they are reportedly fighting? Thus, the two great institutions, the media and the military, have developed a complex and sometimes adversarial relationship over the years. Tom DeFrank, of the *New York Daily News*, claims this is an "insoluble problem," likely to be around as long as conflict and war exist.[121]

As a result of this complicated relationship, governments and military leaders throughout the western world have learned to establish various levels of access to the media with regard to military operations. These stratified access determinations have resulted in frequent and vociferous response from the media and sporadic concern from the public. These various ways to categorize media access to military operations have been developed to include: virtual exclusion of reporters, pooled reporters, embedded reporters, and unilateral reporters who cover the conflict from both sides. Each of these categories could be expanded to include various levels of access and will be discussed later.

Thus, the changing relationship between the media and the military has resulted in a number of ways the two interact on the battlefield. Journalists can act as independents (also known as "unilaterals"), where the journalist is totally divorced from military protection or acknowledgement, or the journalist can decide to engage in a serious relationship with the military and abide by press pools or the embedded arrangement. Some of the benefits and challenges of these arrangements: press pools, embedding and nonembedding, will now be explored.

Press Pools

When the British military responded to the Argentine invasion of the Falkland Islands in the South Atlantic in 1982, they took along 29 British correspondents who were corralled into what they called "press pools." This was considered the first instance of pool reporting where journalists selected by the military were allowed to accompany the troops into battle. The *New York Times* reported that non-British journalists were not permitted to set foot on the Islands during this invasion.[122] The foreign media from the United States and other countries received their information from one of the pooled British Reuters correspondents. The accreditation system for determining which journalists would be selected for this assignment was considered by many, especially non-British, to be flawed. Military censors controlled much of the information disseminated so when journalists accepted the constraints of the pool system, they rejected one of the primary tenets of journalism: independence. Watching the action from another reporter's camera or taking notes from an official televised briefing was not like the work of foreign correspondents of the past.

When the U.S. forces invaded the Caribbean island of Grenada in October 1983, the U.S. military initially did not allow the press access to the invasion at all. During the first 24 hours of the invasion, 600 reporters attempted to gain access to the operation.[123] However, reporters who sought to cover the military action were not permitted to go to Grenada. They were kept on a military base on Barbados, a location more than 100 miles away. After the invasion was completed, the U.S. military created a pool system whereby a limited number of correspondents would be allowed in combat areas accompanied by military escorts. The military eventually allowed fifteen reporters and photographers to travel to the island where the journalists were taken to preselected sites. The pool arrived more than 48 hours after the invasion began. These selected reporters were taken on a bus tour, none of which included areas of fighting.[124]

Another example of the pool system occurred in 1989 when U.S. forces invaded Panama to capture dictator Manuel Noriega. More than 800 reporters eventually arrived to cover the action. However, just 12 members of a pool team landed at a U.S. air base four hours after hostilities began, and these journalists were not allowed to leave the base as it was deemed unsafe for them to travel the streets.[125] The military also refused to take the pool to cover any direct fighting that occurred. The military officers argued that they feared for the journalists' safety.[126] Because of the lack of eyewitness reporting, controversies emerged and protests ensued as a result of the tactics used during the conflict in Panama.

In response to these protests, U.S. General Colin Powell sent a memo to the Joint Chiefs of Staff to outline rules for future engagement with the media:

> The recent DOD [Department of Defense] national media pool deployment to Panama for Operation Just Cause was its first deployment to cover an actual deployment operation. A DOD analysis of the deployment, which included comments from the reporters in the Panama pool and the commands involved and the military escorts, revealed several areas that need to be improved in the operation.[127]

Powell stated that the number of journalists who arrived at the military operations overwhelmed the assets available to support them during both the Grenada and Panama conflicts. However, Powell insisted military operations are not considered successful unless all media aspects are properly handled. He stated, "Commanders are reminded that media aspects of military operations are important."[128] Powell's memo contained specific directives that operation commanders follow in the future to ensure the media are properly accommodated during conflicts.

During the troop buildup for the Gulf War in 1991, more than 1,400 journalists descended on Saudi Arabia in an effort to cover the war. The journalists acquired the bulk of their information from military briefings, interviews arranged with military personnel, or through pooled activity. Only 200 journalists were selected as pool members.[129] Critics of the pool system claimed the pool reports were useless and "90 percent junk."[130]

Embedded Journalists

It seemed no one was pleased with the operation of the press pools during the first Gulf War. So, the U.S. Pentagon developed a system of media access, known as "embedding," in Iraq in 2003. The idea of embedding journalists with the troops was presented to the media by Pentagon spokesperson Victoria Clarke—who remarkably worked for the public relations firm that devised the false baby-incubator story from the First Gulf War.[131] In the Pentagon's "Media Embed Ground Rules" presented on March 3, 2003, the media were promised more uncensored access to the fight if the United States took military action against Iraq.[132] The Ground Rules stated:

> Our ultimate strategic success in bringing peace and security to this region will come in our long-term commitment to supporting our democratic ideals. We need to tell the factual story—good or bad—before others seed the media with disinformation and distortions.[133]

More than 800 journalists signed up to be embedded with military units, anxious to get an opportunity to obtain a close-up view of combat. Most of them did. This embed program allowed media to integrate with military units and supplied the journalists with transportation, escorts, medical attention and rations as well as other amenities. However, embedded media were not authorized to use their own vehicles and were required to stay with their assigned units for the duration of their stay.[134] It has been posited by media critic Douglas Kellner, that the embedded reporters were "gung-ho cheerleaders" who spun the military's war story in Iraq and lost any veneer of objectivity.[135] Other critics referred to the embed program as a Faustian Pact or simply a bargain with the devil. But some journalists reported that there was no other way to safely cover a conflict of this nature. Photojournalist Robert Nickelsberg was reported to be a "fan" of the embedding process. He said:

> If you don't embed, good luck covering a conflict at least where the Americans are involved. And right now in Afghanistan you can't go 100 kilometers from the capitol without being with the military. If you do, you're very lucky. Remember, it's very easy to go half of the journey—out. The toughest part is coming back. They are going to know about it ... whoever may not want you out there. And it's such a risk; it's foolhardy to try it.[136]

The embed program continues to be debated and has left many critics to question whether the journalists' direct connection with the military led to the greatest truth about war or offered the journalists the only alternative to cover the conflict. Iraq has been considered one of the new wars, as it was replete with journalists being deliberately targeted, kidnapped, and executed by insurgents.[137] Examples include *Christian Science Monitor* reporter Jill Carroll and NBC correspondent Ned Colt. This increase in kidnappings led to more journalists working as embedded rather than as unilateral reporters.[138]

CNN consultant and retired general, Wesley Clark, initially favored the embed program, admitting that restricting journalists during the 1991 Gulf War was a "huge mistake."[139] On the other side of the issue was veteran war correspondent Chris Hedges who criticized the embedded program as insidious and predicted it would result in a sense of "false loyalty."[140] Other criticisms focus on the perceived lack of neutrality the embed program presents to civilians and insurgents. This program also begs the question as to whether the journalist traveling with a military unit is protected as a civilian or may be treated as military personnel with regard to the Geneva Conventions. While controversial, this program may have protected and saved the lives of those who reported from this particular conflict. The question remains as to whether the embed program will become the normative way to report from areas of armed conflict when established militaries are involved.

Unilaterals

Journalists and journalism organizations that have concluded that the embed system may be as restrictive as the press pool system have opted instead to report as "unilaterals"—or journalists who travel the countryside of a conflict unencumbered by any relationship to the military. This kind of hardy, rogue journalist, like Harrison Evans Salisbury, has always been around, but the practice of unaffiliated conflict journalism began in earnest during the Gulf War in the 1990s. Many reasons exist for not venturing into dangerous armed conflicts without support. But one of the primary reasons to explore this option refers back to that journalistic tenet of independence and its relationship to truth.

The seriously unstable security situation in Iraq and the wide use of the embed program resulted in fewer independent journalists covering the conflict.[141] Often when unilaterals traveled to the region, they were accompanied by private security firms hired by their news organization. It has been reported that this practice of hiring armed guards can be dangerous for all journalists because armed guards may diminish the veneer of journalist neutrality. During the first month of the Iraqi war, an agent from a private security company accompanying a CNN team to northern Iraq responded with automatic weapons fire after the convoy of several vehicles was shot at on the outskirts of the town. According to Robert Ménard, Secretary-General of Reporters sans Frontières:

> Such a practice sets a dangerous precedent that could jeopardize all other journalists covering this war as well as others in the future . . . there is a real risk that combatants will henceforth assume that all press vehicles are armed. . . . employing private security firms that do not hesitate to use their firearms just increases the confusion between reporters and combatants.[142]

In addition, it has been reported that the guards may not be conversant with international humanitarian law, or may be willing to use force in response to perceived threats.[143]

Not all journalists in Iraq were embedded or unilateral. Andrew M. Lindner argued in 2009 that two distinct alternatives to embedded journalists existed: Baghdad-stationed reporters and complete independents.[144] How this stratification of media access affects freedom of expression or the media's ability to effectively communicate accurate stories of war during conflict continues to be a much debated topic.

The complex relationships surrounding the protection of journalists in armed conflict and dangerous situations will continue to evolve, and new issues will no doubt emerge. Whether or not the presence of women reporters changes the nature of war reporting will continue to be debated. And the relationship between the media and the military will continue to unfold and recoil whenever the two rely on each other. Despite these integral interactions, the question remains how these men and women who report about the world's conflicts should ultimately be protected from risk.

How in the World Do We Protect the Journalists?

Evidence presented above suggests that a free press contributes to the foundation of democracy and, as such, it has an essential role to play during conflicts or during times of turmoil within a country. Subject matter, audiences, transmission devices, ways to tell these war stories, and the complex relationship between the military and the media have evolved and virtually transformed the impact these kinds of stories have on the world. Along the way, the world's journalists have been considered friends as well as enemies. Since the Crimean War, war stories have influenced public opinion about war and therefore the path of conflict. This process has played a profound role in the history of international conflict and thus the history of the contemporary world. Similarly, journalists reporting from local conflicts have altered the way democratic governments have evolved and matured.

The data also suggested that early in the evolution of war stories, rigorous research demonstrated that these journalistic stories could be effective tools for public persuasion, and systematic maneuvers were developed to enhance or mitigate their effect. In addition, Marshall McLuhan, a famous Canadian media critic, remarked about the power of war stories when he proclaimed, "Television brought the brutality of war into the comfort of the living room. Vietnam was lost in the living rooms of America—not on the battlefields of Vietnam."[145] Likewise, when asked what caused the fall of Communism in Eastern Europe, former Polish president Lech Walesa pointed to a television set and proclaimed, "It all came from there ... especially radio (which) brought information prohibited in our country."[146]

New technology played its most felicitous role in bringing the world to action. "Satellites have no respect for political boundaries,"[147] said Newton Minow, former chairman of the U.S. Federal Communications Commission in 1991. "Satellites cannot be stopped by Berlin Walls, by tanks in Tiananmen Square or by dictators in Baghdad. In Manila, Warsaw, and Bucharest, we saw the television station become today's Electronic Bastille."[148]

Despite the spread of information about conflict or the reporting of internal national corruption, the debate continues as to whether reporting about conflict has provoked or prevented wars or if it has saved citizens from hostile regimes such as Egypt. But one indisputable result of the power of journalism in recent decades has been the trend to transform reporters from dispatchers into targets—from government watchdogs to scapegoats.

This chapter explained that the reward of promoting democracy has carried with it the risk of life and livelihood. What is primarily at stake now is how the international community will ultimately devise methods to protect journalists in view of these escalated threats. This critical question is one of paramount importance to all citizens who wish to participate in a world that affirms the democratic process.

The next chapter will explore international humanitarian laws and other policies initiated by governments to protect journalists and thus the spread of democratic values and human rights around the world.

Chapter 2

Measures of Civility: Legal Protections Developed for Journalists Reporting from Danger Zones

Policies and laws dictate behaviors and practice from trade to conflict. These policies and laws originate with international bodies, states, or municipal governments. In the past century, policymakers have taken steps to make the practice of freedom of expression a universal doctrine. Promoting this doctrine around the world has been challenging in many aspects. One particular challenge has been how to protect journalists, who are the prime practitioners of this freedom of expression, when they report from areas of chaos or corruption. Laws, rules, doctrines, and resolutions are explored later in an effort to illuminate what formal procedures have been implemented to protect journalists around the world. These formal laws have faced challenges including: how to define a journalist, what constitutes a journalist's role in conflict, and who is a combatant and who is a civilian during armed conflict. Finally, the vast disparity in how nations appreciate the role of the press in good governance makes the design of universal policies to guard journalists difficult.

The following pages will offer a glimpse at how formal laws, policies, resolutions, conventions, and declarations have been debated and determined with regard to the protection of journalists worldwide. In addition, the authors examine a unique national law recently implemented in the United States that may signal a new bold step in how nations might contribute to formally recognizing protection of press freedom, not only within but also beyond their own borders.

International Humanitarian Law

Combatants engaged in the act of warfare have been limited by codes of conduct for centuries. As early as the sixth century, Sun Tzu in his treatise, *The Art of War,* suggested ethical and moral limitations on how wars should be conducted. These basic thoughts have been reconstructed and developed into codes of practice that fall under the title of international humanitarian law, which is ostensibly the law of armed conflict and its effects. The goal of international humanitarian law focuses primarily on the protection of the two main actors in war: the military and the civilians. These laws strive to limit the brutal effects of war on people and property and are designed to protect vulnerable persons. The codes also ensure protection for those who care for the wounded on the battlefield.

Various national and international humanitarian laws have been devised to protect actors on the battlefield. These laws or codes can take the form of treaties, international agreements, protocols, covenants, conventions, declarations, or resolutions. The countries that sign up to participate in these laws adopt, ratify, and finally become signatories to the agreements. These codes then become binding simply through mutual agreement.

Unfortunately, journalists and media workers are not often directly named as actors in warfare, so they are not eligible for special protection. However, many of these laws have proffered strong suggestions to recognize the journalists who play a unique and essential role during wartime. Despite national differences, the international community has long recognized that accurate and impartial reporting about internal and international conflicts serves fundamental public interest. The information gathered by media workers and journalists during conflicts has had a profound impact on the outcome of the world's conflicts, often by exposing serious abuses of human rights. Recent evidence suggests that the work journalists do during conflict makes them increasingly vulnerable to either governments or nonstate actors trying to silence them.

The paramount challenge for those developing international humanitarian laws remains how to define and categorize the journalist in the battlefield. By the very nature of their work, the categorization of journalists and media workers seems to fall between the two main actors in conflict—soldiers and civilians. As a result, questions have arisen as to whether the journalist should be protected as an innocent bystander or, in fact, a willing participant in the military's purposes. Civilians can be innocent bystanders but may also be used as human shields by opposing forces. Conversely, journalists are not like civilians in that journalists do not run away but toward a conflict situation. But, they are also unlike military personnel because the journalist is not a combatant in the conflict. This confusion over how to categorize the journalist has led to much debate in the international community with regard to how journalists should be protected by international humanitarian law.

The most well known of these humanitarian laws to protect all participants on the battlefield are the Geneva Conventions, first signed in 1864 to formally protect the sick and wounded and those who cared for them under the sign of the Red Cross.[1] Since then the Geneva Conventions have been updated to include significant moral and ethical measures of civility on the world's battlefields. The Geneva Conventions of today have been ratified by 194 states making these rules of conduct on the battlefield globally applicable.[2]

Centuries ago, war correspondents primarily risked being mistaken for spies or shot by a stray bullet. Today, the experience of being a journalist in a conflict region amid the "new wars" of the late twentieth and early twenty-first centuries is significantly different. War correspondents who covered the world wars of the last century faced constraints and censorship from military authorities or the government, but they rarely faced the new form of crude censorship from combatants—harassment, kidnapping, and murder.

While several state solutions to protect journalists who participate in dangerous assignments were introduced as early as the 1920s, those strategies were reflective of the warfare and the media technology in place during the first half of the twentieth century. These solutions did not take into account what has since been learned about the strategic, rhetorical, and political power of the media during conflict. Likewise, no one could predict the enormous transformations that have occurred in the ability to gather and transmit information in this new century.

Given the increased risk for journalists reporting from conflict zones and the increased impact this reporting has had on society, a number of international discussions have focused on the international community's responsibility to protect journalists. Prominent individuals, major journalism protection associations, media companies, and global nongovernmental organizations have recognized the importance of protecting those who gather information about conflict, both regionally and internationally. In order to assess international humanitarian law and how these measures of civility of warfare affect today's journalists, one should examine three things:

- First, one should understand how journalists fit into the components of international humanitarian law protection policies;
- One also should observe how some policymakers have attempted to single out journalists for special protections beyond those humanitarian laws designed specifically for civilians;
- Finally, it is important to discuss the challenges to the development of international humanitarian law to protect journalists in today's conflicts.

Development of International Legal Protection for Journalists

Journalists who follow ethical codes of conduct and pursue stories fairly and accurately should be protected regardless of where they practice their profession. Few would argue that fact. However, because of divergent views on the proper role of the press, the world community has often debated exactly how laws should be developed and implemented to protect journalists who participate, by the nature of their work, in dangerous conflict situations. The following pages explore the evolution of international humanitarian law and how journalists have been included in these laws discussed and developed by states and the international community.

It is important to recognize the distinction between international humanitarian law and international human rights law. The difference is subtle. Despite the concern of both areas for legal protection of human beings, their scope is slightly different. International human rights encompass laws that protect all people, in times of war as well as peace. International humanitarian law applies to specific codes of practice with regard to situations of armed conflict. International humanitarian law aims to limit the suffering caused by war by forcing parties engaged in a conflict to:

- Engage in limited methods and means of warfare;
- Differentiate between civilian population and combatants, and work to spare civilian population and property;
- Abstain from harming or killing an adversary who surrenders or who can no longer take part in the fighting;
- Abstain from physically or mentally torturing or performing cruel punishments on adversaries.[3]

Codes of conduct on the battlefield have been adhered to for centuries but have varied from conflict to conflict, country to country, and century to century. Various treaties and less binding interstate agreements governed how combatants conducted their wars. Then in the nineteenth century the founder of the International Committee of the Red Cross, Henry Dunant, devised a universal code of practice for warfare called the Geneva Convention of 1864. Numerous other Conventions and Additional Protocols have sprung from this original document.

The Hague Convention of 1899 was the first time that the protection of journalists was mentioned under international humanitarian law.[4] These Conventions were primarily concerned with how journalists would be treated if they became prisoners of war, but they also included some guidance on the appropriate treatment for war correspondents. Aspects of the Hague Conventions of 1899 and 1907 which related to journalists were added into the Geneva Convention of 1929, which stated:

> Persons who follow the armed forces without directly belonging thereto, such as correspondents, newspaper reporters, sutlers [vendors], or contractors, who fall into the hands of the enemy, and whom the latter think fit to detain, shall be entitled to be treated as prisoners of war, provided that they are in possession of an authorisation from the military authorities of the armed forces which they are following.[5]

This section of the Convention stipulated that the contemporary journalist was to be considered a quasi member of the armed forces when captured as a prisoner-of-war. However, the journalist at this time would be assured protection only if he or she could present proper identification in the form of a press card. The Geneva Conventions recognized that a journalist covering conflict was not a soldier, but rather a civilian member of the military performing an officially sanctioned role in an organized military force. It was not until 1949 that journalists were no longer required to carry identity cards in order to receive the protection of the law. The legislators relaxed this requirement as they thought it was probable that the journalist might lose the card during the events of the Second World War. Journalists who wished to be "accredited correspondents" still needed permission from the armed forces if they were planning to cover conflict. Captured war correspondents were to be given the same treatment as prisoners of war: they were not required to respond to interrogation, and, if they were sick or wounded, they were entitled to prompt medical treatment.[6]

The international community made great strides to foster freedom of information and open channels of communication when the United Nations proposed, and the world community adopted, the Universal

Declaration of Human Rights in 1948. This multilateral arrangement provided, in Article 19, that all people in the world have the freedom to think and express ideas through any media, regardless of frontiers or situations. Accordingly, the international community proclaimed two fundamental rights used by journalists to be protected by this declaration: the right to communicate information and news and the right to receive information and news.

In the 1970s, the United Nations was again called upon to create special protection mechanisms for journalists in conflict situations, but with mixed results. The French Minister of Foreign Affairs called for the UN General Assembly to review a draft resolution, supported by a number of delegations, which addressed the situations of journalists in armed conflict.[7] The General Assembly subsequently directed the Economic and Social Council and the Human Rights Commission to draft a convention providing for the specific protection of journalists on dangerous missions. The Human Rights Commission requested the International Committee of the Red Cross (ICRC) and other groups to contribute to this discussion. The ICRC developed guidelines it thought would contribute to a solution to the problem of journalists' protection.[8] After reviewing these guidelines, the Human Rights Commission submitted a draft convention which outlined two safety mechanisms to the United National General Assembly in 1971: an identity card and a distinctive armband for journalists.[9] The fundamental idea was to designate a special status for journalists consistent with medical, religious, and civil defense staff, like the Red Cross. The majority of participants from the United Nations Conference of Government Experts welcomed the proposal to provide special protection for journalists. The participants engaged in consensus around the importance of transmitting as much information as possible during armed conflict.[10]

But a significant controversy arose in the committee discussion. One national delegation proposed that the journalists should only be protected if they wore protective gear and visibly displayed an orange armband while covering conflict. Others found this provision absurd. "This proposal was rejected primarily on the basis of the following argument: by making the wearer of the armlet conspicuous to combatants, such means of identification might make the journalists' mission even more dangerous; similarly it was argued that in this way the journalists would be likely to endanger the surrounding civilian population."[11] Debates also ensued with regard to the press identity card, however, little evidence exists except to note that the specific provisions offered by the ICRC and the Human Rights Commission were eventually tabled, and journalists were not given a special status of protection. Despite the disagreements and controversy, a significant section was added to the Geneva Conventions of 1949 that related to the protection of victims of international armed conflict or Protocol I that was titled, "Article 79, Measures of Protection for Journalists."[12]

This section of the Geneva Conventions recognized journalists as civilians, to be afforded only those protections given to civilians in combat zones. Article 79 specifically stated:

- Journalists engaged in dangerous professional missions in areas of armed conflict shall be considered civilians within the meaning of the Conventions;
- Journalists shall be protected as civilians provided that they take no action adversely affecting their status as civilians, and without prejudice to the right of war correspondents accredited to the armed forces to the status provided for in Article 4 (A) (4) of the Third Convention;
- Journalists should obtain an identity card. This card, which shall be issued by the government of the state of which the journalist is a national or in whose territory he resides or in which the news medium employing him is located, shall attest to his status as a journalist.[13]

This international provision clearly designated journalists as civilians and not combatants. Journalists, therefore, would lose protection granted to them under the 1977 Additional Protocol I if they dressed too similarly to military officers in the field as this would blur the principle of distinction on the ground, as defined by Article 48 of Additional Protocol I.[14]

During the early 1980s, significant global discussion occurred about the role of media in society. The United Nations Educational, Scientific and Cultural Organization (UNESCO) convened a panel of distinguished consultants, led by Irish Nobel Laureate Seán MacBride, to analyze the problems of the news and media in modern society.[15] The group addressed myriad issues, including the rights and responsibilities of journalists as well as their protection. The committee envisioned protection of journalists to include physical protection and also cover the protection of the professional independence and integrity of those involved in the collection and dissemination of news, information and views to the public.[16] While this discussion and resulting text signaled the beginning of the New World Information Order, the debate did not materially affect the protection of journalists in reporting from dangerous situations.

Under the Geneva Conventions today, journalists are entitled to the same rights and protections granted civilians in armed conflicts—no more, no less. This protection helps journalists because attacks directed against civilians or civilian objects are considered illegal under international humanitarian law. This is known as the principle of distinction and forms the foundation of international humanitarian law.[17] The Geneva Conventions insist that a variety of precautionary measures must be taken in military operations to spare civilians and civilian objects from indiscriminate attacks.[18] This means that journalists cannot be used as hostages or human shields,[19] nor can they be made the object of reprisals.[20]

Journalists and media workers are considered protected as civilians as long as they do not take part in direct hostilities. Civilians, and thus journalists by extension, also have the added protection of the Rome Statute of the International Criminal Court. The ICC was established in 2002 as the first court of its kind designed to end impunity for perpetrators of the most egregious crimes of concern to the international community. The International Criminal Court counts 113 nations among its state parties who agree to abide by the Rome Statute—the United States not among them. The ICC is not part of the UN but maintains a close relationship with it. Article 68 (1) of the Rome Statute provides that the Court shall take appropriate measures to protect the safety, physical and psychological well-being, dignity and privacy of victims and witnesses and holds that any direct action against civilians constitutes a war crime, whether the armed conflict occurs in an international or an internal dispute.[21]

Although the Geneva Conventions and their Additional Protocols contain only two explicit references to media personnel—Article 4A of the Third Geneva Convention and Article 79 of Additional Protocol I—ICRC Legal Adviser Robin Geiss asserted that if one reads these provisions in conjunction with other humanitarian rules, it shows that existing law is quite comprehensive for the protection of journalists.[22] According to Geiss, the most important section is Article 79 of Additional Protocol I, which provides journalists entitlement to all rights and protections granted to civilians in international armed conflicts.[23]

However, not everyone is convinced that this legal protection translates into practical protection on the ground. At a media workshop on international humanitarian law in Nigeria in 2000, arguments raged among participants over whether two Nigerian journalists, murdered in 1990, could have been saved if the Geneva Conventions of 1949 and the two 1977 Additional Protocols had designated a special status for journalists. The workshop was organized by the Nigerian Red Cross Society in conjunction with the ICRC and ended with journalists unanimously agreeing that international conventions and protocols do not protect war correspondents in any practical manner. ICRC's Chief of Information, Alain Modoux said, "States do not feel that journalists require any special privileges and/or special guarantees to enable them to do their work in spite of the fact that their profession is dangerous."[24] Modoux asserted that journalists have an especially important role in ensuring greater respect of international humanitarian law through their reports and broadcasts about the horrors of war, and, as such, deserve better protection. However, Patrick Megévand, a Dissemination Delegate of the ICRC and Abdullahi Bawa, a National Dissemination and Information Officer of the Nigerian Red Cross Society, asserted that establishing a special status would be counterproductive. He claimed that such a designation of special protection as afforded by an emblem, would lead to easy identification by belligerents intent on silencing journalists. Therefore, it was determined to be unlikely that the two Nigerian journalists, who were killed covering the Liberian crisis, would have been saved with a special status, considering the slant of the Nigerian press coverage of the Liberian war.[25]

As current humanitarian law now stands, journalists seeking to uncover the truths of war are considered like any other civilian in an armed conflict. No added protection under international humanitarian law is afforded the journalistic function of seeking accounts of war. However, within the last few decades, international initiatives such as declarations and resolutions have been introduced by policymakers around the world in an attempt to address what they consider this shortcoming in the law.

Other International Initiatives

In addition to formal treaties calling for multilateral participation, other international initiatives have been introduced to offer protection for journalists in conflicts. These initiatives do not carry the full weight of signed treaties, but represent concerted efforts of national and international policymakers to design legally binding protections for journalists and media workers.

Declarations

Although the United Nations Treaty Reference Guide describes a declaration as an international instrument that is not always legally binding, declarations can be considered treaties in the generic sense and are often intended to be binding as international law.[26] Declarations tend to draw attention to various issues and problems that organizations believe need to be addressed by the international community.

Several organizations have advocated for increased press protection through written declarations. In 1996, on World Press Freedom Day, the Council of Europe adopted a declaration and recommendation on the protection of journalists in situations of conflict.[27] In this declaration, the Committee of Ministers of the Council of Europe reaffirmed that all journalists have rights that should be upheld during war. It also advocated for survival or specific hostile environment training and equipment like flak jackets and helmets for the physical protection of journalists.[28]

Four years later, during a roundtable discussion arranged by the Organization for Security and Cooperation in Europe (OSCE), the Berlin Declaration was estabilshed.[29] This declaration pressed for enhanced efforts by governments to investigate the murders of journalists and reaffirmed that targeting journalists is unacceptable. At the forum, participating media professionals and officials encouraged news organizations to provide insurance, safety training, and equipment for their staff. Participants agreed to continue discussing media safety with the OSCE, UN, and the Council of Europe in addition to other relevant international organizations.[30]

Three years later, in 2003, Reporters sans Frontières (RSF) advocated for a declaration on the safety of journalists and media personnel in situations of armed conflict. The declaration reaffirmed basic principles of international humanitarian law and stressed that journalists should be protected as civilians in wartime and that media equipment should not be attacked.[31]

During World Press Freedom Day in 2007, the international community specifically addressed press freedom, safety of journalists, and impunity for those who target journalists. It was the 10th anniversary of the UNESCO/Guillermo Cano Press Freedom Prize, so this year

World Press Freedom Day was celebrated in Medellin, Columbia, to honor Guillermo Cano. Cano was assassinated in 1986 by hired killers for his fearless denunciation of drug trafficking mobsters.[32] On this day, the United Nations Educational, Scientific, and Cultural Organization (UNESCO), created the *Medellin Declaration* committed to securing the safety of journalists.[33] This *Declaration* addresses concerns regarding attacks on freedom of the press including murder, abductions, hostage taking, intimidation, and illegal arrests and detention of journalists, media professionals, and associated personnel. It also calls on news associations to promote actions that secure the safety of journalists, including access to safety training, health care and life insurance for freelancers and staff.[34]

Resolutions

Whereas declarations serve as a call to action, resolutions are considered a formal expression of opinion, will, or intention by an official body and are often legally binding.[35] Prior to resolutions being implemented, organizations request these resolutions from international governmental bodies. The resolutions are then discussed by experts and brought to a larger body for a vote.

In 2003, the International Federation of Journalists (IFJ) called for a United Nations resolution that would provide the same protections to journalists as currently exist for aid workers. The IFJ argued that this resolution was necessary to modify the Geneva Conventions and Additional Protocols to make the targeting of journalists a specific war crime.[36]

The IFJ revisited the possibility of a resolution again in November 2005 in a draft text presented to UN Secretary-General Kofi Annan at the World Electronic Media Forum. The resolution requested Annan to:

> Address in all his country-specific situation reports, the issue of the safety and security of journalists, media staff and associated personnel including specific acts of violence against such personnel, remedial actions taken to prevent similar incidents and actions taken to identify and hold accountable those who commit such acts, and to explore and propose additional ways and means to enhance the safety and security of such personnel.[37]

In the following year, two international resolutions that are most prized for their attention to journalists' protection were subsequently adopted. In December 2006, the United Nations Security Council unanimously adopted *Resolution 1738*. In this resolution, the Security Council formally condemns attacks on journalists in conflict situations.[38] This resolution calls on countries to put an end to deliberate attacks on the news media in armed conflicts and urges an end to impunity for those who kill journalists. Specifically *Resolution 1738*:

1. *Condemns* intentional attacks against journalists, media professionals and associated personnel, as such, in situations of armed conflict, and calls upon all parties to put an end to such practices;
2. *Recalls* in this regard that journalists, media professionals and associated personnel engaged in dangerous professional missions in areas of armed conflict shall be considered as civilians and shall be respected and protected as such, provided that they take no action adversely affecting their status as civilians. This is without prejudice to the right of war correspondents accredited to the armed forces to the status of prisoners of war provided for in article 4.A.4 of the Third Geneva Convention;
3. *Recalls also* that media equipment and installations constitute civilian objects, and in this respect shall not be the object of attack or of reprisals, unless they are military objectives;
4. *Reaffirms* its condemnation of all incitements to violence against civilians in situations of armed conflict, further reaffirms the need to bring to justice, in accordance with applicable international law, individuals who incite such violence, and indicates its willingness, when authorizing missions, to consider, where appropriate, steps in response to media broadcast inciting genocide, crimes against humanity and serious violations of international humanitarian law;
5. *Recalls its demand* that all parties to an armed conflict comply fully with the obligations applicable to them under international law related to the protection of civilians in armed conflict, including journalists, media professionals and associated personnel;
6. *Urges* States and all other parties to an armed conflict to do their utmost to prevent violations of international humanitarian law against civilians, including journalists, media professionals and associated personnel;
7. *Emphasizes* the responsibility of States to comply with the relevant obligations under international law to end impunity and to prosecute those responsible for serious violations of international humanitarian law;
8. *Urges* all parties involved in situations of armed conflict to respect the professional independence and rights of journalists, media professionals and associated personnel as civilians;
9. *Recalls* that the deliberate targeting of civilians and other protected persons, and the commission of systematic, flagrant and widespread violations of

international humanitarian and human rights law in situations of armed conflict may constitute a threat to international peace and security, and *reaffirms in this regard its readiness* to consider such situations and, where necessary, to adopt appropriate steps;

10. *Invites* States which have not yet done so to consider becoming parties to the Additional Protocols I and II of 1977 to the Geneva Conventions at the earliest possible date;

11. *Affirms* that it will address the issue of protection of journalists in armed conflict strictly under the agenda item "protection of civilians in armed conflict;"

12. *Requests* the Secretary-General to include as a sub-item in his next reports on the protection of civilians in armed conflict the issue of the safety and security of journalists, media professionals and associated personnel."[39]

Resolution 1738 marks a concerted effort by the international community to address the plight of media workers in conflict situations. According to the International News Safety Institute (INSI), proposals from the International Federation of Journalists (IFJ), the European Broadcasting Union (EBU), and the International News Safety Institute led to the drafting and passing of this Security Council Resolution.[40] In addition, Reporters sans Frontières acknowledged the efforts by the French Foreign Minister and French diplomats in initiating and securing the passage of the resolution.[41]

Less than a month later, the Council of Europe passed a similar resolution, known as *Resolution 1535: Threats to the lives and freedom of expression of journalists,* which addressed safety of journalists in peacetime as well as war. In this resolution, the Council of Europe called on national parliaments to respect freedom of expression and to protect journalists from intimidation and political threats. The Council resolved to establish a specific monitoring mechanism for identifying and analyzing attacks on the lives and freedom of expression of journalists in Europe as well as the progress made by national law enforcement authorities and parliaments in their investigations of attacks made against journalists.[42] This resolution states: "The Assembly believes that fully representative, independent organisations and unions of journalists are an important form of protection for freedom of expression and rejects any concept of state licensing or control over the profession of journalism."[43]

Most recently, in March 2010, a resolution was adopted by the UN Human Rights Council reaffirming the role of journalists and media workers in conflict and addressing the increasing numbers of press workers killed and injured while working in conflict.[44] The resolution, co-sponsored by Egypt, Mexico and Bangladesh, called for a panel discussion to be held during the Human Rights Council's Fourteenth Session in June 2010. The purpose of the panel was to:

- Draw the international community's attention to the dangers faced by journalists in armed conflicts;
- Take an "inventory" of existing international agreements and whether they were implemented; and
- Contribute to the development of a response by the Human Rights Council.[45]

The panel began with the United Nations Deputy High Commissioner for Human Rights, Kyung-wha Kang stating that despite international law protection of journalists in armed conflict, journalists continue to be targets of abuse by actors who enjoy impunity.[46]

This was the first time since the 1970s that such a formal discussion was convened to address specifically the protection of journalists in conflict. Members of the international panel included Frank La Rue, the Special Rapporteur on the promotion and protection of the right to freedom of opinion and expression; Robin Geiss, Legal Adviser to the ICRC; Mogens Schmidt, Deputy Assistant of the Director-General for Communication and Information and Director of the Division for Freedom of Expression, Democracy and Peace, at UNESCO; Osama Saraya, Editor-in-Chief of *Al Ahram* Newspaper; Omar Faruk Osman, President of the Federation of African Journalists; and Hedayat Abdel Nabi, President of Press Emblem Campaign.[47]

LaRue said that states have a threefold obligation to respect, protect, and fulfill the right of freedom of expression. He added, "Preventing impunity functions as the most important deterrent against the repetition of attacks on journalists, and effective investigation of attacks and prosecution of persons responsible is in itself a means of protecting journalists."[48]

Geiss said that the ICRC remained deeply concerned by the high number of violent and deliberate attacks against journalists, media professionals, and associated personnel in international and noninternational conflicts.[49]

Another panelist at the June 2010 meeting, Omar Faruk Osman, said that African journalists' predicament today was complicated by the fact that in many conflict and nonconflict countries, reporters encounter not only repressive national governments but also armed gangs and militias. "The Horn of Africa was a place where to choose to become society's messenger was often equated with choosing martyrdom," he said.[50] He called on the Human Rights Council to send a clear message that it would not remain idle while journalists continued to be subjected to violent and unjustified attacks.[51]

Hedayat Abdel Nabi, President of the Press Emblem Campaign, requested that a working group be convened to develop guidelines that would lead to a global compact for the promotion and protection of journalists. Such guidelines would seek to guarantee unhindered, unfettered, and uninterrupted Internet services anytime and under all conditions and circumstances. The PEC retained the belief that a protective emblem for journalists is necessary to show that journalists are protected by international law. Such an emblem would carry with it the right for compensation and combat impunity.[52]

Throughout the panel discussion, speakers emphasized the changing nature of warfare and the need to reevaluate norms and standards, to redesign aspects of international humanitarian law and for the international community to consider seriously what could be done to afford journalists greater protection. The panelists emphasized the importance of establishing prevention mechanisms to support the safety of journalists and criminal justice reform to support effective investigations and prosecutions of attacks and killings against journalists. They noted that putting an end to impunity might be the best way to protect journalists and media professionals, and they said they hoped that holding an international discussion of this nature at the Human Rights Council, would send an important message to journalists working in conflict zones that the international community is working to address this problem. Moreover, the speakers said they believed that the Human Rights Council should help countries emerging from conflict to create conditions which would lead to greater respect for freedom of speech and expression.

Complementary Initiatives

In addition to formal resolutions and discussions at the international level, other intergovernmental and nongovernmental organizations have devised unique strategies to promote the protection of journalists in dangerous situations.

In 2007, the International Committee of the Red Cross and the Red Crescent held the Thirtieth International Conference where ICRC participants were invited to voluntarily sign individual or joint humanitarian commitments in the form of pledges. These commitments entitled, *Journalists and Other Media Professionals in Armed Conflicts* are nonbinding declarations that require the entities that signed them to take several steps to ensure the protection of journalists.[53] The pledges are effective until 2011 and require signatories:

- To take all necessary steps to ensure that civilian journalists, media professionals, and associated personnel working in armed conflicts enjoy the respect and protection granted to civilians under international humanitarian law for so long as they are entitled to such respect and protection;
- To promote international humanitarian law principles and rules applicable to journalists, media, professionals, and associated personnel working in armed conflicts, through, inter alia, the provision of training to members of the armed and national security forces, both in peace and war times;
- To provide all members of the armed and national security forces with adequate information on the rights and professional principles of journalists, media professionals and associated personnel, including on the need to preserve their independence;
- To ensure that those responsible for serious violations of international humanitarian law against journalists, media professionals, and associated personnel are prosecuted and brought before a competent and impartial tribunal.[54]

By signing these pledges, the states "commit themselves to taking the steps necessary to ensure that media professionals working in armed conflict enjoy the respect and protection granted to civilians under international humanitarian law, and to promoting the rules and principles of international humanitarian law that are applicable to journalists."[55]

The Press Emblem Campaign (PEC) launched another ambitious effort in December 2007. The initiative, known as the "International Convention to strengthen the protection of journalists in armed conflict and other situations including civil unrest and targeted killing" seeks to protect journalists from attack.[56] The general provisions of the PEC Convention proclaim that:

1. Any deliberate attack or aggression, threats, kidnapping, or detention directed against a journalist while carrying out his or her functions is prohibited, whenever and wherever it may take place, provided that the

journalist takes no action adversely affecting his or her status as a civilian and does not directly contribute to military operations. These provisions and those following apply to all authorities representing a State as well as all representatives and so-called nonstate actors of the civil society, such as criminal networks;

2. Any attack against media installations and equipment is prohibited, unless their use for military purposes by armed groups is clearly demonstrated;

3. Any attack against the life and physical and moral integrity, notably killing, cruel and inhuman treatments, torture, hostage taking involving journalists are prohibited at all times and in all places and constitute a war crime as defined in applicable international law and shall lead to the consequences provided for under such applicable international law;

4. Internet services must be guaranteed full operation anytime by the concerned authorities;

5. All incitements by all media to violence, genocide, crimes against humanity, and serious violations of humanitarian law are prohibited;

6. A journalist wishing to benefit from the protection accorded to civilians must never be armed nor contribute in any way to the hostilities. Journalists are allowed to be escorted by military personnel or armed guards, for self-protection and the protection of the media installation.[57]

The PEC Convention claims its provisions apply to all journalists and media workers covering conflict, whether they are embedded, independent, unilateral, or freelance. The Convention also calls for state parties to adopt a press emblem to strengthen their protection and facilitate their protection in zones of fighting. The PEC proclaims that in order for the Convention to be ratified or entered into force, five United Nations member states would be required to move the Convention forward to the Secretary General.[58] To strengthen its efforts, the Press Emblem Campaign acquired Economic and Social Council (ECOSOC) consultative status to the United Nations as a nongovernmental organization in July 2010, which enables the PEC to more actively participate through written and oral statements in UN meetings and HRC sessions.[59]

Despite journalists and media workers not being designated for special protection under current international humanitarian law, a number of herculean efforts have been advanced to address the need to provide journalists with some version of legal safety measures. Organizations like the ICRC and the PEC have devised unique proposals in an attempt to enhance the accepted legal protection provided by the Geneva Conventions, but the question remains how effective these formal and informal provisions might be in protecting the journalists and media workers in the field.

National Efforts to Protect Free Expression Around the World

In addition to being concerned with the protection of journalists in dangerous situations, the international community has also been focused on protecting the universal and fundamental right of free expression, which directly corresponds with protecting journalists. In an effort to more closely monitor press freedom issues, the U.S. Congress introduced legislation in 2010, known as the Daniel Pearl Freedom of the Press Act, that would ostensibly offer the U.S. State Department as a helpful outlet for protecting global press freedoms. In the video that depicted his gruesome murder, Pearl famously said, "My name is Daniel Pearl. I am a Jewish American . . . My father's Jewish, my mother's Jewish, I'm Jewish. My family follows Judaism."[60] In this statement, Pearl was not only declaring his rights as a journalist to speak out but also his universal right to speak as a member of a particular religion.

Freedom of expression is a priority in the United States but also serves as a priority for its many embassies around the world. The Daniel Pearl law requires the State Department to document the independence of foreign media and to identify nations where journalists are attacked, intimidated, or censored. The annual report would establish whether foreign governments participate in the abuse and document what steps have been taken to preserve the safety and independence of the media. The law covers both traditional reporters and Internet bloggers. The bill unanimously passed the U.S. Senate where the bill's sponsor, Senator Christopher Dodd, said:

> In many parts of the world, the freedom of the press is the last—or even the only—safeguard against the complete erosion of all other human rights. The horrific murder of Daniel Pearl that shocked the world also opened our eyes to the abuse and harassment that many journalists face, too often at the hands of government authorities. With this bill, we pay tribute to Daniel's life and his work by shedding a bright light on this repression, and hope to prevent this sort of tragedy from ever happening again. Freedom of expression cannot exist where journalists are not safe from persecution and attack. Our government must promote freedom of the press by putting on center stage those countries in which journalists are killed, imprisoned, kidnapped, and threatened or censored.[61]

When he signed the Daniel Pearl Act on May 17, 2010, U.S. President Barack Obama observed:

All around the world there are enormously courageous journalists and bloggers who, at great risk to themselves, are trying to shine a light on the critical issues that the people of their country face; who are the frontlines against tyranny and oppression. And obviously the loss of Daniel Pearl was one of those moments that captured the world's imagination because it reminded us of how valuable a free press is, and it reminded us that there are those who would go to any length in order to silence journalists around the world.[62]

Through this legislation, journalists from around the world can report violations of press freedoms to the U.S. Embassy in their country; the embassy is required to identify the country publicly and report these abuses. A recent example of how this law has been implemented occurred late in 2010 when officials at the U.S. Embassy in Pakistan said they interviewed a Pakistani journalist, Umar Cheema, after he was attacked, beaten, and stripped naked. Cheema's head and eyebrows were shaved, and he was videotaped in humiliating positions by assailants who he and other journalists believe were affiliated with the country's powerful spy agency.[63] The U.S. Embassy sent a report of his account to the U.S. State Department, however, it is unclear what, if anything, has resulted from this documentation.[64]

Effectiveness of International Humanitarian Law in Protecting Journalists and Media Workers in Conflict

During the last decades of the twentieth century, a new type of organized violence developed in Africa and Eastern Europe. This "new war" consists of a blurring between traditional distinctions of violence among states or organized political groups for political motives. It is characterized by violence joined with organized crime, or violence undertaken by privately organized groups for private purposes, such as financial gain and large-scale violations of human rights.[65]

International humanitarian law was founded on the fundamental assumption that war continues a conflict among states; however, today's conflicts offer a number of challenges to this assumption.

One challenge is that today's conflicts represent disputes where the states or combatants are not militarily equal. This inequality results in the entitle with the stronger military employing its law and customs of war with less risk to its soldiers or civilians. While the weaker group, in order to remain a viable opponent, may decide to resort to tactics that violate international humanitarian law.

The second challenge is the impact of modern warfare on the fundamental tenets of international humanitarian law. One of the leading principles of the law is that all parties clearly distinguish between civilians and military targets. However, with the traditional approach of military against military increasingly replaced by guerrilla warfare, this distinction becomes more difficult to manage.

The third challenge focuses on the ultimate goal of the combatants in today's conflicts. In conventional or traditional conflicts, the ideal outcome was to capture territory. However, in guerrilla warfare, the main objectives is to frighten, intimidate, or circumvent the stronger military force. In today's wars, the victory is not won by acquiring territory, but by gaining real or imaginary control over the population. This guerrilla warfare introduced by Mao Tse-Tung and Ernesto "Che" Guevara, focuses ostensibly on capturing "hearts and minds," not geography.[66] Guerrilla fighters today have learned to control the masses by controlling the messages. As a result, journalists, with their sole ammunition of words, become primary weapons and sometimes targets of these combatants. These tactics also cause a dramatic increase in violence directed at civilians. At the turn of the century, the ratio of military to civilian casualties in wars was 8:1. Today, this ratio is reversed.[67]

Classic rules of warfare were codified during the late nineteenth to early twentieth century. Yet the battlefields have changed. Warring parties often deliberately strike at civilian populated areas. In addition, these armies are often not wearing military uniforms, blurring the distinction between civilian and military operatives. In addition to civilian targets, tactics of moderns conflicts increasingly include attacks on businesses and historic artifacts and monuments.

However, the fundamental problem is the difference between civilians and journalists and how to address this distinction with regard to international humanitarian law. The discussion about press protection that occurred in the 1970s resulted in meager progress for journalists' protection. State delegates involved in the process could not agree on who deserved this special protection. With the onset of digital technology and proliferation of citizen journalists in conflict areas, this distinction has been blurred even further. In order for a multilateral consensus to be determined as to how to protect journalists in conflicts, a definition of who is a journalist must be ascertained and agreed upon by an array of entities holding divergent opinions of free expression and freedom of press. Determining this definition may be the paramount challenge for international humanitarian law in this instance.

Finally, getting these various state actors to agree on methods of promptly investigating and prosecuting those who target journalists may also be a daunting challenge for the international humanitarian law community. Unfortunately, in some cases where the government is corrupt, the journalists are attacked by the state or direct representatives of the state. Killing journalists is the more effective way of killing the truth in these environments. It may be difficult to ask these states to address fair-trial standards and justice reforms in order to protect the journalists. These requests may cause significant disruptions in their corrupt or hostile regimes and may be impossible to enforce.

These challenges leave journalists on the ground more vulnerable to attacks and with virtually no additional international protection than civilians on the ground. While trying to determine the causes and effects of the conflict, the journalists are increasingly becoming collateral damage in the new wars.

However, these challenges do not mean that international humanitarian law or other international policies are no longer viable. In the past, international humanitarian law faced challenges which have led to a strengthening of the laws in the current environment. For example, the Geneva Conventions of 1949 had to assimilate experiences from World War II. Similarly, the first Additional Protocol, adopted in 1977, had to consider "liberation movements that had obtained *de facto* authority in their respective territories;" otherwise they would not be held accountable by international humanitarian law.[68]

In September 2010, the International Committee of the Red Cross (ICRC) announced it had completed a two-year internal study focused on identifying and understanding the humanitarian problems arising from armed conflict and devising possible legal solutions to them in terms of legal development or clarification.[69] More than 30 issues of concern were analyzed. According to ICRC President, Dr. Jakob Kellenberger, the ICRC chose to first assess the actual humanitarian needs, drawing on its own experience and that of other organizations. Then, the ICRC evaluated the responses provided by humanitarian law to identify whether there were gaps, or whether existing law was sufficient.[70] The study concluded that in most circumstances greater *compliance* with international humanitarian law is necessary, rather than a significant reworking of its provisions. To this end, greater codification of humanitarian law may help prevent legal gaps in practice.[71] Kellenberger said:

> One can say with some certainty that if all the parties concerned showed perfect regard for humanitarian law, most of the humanitarian issues before us would not exist. All attempts to strengthen humanitarian law should, therefore, build on the existing legal framework. There is no need to discuss rules whose adequacy is long established.[72]

Kellenberger added that the study showed that humanitarian law does not always respond fully to actual humanitarian needs, so the challenges in protecting persons and objects during armed conflict are the result of gaps or weakness in existing law, and thus require greater development or clarification.

Kellenberger outlined four specific gaps in international humanitarian law's current state, and especially in noninternational armed conflict. These gaps included the following:

- Protection of persons deprived of liberty;
- Implementation of humanitarian law and reparation for victims of violations;
- Protection of the natural environment; and
- Protection of internally displaced persons.

The primary element that related to strengthening protection of journalists was the implementation of humanitarian law and reparation for victims of violations. Although in recent years there has been a plea to develop criminal law procedures to prosecute and punish those who have committed serious violations against journalists covering conflict, the means to halt and redress violations have not yet been devised. In international armed conflicts, procedures to supervise belligerent parties have not been used in practice because the belligerents do not commit to the provisions of the law. Likewise, in noninternational armed conflicts, Kellenberger again admitted that procedures for addressing belligerent parties do not yet exist.[73]

International humanitarian law has had success, albeit some might consider it negligible, protecting soldiers and civilians during combat in the last few centuries. But even critics must admit that without these codes of good practice, war would likely be much more brutal and uncivilized. International humanitarian laws have adapted to numerous challenges and evolved not just to protect combatants but also to protect wounded and sick soldiers as well as civilians, to outlaw torture, and to provide rules for prisoners of war. There may be good reason to be optimistic that provisions to protect the chronicler of the battle may soon be forthcoming. The Daniel Pearl Freedom of the Press Act initiated by the United States may be an effective way to build momentum for international support in states' national legislation.

However, these laws may have limited value if journalists are not aware of the protective measures these laws encompass and if the belligerents involved in the world's conflicts choose not to abide by these codes. Various journalism organizations and advocacy groups, including the U.S. Society of Professional Journalists, have attempted to tackle the first limitation by publishing on its website a clear and comprehensive reference guide to the Geneva Conventions.[74] Prosecuting violators of these laws proffers a way to address the belligerents who do not abide by these codes.

Although mechanisms for monitoring armed conflicts and prosecuting those who target journalists are considered by some to be ineffective, these mechanisms do exist within the framework of the UN Security Council, the International Criminal Court, and the UN Human Rights Council as well as in regional human rights systems and national legislation. While these mechanisms apply to all forms of armed conflict—both international and noninternational—and can be used without prior consent of parties in the conflict, recent monitoring focused on the responsibilities of states and nonstate actors. This is unfortunate as noncompliant state or nonstate actors often cause the attacks.

Another mechanism of protection that has been previously untapped but may be useful to add to journalists' protection would be to formally proclaim attacks on journalists as "hate crimes" within the scope of international law. Hate crimes have been widely discussed, and significant provisions have been introduced to prevent these crimes and to prosecute those who engage in these acts. Unlike traditional victims of these hate crimes, journalists and media workers who are attacked may not be victims of discrimination but people who attack journalists are, indeed, making efforts to terrorize a specific group. Thus, as a group, journalists have been singled out as victims because of what they represent rather than who they are. If the international community can include provisions and mechanisms to protect journalists from being attacked as victims of hate crimes, this broader umbrella of protection may have some benefit.

International humanitarian violations must be prosecuted, and international humanitarian law must adapt to today's changing conflict environment if it is to retain its relevance and value. The ICRC's suggestion to enhance existing international humanitarian law and to include a section on the implementation of reparation for victims, such as journalists, is a needed first step. Freedom of expression violations require deeper and more sustained attention within stable and nonstable governments. As it is ultimately up to the states to influence the evolution of international law, a national law like the Daniel Pearl Freedom of the Press Act in the United States offers a template from which to start. Nations that agree there is a positive role for the free press to play should initiate similar legislation and agree to protect journalists within their country and to encourage other states to demand the same protection. These countries should act swiftly and strongly to bring nonstate actors to justice. National and international laws may be flawed and limited, but they represent a necessary element for the protection of journalists worldwide.

The next chapter will describe how numerous nonstate organizations have devised strategies and tactics to pressure states to uphold international humanitarian law and to protect journalists in dangerous situations.

Chapter 3

From "Name and Shame" to Media Literacy: Nonstate Strategies and Tactics to Protect Journalists

The previous chapter explored various state and international governmental solutions designed to protect journalists working around the world who may be subjected to dangerous situations. During the past 30 years, other international stakeholders have addressed this issue with vigor. Rich discussions among these stakeholders have led to various actions beyond legal initiatives. These nongovernmental organizations and other entities have developed a wide range of projects and processes that could be enlisted to protect journalists engaged in dangerous missions. Prominent individuals, major press associations, media companies, unions, international and various other organizations have forged unique journalistic tactics to address the dangers faced by those who report about conflict. The tactics these organization have devised to protect journalists in danger encompass the following:

- Advocacy groups that expose and report the mistreatment of media workers around the world;
- Protection organizations, international initiatives and foundations that promote training and education for journalists and media workers;
- Protection organizations that have introduced emblems for journalists to wear as symbols of protection similar to the Red Cross; and
- Specific journalism education tactics designed to offer media education and alternative ways to tell the stories of conflict.

In addition, international organizations have determined that journalists who cover conflict may experience some psychological damage as a result of bearing witness to atrocities. These organizations have researched and offered protective mechanisms to guard against personal mental damage before, during, and after journalists participate in the coverage of conflict. One long-term strategy has been media literacy projects that enhance civilian knowledge and appreciation of journalistic practices.

The protection of journalists on dangerous assignments is a complex goal, and no one method of protection will accomplish that outcome for all journalists working in all risky situations. However, this chapter will highlight an array of tactics and strategies designed to address the issue of journalists' protection that are in place around the world. Some of the protection strategies are designed for specific situations and unique perspectives. Many of the suggestions are controversial, while others are basic principles of good practices. This chapter will also explain the psychological hazards that reporters may endure when covering conflict, and the way the journalistic community is coming to grips with and addressing these issues in order to protect journalists' minds as well as their bodies. The authors explore efforts developed by stakeholders to revise fundamental practices of conflict reporting which could eventually mitigate the targeting of journalists in the field. Finally, the strategy of media education as a means of protecting journalists today and in the future will be explained. All of these strategies and methods demonstrate the exceptional efforts many people around the world have made to develop and promote effective ways to protect those who risk their lives to tell the stories of conflict.

"Name and Shame": Advocacy Groups and Their Strategies

The most prominent advocacy organizations that focus on the protection of journalists include the Committee to Protect Journalists (CPJ), Reporters sans Frontières (RSF), and the International News Safety Institute (INSI). They were developed to shine a harsh light on constraints facing journalists around the world. These organizations are active and reactive. These groups not only deal with journalists who are targeted by combatants, but they also defend journalists who are censored or persecuted by their own governments. These organizations collect and disseminate facts and figures pertaining to the mistreatment of journalists, offer safety training for new and seasoned journalists, and promote freedom of expression for all global citizens. Their tactics are similar as each organization works unapologetically as an advocate for journalists' protection. Conversely, each organization has what it considers a unique rhetorical stance and a specific way to approach its advocacy function.

Committee to Protect Journalists

Founded in 1981, CPJ[1] is an independent, nonprofit organization developed by a group of U.S. correspondents who were working abroad. The organization functions under a 35-member board made up of prominent journalists from around the world. The full-time staff in New York City supervises research and reports on hundreds of attacks on the press each year. CPJ classifies the attacks on the media into eleven different categories: abducted, attacked, censored, expelled, harassed, imprisoned, killed, killed with motive unconfirmed, legal action, missing, and threatened. The Committee to Protect Journalists derives its funding from individuals, corporations, and foundations; it does not accept any government funding.

A unique feature of CPJ is the way it reports the number of journalists killed:

> When CPJ publicizes journalists killed on duty; it cites only those cases in which the motives have been "confirmed." Lists compiled by other organizations may include journalists whose killings CPJ has not connected to their work with reasonable certainty. Other organizations may also list media support workers, such as drivers and interpreters. CPJ maintains a separate list of media support workers killed on duty.[2]

The Committee has also directly addressed the issue of greater prosecution of those who target journalists during war. CPJ has described murder of a journalist as the ultimate form of censorship. In 2005, CPJ suggested that the best way to curtail the abuse of journalists is for journalism organizations to push governments to aggressively investigate and prosecute those who commit acts of violence. The report stated, "Press freedom groups and journalists around the world need to draw attention to the killings and make the argument that the murder of a journalist is an attack on the collective right of a society to be informed."[3]

CPJ is proud of its "name and shame" record, citing that this strategy has been a hallmark of the international human rights movement and worked exceptionally well in the 1970s through the 1990s. Joel Simon, the Executive Director of CPJ stated:

The guiding premise is that even the most brutal leaders want to hide—or at least justify—their repressive actions. If abuses could be exposed through meticulously documented reports, and if those reports could generate coverage in major international media outlets, governments would be compelled to cure their most egregious behavior.[4]

Simon added that while this strategy continues to be an effective one, it has been modified to fit the current fragmented and diffused media landscape.[5]

In addition to collecting and disseminating data about journalists in danger, CPJ has initiated other successful projects in the past few years. For example, in 2005, CPJ witnessed more than a dozen newspaper publishers and editors imprisoned in Ethiopia. After trying several options, an international mission in 2006 managed to secure a visit with several prisoners. Through this effort, CPJ delivered modest but steady sums of money to the most destitute family members of the imprisoned editors. They also sent reading material. CPJ subsequently learned that every effort in this case had made a difference. The visits had led to improvements in prisoners' treatment; the reading materials that were received had lifted spirits, and some journalists told CPJ they felt enormous relief knowing their families were given needed funds.[6]

Reporters sans Frontières

Reporters sans Frontières[7] enlists more than 120 correspondents worldwide who work closely with local and regional press freedom groups to "investigate, expose and support" journalists around the world. The organization was founded in 1985 and is registered in France as a nonprofit organization with consultative status at the United Nations. The organization is largely funded by the sale of its biannual albums of photographs as well as calendars, auctions, donations, member dues, public grants, and partnerships with private firms.

Reporters sans Frontières gathers information about press freedom abuses from its correspondents around the world, including Afghanistan, Bangladesh, Belarus, Burma/Myanmar, Colombia, Democratic Republic of the Congo, Eritrea, Kazakhstan, Pakistan, Peru, Romania, Russia, Somalia, the United States, and Tunisia. In addition, it organizes publicity campaigns, with the help of public relations firms, to pressure governments and to inform the public about the misuse and the value of free expression. The organization sponsors a number of annual events and online presentations, including its comprehensive Worldwide Press Freedom Index that uses various survey data to measure the degree of freedom journalists and media operations have in more than 160 countries. The data used to determine this degree of freedom includes reports and interviews with journalists in each of these countries.

RSF also prides itself on training initiatives. In 2006, RSF published a *Handbook for Journalists* in conjunction with UNESCO that has been made available online.[8] The handbook includes basic information about the principles of press freedom and the international documents that address this issue. In addition, the handbook offers guidelines and procedures for protecting journalists and how to report abuses of press freedom. In the appendices, there is useful material about insurance policies for freelance journalists and photographers as well as a form to request the loan of a bulletproof jacket from RSF.

An example of a successful project initiated by RSF includes a recent initiative to assist a Mexican journalist who had been covering the bloody war being waged by Mexico's main drug cartels in Ciudad Juárez, and who had fled his country after drug traffickers repeatedly threatened and harassed him and his family. RSF gave him money and assistance with official paperwork.[9] RSF has also recently provided financial support to three independent newspapers—*Shamal*, *Salam*, and *Chand*—in one of the worst hit flood areas of Pakistan.[10]

The International News Safety Institute

Another of the journalists' advocacy groups, INSI[11] was established in 2003, "... to promote best safety practices in news coverage including journalists' training, operational procedures, equipment provision and health issues."[12] The organization was developed through a joint initiative by the International Federation of Journalists and the International Press Institute, in addition to a number of other news organizations, professional and press freedom groups, humanitarian organizations, and interested individuals. It was officially launched on World Press Freedom Day in 2003. INSI is a not-for-profit organization that is supported primarily by contributions.

INSI is best known for its safety training initiatives—it has established its own Safety Code and works to investigate, develop, and promote better safety services, including insurance. In addition, INSI offers "training for the brain" as it collaborates with mental health care professionals to assist frontline journalists in addressing the mental health hazards of reporting about conflict.

INSI takes a slightly different approach when reporting how many media workers have been attacked during any given time or in any given region because it monitors and reports about places where all members of the news media are in danger at work, whether from conflict, disaster, disease, hostile regimes, or other violent elements. Thus, INSI reports on intentional and accidental deaths of journalists and media workers.

In March 2007, INSI released a report entitled, "Killing the Messenger: Report of the Global Inquiry by the International News Safety Institute into the Protection of Journalists."[13] The 18-member Global Inquiry Commission undertook an investigation into the "legal, professional and practical issues related to covering the protection of journalists in dangerous situations." The report concluded that more than 1,000 news media personnel had died trying to cover news around the world in the 10 years the report covered. From 1996 until 2006, at least 657 men and women were murdered while reporting the news in their own countries, and in two-thirds of the cases where media workers were killed, the killers were not identified or even pursued. The Chair of the Inquiry, BBC Global News Director Richard Sambrook, said:

> In many countries, murder has become the easiest, cheapest and most effective way of silencing troublesome reporting, and the more the killers get away with it the more the spiral of death is forced upwards. Impunity for killers of journalists, who put themselves in harm's way to keep us all informed, shames governments around the world.[14]

The report included recommendations for war assignments to be strictly voluntary, and it encouraged employers of journalists to provide hostile environment and risk awareness training, as well as seminars on international humanitarian law.[15] INSI also called on employers to cover all journalists with insurance against personal injury and death and provide free counseling to war journalists and their families.[16]

Another highly successful effort of INSI was a project it initiated in November 2010 where 46 Sinhalese and Tamil journalists in Sri Lanka were given free journalism and trauma training, in collaboration with the Dart Center for Journalism and Trauma and local partners at the Sri Lanka Press Institute and the Sri Lanka College for Journalism. Of the 46 journalists who attended the workshops, 11 were women. The courses were aimed to increase the participants' awareness of trauma across a broad spectrum of story areas, ranging from family violence to large-scale disasters, teaching them how to deal with issues of trauma as a journalist, but also to understand the effect of reporting on those involved. The Norwegian Ministry of Foreign Affairs funded the training.[17]

These three internationally-recognized advocacy organizations are prolific and resolute about disseminating news releases, articles, and their annual reports to international news outlets and the public. They are unrelenting in the strategy of naming and shaming. Each of these organizations also enlists seasoned spokespersons to write regular opinion pieces and speak at international journalism conferences to garner prolonged, positive attention and support for the issue of protection of journalists in conflict. These organizations also formally challenge the UN, international development institutions (such as the World Bank and International Monetary Fund), national governments, military and security forces, news organizations, and individual journalists to support measures that will improve the safety and security of journalists around the world.

The unresolved issue of impunity for those who target journalists has become a prolonged topic of attention among these groups. They each believe that impunity for those who commit crimes against journalists and media workers demonstrates an egregious affront not only to the individual, but also to the ultimate goal of free expression and democracy. While their data and statistics do not always align, their ultimate missions—as Rodney Pinder, Director of the International News Safety Institute, put it, "is to help you [journalists] survive the story."[18]

These organizations have been effective in bringing attention to the issue of journalists being targeted while doing their jobs in conflicts. They have been instrumental in forging international humanitarian law, multilateral declarations, resolutions, and policies to address protection of journalists and to bring attention to the lack of prosecution for those who deliberately attack the press. They have initiated systematic data collection and offered prolonged reporting of these attacks on journalists. They have also developed educational and training practices for journalists who work in conflict areas. Overall, their rhetorical strategies have been highly successful at bringing attention to this issue. But there may be another strategy they might consider.

While successful at naming and shaming, these organizations have concentrated little on educating the nonjournalists about the ultimate threat to liberty that ensues when journalists are threatened. They may consider this educational initiative outside of their missions, but with such worldwide name recognition, an effort directed at the general public might be highly effective. With the exception of the *Handbook for Journalists* published by RSF, these organizations have concentrated on the ultimate effect of belligerents' actions on journalists without dealing with the faulty reasoning and assumptions the perpetrators use when performing their acts of violence against journalists. In fact, if one of the primary reasons journalists are targeted in the field is that the attackers perceive journalists to be mouthpieces of the enemy, then all three of these organizations should consider implementing projects that foster educational media literacy programs for all people and institute programs that explain the fundamental goals and effects of critical, objective journalism. People around the world need instruction to realize that words are not weapons, but can be used to illuminate and inform— when truthful and critically evaluated. Each organization would be well served to design programs that teach the value of freedom of expression and critical analysis as well as the importance of unfettered journalism in open societies.

Other Advocacy Groups

Several other organizations have initiated missions to support the general notion of freedom of expression and protection for the media specialists covering armed conflict. These organizations are more specialized in their membership, but demonstrate that there is a broad interest in the protection of journalists and journalism, both foreign and domestic.

- International Media Support (IMS) is primarily funded by the Danish Ministry of Foreign Affairs.[19] This group, founded in 2001 in Copenhagen, works to support local media in more than 30 countries affected by armed conflict, human insecurity, and political transition. The organization has provided support for journalists in Afghanistan, Sudan, Zimbabwe, Ukraine, the Caucasus, Sri Lanka, Burma /Myanmar, and the Maldives.
- The International Covenant for the Protection of Journalists (ICPJ)[20] was founded in 2007 and adopted to assist media associations and journalists who face extreme duress in their working conditions. The organization was begun in partnership with the Press Emblem Campaign. It was founded by members of the media primarily from the Middle East and

Africa including the UAE Syndicate of Journalists, the Iraqi Syndicate of Journalists, the International Union of Somali Journalists, the Sudan Syndicate of Journalists, the Iran Syndicate of Journalists, and the Mingora Union of Journalists.

- International Federation of Journalists (IFJ)[21] was first established in 1926, relaunched in 1946 and then again in 1952. The organization boasts the largest membership of journalists from around the world, with more than 600,000 members from 100 countries. The IFJ represents journalists within the UN system and within the international trade union movement. The organization is based in Brussels with regional offices in Caracas, Dakar, and Sydney. The IFJ publishes a safety fund report annually that heralds those journalists and media workers killed while reporting from danger zones. The IFJ was one of the founding members of the International News Safety Institute.

- The International Press Institute (IPI)[22] was born in 1950 when a group of journalists formed a global organization dedicated to the promotion and protection of press freedom. The organization, with headquarters in Vienna, now has members in 120 countries and believes that "freedom of expression is the right that protects all other rights and this freedom needs to be promoted and defended."[23] The IPI also maintains a "Death Watch" on its website, indicating how many journalists and media workers have been killed during the year. In addition, the IPI investigates incidents where journalists are targeted or imprisoned for their work. This "Justice Denied Campaign" works to ensure visibility for these injustices as well as encourage policymakers to address these problems.

- ARTICLE 19: Global Campaign for Free Expression[24] was established in 1987. The organization derives its name from the number of the article in the 1948 Universal Declaration of Human Rights that promotes free expression for the global community. ARTICLE 19 is a nonprofit, advocacy organization with headquarters in London and field offices in Senegal, Kenya, Bangladesh, Mexico, and Brazil. ARTICLE 19 monitors, researches, publishes, lobbies, campaigns, sets standards, and litigates on behalf of freedom of expression wherever it is threatened.

Criticism of these advocacy organizations is difficult to muster because they all promote a mission that fundamentally generates positive public and government opinion to protect journalists in conflict. Despite slightly different tactics, they have experienced success for their cause; however by working together more frequently, they could bring greater attention and action to key issues facing journalist protection.

Burgeoning Partnerships Among Advocacy Groups

Since 2009, several of these advocacy organizations have joined in a coordinated effort to build partnerships to act on free expression and journalists' protection strategies around the world. The first meeting was initiated by the International Media Support organization and was held in Copenhagen in September 2009. Representatives from 21 international media support and press freedom advocacy organizations met to assess the concept of working together in partnerships and exploring ways to further improve collaborative support to journalists and media workers in countries affected by conflict, human insecurity, and political transition. The group met to coordinate partnerships among national, regional, and international organizations in order to increase the impact of their activities and avoid duplication in a specific country or around a certain theme.[25]

The participants in the Copenhagen meeting developed three types of partnerships, which could form the basis for enhanced collaboration:

Advocacy Partnership–aimed at pursuing lobbying and advocacy related objectives with national or third party governments, or multilateral bodies. Such processes are normally focused on freedom of expression, press freedoms and safety issues.

Emergency Partnership—aimed at providing rapid and flexible support to a media community as a result of conflict or natural disasters. Such processes could have a broad range of focuses, including conflict mitigation, infrastructural/professional support, raising awareness, humanitarian information and so forth.

Media Development Partnership—aimed at building holistic broad-based support for the development of a media community over a longer timeframe. Such processes could target media policy and institutional building, as well as professionalization and sustainability issues.

It was noted that these three types of Partnerships are not mutually exclusive, but rather in any given country they may run in conjunction or in parallel with one another.[26]

A fourth collaboration: *Thematic Partnerships*, was introduced at a follow-up meeting in New York City in January 2010, hosted by the Open Society Foundations (formerly known as the Open Society Institute). According to the minutes of the meeting, "Thematic Partnerships are not related to a specific country, but are rather shared themes, such as testing of the UNESCO media development indicators in a particular country or participating in global initiatives around network communication environments."[27]

At this meeting, 30 representatives were present. The group determined that for this advocacy partnership to work, international and national media support organizations must agree on the issue they would like to address and be willing to work together. The government in a country must be receptive to discussing freedom of expression in order for the partnership efforts to have any influence or impact. Finally, the capacity of national organizations to take ownership of the process to ensure a long-term effect must be established. The final document from this meeting included specific action plans for building regional, national, and international partnerships to address nine specific countries currently considered in peril with regard to freedom of expression issues.[28] The nine selected countries included Afghanistan, Azerbaijan, Haiti, Nigeria, Pakistan, Philippines, Uganda, Venezuela, and Yemen.[29]

This second International Partnerships meeting concluded by appointing a strategic working group to build on the discussions in Copenhagen and New York. The working group will also look closely at how the organizations may collectively develop various partnerships and tailor them to the specific circumstances of each country. This collaborative effort among more than 40 international media support and advocacy organizations is a significant step toward promoting free expression and protecting journalists around the world.

"Be Prepared": Pragmatic Tactics that Include Safety Training and Other Protection Mechanisms

In addition to the efforts of these advocacy organizations, a number of pragmatic strategies to protect journalists gathering information in dangerous situations have been introduced by a wide array of individuals and organizations. These strategies include proposed safety guidelines and protective equipment, as well as specific identity badges to be worn by working journalists and media workers in conflict. Several of these strategies have been embraced or summarily dismissed by the journalistic community, while other suggestions have evoked controversy among journalists and stakeholders.

Memo on the Protection for Journalists

Daniel Pearl, the *Wall Street Journal* correspondent who was kidnapped and killed in Pakistan in 2002, had addressed the issue of journalists' safety years before his death. His wife, Mariane Pearl, reported in her book, *A Mighty Heart*, that before Daniel Pearl ever went to Pakistan he was commended for his coverage of Kosovo in 1999 and he was told by his editors, "We'll keep you in mind for the next war."[30] Mariane Pearl added that this was not what her husband was looking to hear. As soon as he returned to Paris from the Balkans in 1999, he composed a detailed document titled: "Memo on Protection of Journalists." This report offered a number of safety measures to manage risk for journalists and editors covering conflict. These recommendations included checking in routinely with fellow reporters and editors, maintaining a standard account of $5,000 to $6,000 for each trip in order to avoid taking unnecessary risks in dangerous situations, using the right equipment such as properly fitted flak jackets, and seeking advanced security training by specialty training organizations. In his memo, Pearl mentioned training organizations such as Centurion Risk Assessment Services in the UK (used by the *New York Times*) and Andy Kain Enterprises also in the UK (used by CNN and BBC) were well worth the approximately $500 per day for the courses. Mariane Pearl noted in her book that, unfortunately for Daniel, these suggestions were not adopted.

Building Safety Guidelines

Chris Cramer, global editor for multimedia at Reuters and formerly director of the world's largest newsgathering organization in the world, the BBC, described his epiphany about journalists' protection when his staff was covering the siege of Dubrovnik in 1991. The staff had made the decision to pull out of the city because of the severe conditions including constant bombing. The staff felt they were risking their lives if they stayed. Cramer noted, "Back behind my desk in London, I was furious that our competitors had decided to stay—and likely pick up all those broadcast awards."[31]

But Cramer admitted that his shortsightedness made him a lousy manager. He proceeded to convene a working party to draw up some operating guidelines for future staff members working in hostile environments. Cramer published these guidelines for the BBC staff:

- No story was worth a life;
- No picture sequence was worth an injury;
- No piece of audio or video was worth endangering our staff members.[32]

Even though these guidelines seem rather simple now, Cramer said at the time (early 1990s) they caused quite a stir at the BBC. Journalists were outraged that their autonomy had been compromised.

> We were simply stating the obvious to reporters and those who worked with them: we don't expect you to go off and get killed or injured for the sake of the story; it is okay to say 'no': when we say it's voluntary, we mean it; that is not some weasel management phrase designed to stop you suing us.[33]

Cramer explained that his organization went even further to provide their reporters with the best equipment, the best training, the best vehicles, and the best insurance for staff and freelancers on the payroll who were reporting from dangerous areas.

Soon after the murders of Miguel Gil Moreno of Associated Press Television News (APTN) and Kurt Schork of Reuters in May 2000 in Sierra Leone, the Freedom Forum European Centre brought together representatives from three major news broadcasters and two major television news agencies to establish common guidelines for their journalists working in war zones. CNN, BBC, ITN, Reuters, and APTN published their joint code of practice document at the News World Conference in Barcelona in November 2000. The guideline proposed:

(1) The preservation of human life and safety is paramount. Staff and freelancers should be made aware that unwarranted risks in pursuit of a story are unacceptable and must be strongly discouraged. Assignments to war zones or hostile environments must be voluntary and should only involve experienced newsgatherers and those under their direct supervision.
(2) All staff and freelancers asked to work in hostile environments must have access to appropriate safety training and retraining. Employers are encouraged to make this mandatory.
(3) Employers must provide efficient safety equipment to all staff and freelancers assigned to hazardous locations, including personal issue kevlar vests/jackets, protective headgear, and properly protected vehicles if necessary.
(4) All staff and freelancers should be afforded personal insurance while working in hostile areas including cover against death and personal injury.

(5) Employers to provide and encourage the use of voluntary and confidential counseling for staff and freelancers returning from hostile areas or after the coverage of distressing events. (This is likely to require some training of managers in the recognition of the symptoms of post traumatic stress disorder.)

(6) Media companies and their representatives are neutral observers. No member of the media should carry a firearm in the course of their work.

(7) We will work together to establish a databank of safety information, including the exchange of up to date safety assessments of hostile and dangerous areas.

(8) We will work with other broadcasters and other organizations to safeguard journalists in the field.[34]

Speaking on behalf of the group, Richard Sambrook, Deputy Director of BBC News (at the time) said: "This agreement represents unprecedented co-operation between competitors in the broadcast news industry to try to protect all journalists, staff and freelance, working in dangerous conditions. It's a starting point, not a final position. Our aim is to limit risk and to take responsibility for anyone working on our behalf in war zones or hostile environments."[35]

IFJ Codes of Good Practice

The International Federation of Journalists is one of the world's largest journalism trade unions, which routinely addresses the issue of good practice when it produces its report on journalists in conflict. IFJ[36] promotes and publishes a standard of professional conduct for its members to follow when practicing journalism around the world. The IFJ's annual report of journalists and media staff killed during the year includes a page titled, "International Code of Practice for the Safe Conduct of Journalism."[37] The specific elements of the IFJ code are as follows:

- Journalists and other media staff shall be properly equipped for all assignments including the provision of first-aid materials, communication tools, adequate transport facilities and, where necessary, protective clothing;
- Media organisations and, where appropriate, state authorities shall provide risk-awareness training for those journalists and media workers who are likely to be involved in assignments where dangerous conditions prevail or may be reasonably expected;
- Public authorities shall inform their personnel of the need to respect the rights of journalists and shall instruct them to respect the physical integrity of journalists and media staff while at work.

- Media organisations shall provide social protection for all staff engaged in journalistic activity outside the normal place of work, including life insurance;
- Media organisations shall provide, free of charge, medical treatment and health care, including costs of recuperation and convalescence, for journalists and media workers who are the victims of injury or illness as a result of their work outside the normal place of work;
- Media organisations shall protect freelance or part-time employees. They must receive, on an equal basis, the same social protection and access to training and equipment as that made available to fully employed staff.[38]

The IFJ suggests that while journalists may be targeted in conflict situations, they, along with their principal employers, should take these steps to minimize the dangers to media organizations and their staffs.

Training Camps

In 2002, the U.S. Department of Defense (DOD) took direct action to protect journalists covering conflicts when, in a move to foster a more convivial relationship between the media and the military, the DOD offered war correspondents a week-long media boot camp at the Quantico Marine Corps Base in Virginia.[39] The program was designed in response to journalists' protests that they were kept away from previous conflicts. This project was developed by the military to address complaints about previous journalistic restrictions and to prepare journalists to operate safely on the battlefields with frontline units in Iraq and subsequent conflicts. Journalists learned about camouflage and combat first aid, minefield diction, and protection from chemical and biological weapons. The journalists at the camp received Marine Corps training manuals that advised them what to do if captured.

The British Ministry of Defence took a different approach to journalists' safety in 2006 when it added material that directly addressed journalists' safety issues to its "Green Book" manual for military-media operations.[40] The document ostensibly outlined, "What editors can expect from MOD and what the MOD seeks from the media."[41] The 27-page document included information on how media personnel would be treated on the battlefield and how the embed and pool systems would work. In addition, the MOD Green Book included "Safety Advice" for correspondents working in operational areas and other hostile environments. This portion of the document clearly stated that the UK Forces would "never deliberately target either individual correspondents or civil media facilities."[42]

ICRC Hotline

The primary leader in international humanitarian law and humanitarian efforts worldwide, the International Committee of the Red Cross (ICRC), has developed an initiative to assist media professionals who are directly attacked, or who disappear or are taken captive in wartime or in other violence. The ICRC began this media safety project in 1985 by offering a permanent hotline (+41 79 217 32 85) available to journalists who find themselves in trouble in armed conflicts. This service is not only for journalists, but also their employers and relatives who can report a missing, wounded, or detained journalist and request assistance. The services provided by the ICRC range from seeking confirmation of a reported arrest, obtaining access to persons arrested, providing information on a journalist's whereabouts for relatives and employers, maintaining family links, and actively tracing missing journalists, to carrying out medical evacuations of wounded journalists. The ICRC also offers training in international humanitarian law and provides support for National Red Cross and Red Crescent Societies offering first aid courses for journalists.

The Press Emblem

Another strategy proposed by a group of journalists in Geneva has been hotly debated among the journalistic community. The Press Emblem Campaign (PEC) was organized in 2004 to protect journalists and was developed in reaction to events during the Iraq and Afghanistan wars. The PEC proposes an internationally recognized symbol or badge which journalists would wear in combat zones to distinguish them from the military. Since its introduction, this campaign has represented one of the most hotly debated projects in the international community aimed at the protection of journalists. Below are some of the mixed reviews from other protection organizations and journalists.

The PEC proposed a convention symbol similar to the established International Committee of the Red Cross Convention, which declared the Red Cross as a protected emblem. Similarly, the PEC emblem would require full support of governments in upholding international law to ensure journalists have the same legal protection afforded to humanitarian workers. In addition, the convention stressed that those who harass or harm media workers wearing the emblem, would be held accountable for their aggressive actions.[43] The strategy to protect journalists with an emblem is not new. A proposal to create a special international badge for journalists in conflict was introduced at the United Nations in the late 1980s. Government officials blocked this proposal because journalists felt it would lead to licensing of journalists.

The Broadcast News Security Group, consisting of major networks and news agencies across the world, including the BBC, CNN, ITN, Reuters, and Sky News, expressed its negative opinion about the PEC proposal in a 2008 news release. The organization posted this release on the International News Safety Institute's website and declared: "The PEC is at best irrelevant and at worst dangerous."[44]

In a 2006 interview, the Committee to Protect Journalists' Washington, DC representative, Frank Smyth said, "Placing an emblem on journalists doesn't provide a guarantee that they won't be targeted, as they are still being killed in target zones. We don't believe it [the Press Emblem] will be effective in protecting journalists."[45]

The supporters of the Press Emblem Campaign dispute Smyth's comments on the PEC website:

> We can reduce the probability to be mistaken with a military target by avoiding looking like one: a camera can appear as a weapon if the journalist is close to a strategic target. If such an 'incident' happens, it will no longer be possible to say: "We didn't know that X was a journalist"—if we are wearing a press emblem.[46]

PEC Secretary-General and cofounder Blaise Lempen does not deny the existence of targeted attacks, but believes an internationally recognized press emblem will help. "The emblem is necessary to avoid any mistake on the identification of journalists. It is too simple to say, 'We didn't know he was a journalist.' "[47]

Some critics reported that journalists already carry a protective symbol of sorts. The PEC recognized these concerns and maintained that current protection through identification is simply not enough because journalists are considered civilians in conflict situations despite significant added responsibilities and hazards. The organization said on its website that it believes current armbands and distinctive self-made signs do not have legitimacy because they are not harmonized or internationally recognized by international law.

Supporters of the PEC suggested that government and states should and would legally maintain this emblem if it carried the weight of international humanitarian law. The PEC convention would provide an obligation on states to protect journalists and an obligation to inquire about abuses.[48] If the convention were adopted, these obligations would subsequently be upheld through independently led investigations and proceed to prosecution of those responsible for any abuses, with any necessary reparations made to journalists' families.

The International Committee of the Red Cross disagreed with the PEC's view that adding to the existing Geneva Conventions would lead to strengthened journalist protections. Knut Dörmann, former legal adviser in the Legal Division of the ICRC and member of the ICRC delegation to the Preparatory Commission for the International Criminal Court, said, "Making a new convention wouldn't solve the existing problems."[49] Instead, Dörmann said, the new convention would experience the same problems that exist with the old convention. Any attempts to change the current conventions would send a dangerous signal to the international community that the present conventions are not enough. In the ICRC's view, international humanitarian law already provides protection to journalists. Dörmann said he believed a new convention may create more visibility with regard to the issue of journalist protection, but these new conventions may not be as strong in the long run. Changing the existing convention would essentially mean going through the document and replacing the term "civilian" or "person" with "journalist." Dörmann said, "Article 79 shows that journalists already have protection and they are to be granted the same protection as civilians in times of conflict."[50] According to the ICRC, it is up to each nation-state to protect its people and make sure that international humanitarian law is respected. Enforcement of international humanitarian law is "still dependent on the political will of the state for investing or referring to the international court."[51]

However, the PEC maintained the current protection for journalists, afforded under Article 79 of the Geneva Conventions, does not provide enough protection. Instead, the PEC differentiates between the role of the journalist and the civilian in times of conflict. "They [journalists] have to take risks to report a situation by going to dangerous places on behalf of people's right to information," the PEC stated on its website in 2008. The PEC reported that it thinks it is this mission of informing the public that justifies journalists having special protection. But, to achieve distinction as a journalist, one must first be defined as a journalist under any newly proposed strategy. This leads to the issue of licensing, which is worrisome for some journalists and journalism organizations.

Rodney Pinder of INSI said, "Another issue which gives enormous concern is who issues the emblem, and who decides who is a journalist? Is this power given to the government or military?"[52] CPJ's Smyth added that this issue of licensing could be immensely problematic, because a licensing regime to establish journalistic identification cards would restrict press freedom.[53]

The PEC responded to this concern by maintaining that international, national, and regional journalist organizations would, indeed, be the primary parties involved in the licensing process. The PEC posited that this would help limit government influence; however, the PEC admitted that licensing may also afford a government the ability to know where a journalist is located, which could result in increased government control of the media. Lempen said his organization would need the cooperation of various government agencies in order to formally propose the PEC convention, because governments are ostensibly responsible for law and order. However, Lempen added, the licensing itself would not be conducted by the states. "The emblem will be given by the journalists' associations as it is now for the press cards. There will be no control of the distribution of the emblems by any state or government office."[54]

Journalist Thorne Anderson countered this argument by stating that even if the licensing process was separated from the government and regulated through a liaison body (i.e., journalist association) it would be limited in its ability to provide protection for those journalists who wish to remain anonymous. "There will always be journalists who choose to not publicly identify themselves as journalists."[55]

The fervor surrounding the PEC also included the issue of impunity and enforcement of international humanitarian law. INSI's Pinder noted that what was most appalling about the lack of journalists' protection is the issue of impunity for those who target journalists in conflict. He said, "Ninety percent of these cases haven't been brought to justice."[56]

"Those who kill journalists don't care about legal framework," said Jean-François (Jef) Julliard, Paris representative of Reporters sans Frontières.[57] Journalist Anderson added, "The greatest threat doesn't come from state sponsors, but from small, non-state actors that are not intimidated by international law in the first place."[58]

PEC's Lempen said that international humanitarian law has no provisions to conduct inquiries, to sue those responsible for breaches, or to put sanctions on states or actors violating the Geneva Conventions.[59] Lempen added that a proposed convention on the protection of journalists would complement the Geneva Conventions. "It will create mechanisms of enquiry, sanctions and follow-up."[60] Others, such as the representatives from the ICRC, remain unsure about this PEC convention adding prosecution for those who target journalists. "Would new rules make a difference in the field?" asked ICRC's Dörmann.[61]

The Press Emblem Campaign, while controversial, responds directly to one of the primary challenges that confront those trying to draft international humanitarian law to protect journalists in conflict with an international treaty: how do we distinguish journalists from all the other actors in the battlefield and grant them special protection? While critics are quick to point out the flaws to the project, the debate signals a need to address the controversial concerns like journalists' licensing and special protections.

"Be Prepared": International Crisis Training

Organizations that focus on international journalists traveling to dangerous areas routinely mention the need for these kinds of journalists to obtain some kind of safety training or hostile environment training before entering any area where conflict may erupt. Militaries spend a great deal of time, money, and energy preparing their soldiers for all contingencies. A number of operations around the world supply a similar form of training not only to journalists, but also to government officials, nongovernmental organizations, and business people. This type of training can range from basic first aid to combat training; it can be conducted in-house or with the aid of professional training operations. The training can also last from a few hours to several days, and the cost of it varies as well. The idea of preparing journalists for work in the field is nothing new. Journalism schools have routinely offered students basic journalism training in gathering information during difficult assignments. This specialized training for journalists and media workers now, however, takes on a new meaning in the dangerous environment of today's conflict areas.

The notion of initiating special crisis training for international journalists and media workers reporting from war zones was on Daniel

Pearl's mind even before he was captured and killed. The two organizations he mentioned in his 1999 memo were Centurion Risk Assessment Services in the UK and Andy Kain Enterprises in the UK, which continue to offer training for journalists and others who find themselves working in conflict zones. Another organization, Dynamiq, from Australia also offers hostile environment training for journalists and other professionals in conflict.

"Conflict has become more sophisticated and unpredictable," said Mark Thompson, managing editor for multimedia at Reuters news agency. Reuters has been providing hostile environment training (HET) to expatriate and locally engaged staff, along with contracted freelancers, for 15 years. Many other major media organizations do the same. Normally lasting five days and organized at central locations or on-site, the course may be followed by a refresher after three years.[62]

The British-based company Andy Kain Enterprises, or AKE, pioneered such specialized expertise in hostile environment training. Founded in 1991 by a former member of Britain's elite Special Air Service, it has been offering HET courses since 1993. The core five-day residential course costs about $5,100.[63] AKE provides specialized training for journalists around the world and in 2010 traveled for the first time to Beijing, to provide a tailored HET course for Chinese television journalists.

Another organization from the United States that focuses on security training people for difficult assignments abroad is Crisis Consulting International. While this organization's main constituents are faith-based entities, cofounder Robert "Bob" Klamser suggested that journalists have much in common with the health care workers he instructs because constant and intense interactions with people are vital to both professional pursuits.[64] "Yes it's risky out there but what you're doing, there is no other way to do it. They [journalists] can't surround themselves with bodyguards or be in armored cars and live in compounds. They might as well stay home," he said.[65] Klamser explained that he believed one of the key elements to avoiding risk is to have current information about the specific situation and environment you are about to encounter. He added:

> I think journalists are always going to take risks. I see people getting in trouble because they didn't fully understand the risk and they were too casual about the implications of the risk. I don't think journalism can be a risk-free industry or profession; on the other hand I think risk can be managed in journalistic pursuits just as it can everywhere else. Having current local accurate information is the key. You can't get that from

Washington, you can't get that from a capital. You've got to develop sources that are focused on gathering that information locally.[66]

News organizations around the world insist upon crisis training for their operatives who take on dangerous assignments. Deputy Head of Newsgathering at BBC News, Sarah Ward-Lilley said the BBC enlists some very stringent measures to ensure they have tried to mitigate against risk as much as possible before anyone from the BBC is deployed to a dangerous area. She explained the BBC training strategy:

> We in the BBC, like many other media organizations, have a very strict policy in terms of safety training. No one from the BBC is allowed to go to what we term a hostile environment or a war zone or anything resembling a war zone—what we classify as risk category one—in any capacity without having been on a six-day residential hostile environment safety course. They come out of that as qualified first aiders but they also have been through some solid training in watching out for risks and potential risks, how to deal with check points, how to spot where there might be a land mine risk, how they might appear to others in silhouette and all sorts of other risks and consequences. So they are all carefully trained and they work in teams—we try to team up less experienced people with the more experienced to try to minimize risk. And we also have a very rigorous risk assessment process. Detailed forms have to be completed with emergency evacuation plans, next of kin details and other practical information. These assessments have to be checked and signed off at a very senior level before anyone leaves on a high risk deployment.[67]

Senior Managing Editor for the Associated Press, John Daniszewski, explained how the Associated Press treats the issue of journalists' training:

> At the AP we tend to send people into these assignments who have the training and background that will help them—whether experience covering hostile situations before or perhaps some military experience in their background . . . and those who are physically fit enough to put up with the elements of a conflict situation. We also have a global vice president from security and regional security officers who monitor the threat level in different places and also give us advice about what is safe and not safe to do. And for people who are going to be in those conflict situations, we also provide access to post-traumatic stress counseling and training on a case-by-case basis. We provide body armor and, where appropriate, gas masks for demonstrations and things like that. And we implement

procedures to help us keep track of our people when they are in the field so when there is a problem we can respond as quickly as possible.[68]

At the Australian Broadcasting Corporation, the news organization is famous for its groundbreaking program to prepare journalists and crews for covering potentially traumatic events. The ABC program takes a three-tier approach: peer support group training, manager awareness training, and staff awareness training. Manager of Staff Development from the ABC, Heather Forbes, explained that the journalists and media workers at the ABC also participate in "hostile environment courses" prepared by Dynamiq. She said:

> These courses are five days in duration and they take journalists through every sort of likely scenario. They take them through kidnapping and through hostage situations. They take them through weapons recognition and the reporters learn how to recognize what kind of gun is being used. They learn to recognize whether it's a gun used by the Australian or the American military or whether it's a gun used by others, like AK47s, which are pretty common. AK47s are mainly used by just about every kind of guerrilla terrorist group in the world. We give them flak jackets and helmets and gear like that. We give them satellite phones and part of the instruction is that they are not allowed to go anywhere without telling people where they are going. And when they are on a dangerous assignment they have to check in every hour to tell us that they are safe.[69]

Forbes explained that she was disappointed that more global media organizations have not instituted a formal safety and trauma training for their journalists in the field. She said there are a number of reasons that the ABC believes this kind of expensive training and equipment is worth the enormous expense to its news department:

> We reached this view that no story is worth a life. We value our staff. We don't want them dead. We want them alive and the only way to keep them alive is to give them as much training as we are able to and to provide them with all the safety gear that they should have so that our journalists are in a position to make very, very good decisions about what to do when they are on the ground. And they are told that if they want to pull out they can come out. And that's really psychologically important.[70]

A Reuters journalist, Vivek Prakash, detailed on his blog the four-day hostile environment training course he participated in conducted by the

Australian company, Dynamiq, in 2008 in Bangkok.[71] He explained how he and his fellow journalists were informed about correct bandaging techniques in the case of snake bites, fractures, shrapnel and chest wounds as well as what to do in case of a vehicle accident–one of the most common ways in which journalists are injured. The course also included correct procedures for traveling in a convoy, how to read and give GPS coordinates, how to select a hotel room least exposed to dangers such as explosions, flying shrapnel and stray bullets, and how to backtrack out of a minefield. Prakash also said he "learned how to put together a basic med [medical] kit; what to keep in a go-bag and, most importantly, how to assess every situation for potential safety threats, letting colleagues you trust know what you're doing every step of the way." He added:

> It brought home just how much difference preparation and training can make to anyone working in an unsafe environment. Getting the story and covering it effectively is one thing but we need to do that without jeopardizing our safety or that of our colleagues, eliminate completely unnecessary risks always thinking ahead to the next step and the way out.[72]

Attending to the Needs of the Forgotten Freelancer: The Rory Peck Trust

The cost of hostile environment training may be well beyond the means of freelance journalists or local, indigenous journalists on the ground. An organization established in the UK in 1995 has developed a unique mission to raise the profile of freelance journalists who continually risk their lives in conflict situations. The Rory Peck Trust provides assistance to freelance journalists around the world that includes grants for training as well as information and advice on insurance, trauma counseling, safety, and other issues. This completely independent organization was established to help freelance journalists and their families in need by providing assistance to the dependents of journalists who have been imprisoned or killed while working. The unique organization also honors the work of news cameramen and women through annual awards. Much of the funding for the Rory Peck Trust comes from major media organizations that recognize the need to offer superior training to freelancers who do the majority of the dangerous assignments in today's conflicts.

The Rory Peck Trust was established for Rory Peck, an esteemed freelance television cameraman who died while filming the attempted coup against Boris Yeltsin on October 3, 1993. Peck was just 36 but a veteran of the first Gulf War, Bucharest, Afghanistan, and Bosnia. Peck, who once carried a dying man over remote mountains for several days, was cut down in crossfire outside a Russian TV station. He was post-humously awarded Russia's highest civilian honor, the first time it had been bestowed on anyone outside the country. When Rory Peck died there were no rules and no structures about what to do if a freelancer is killed. So Peck's family and close friends set up the Rory Peck Trust to address this gap.[73]

Much of the work of the Rory Peck Trust involves the distribution of bursaries or donated funds to freelancers for industry-recognized safety training courses. The bursaries allow freelancers the chance to take part in the same training that media organizations use for staff training for those preparing for work in hostile environments. The Trust also offers help to freelance journalists who get into dangerous situations while reporting in a country. Director of the Rory Peck Trust, Tina Carr, said, "What we primarily do as well as safety training is to give charitable grants to freelancers in trouble or their families."[74]

Crisis Training for the Mind

Chris Cramer noted on the INSI website that in addition to safety train-ing, journalists who report from conflict areas should participate in "cri-sis training for the mind."

One can find few medical research studies on the psychological toll journalists face in conflict despite data on the increase of journalists being targeted in these conflict zones. One of the few medical researchers who have focused on this area of psychoanalysis has been Dr. Andrew Feinstein, a psychiatrist from Canada. Dr. Feinstein said journalists and their organizations need to be aware that there are more than physi-cal risks when one chooses to pursue a story in a dangerous environ-ment. He added:

> Journalists need to understand the psychological risks of doing very dan-gerous work ... education is very important. So that should a journalist develop symptoms of emotional distress in response to the danger that they confront, they are able to recognize what is going on and have an appreciation of what needs to be done. And certainly news organizations need to know this ... I think these organizations are bound to look after the health of their journalists. I think it's one thing to send someone into a war zone but I think if you do so you need to have the responsibility of

care that should the journalist get into difficulty whether it be physical or psychological that there is a mechanism in place to help the journalist.[75]

Dr. Feinstein has been working with journalists for more than 10 years, and he has conducted one of the few research investigations on the affects of war reporting on the psyches of journalists.[76] He has found that the personal costs for those who cover conflict may be high. Dr. Feinstein said:

> The longer you are exposed to grave danger the chances of you developing some psychological problems become fairly significant . . . The first group of journalists that I studied had been doing front line war reporting for 15 years . . . a long time. . .and they really defined their careers by war reporting . . . the rates of post traumatic stress disorder in this group were high, about one in four journalists over the course of that period developed post traumatic stress disorder–which was very high, relative to the general population where the rates were four to five percent. Going into war zones and confronting danger and getting shot at and maybe getting wounded or having friends killed—for many journalists comes at quite a cost.[77]

Dr. Feinstein said that, for the most part, journalists are a resilient group and many who report from dangerous areas manage to do so without any psychological damage. Feinstein's research suggested that while a minority of journalists suffers from emotional distress, it is not an insignificant minority.[78] As a result of Dr. Feinstein's research findings, organizations like the Dart Center for Journalism and Trauma have focused on the possible damage war reporting could possibly have on the minds of journalists in the field.

While the Dart Center's mission focuses ostensibly on improving media coverage of trauma, the organization has likewise encouraged research on the impact of reporting traumatic events on those whose responsibility it is to follow these events closely. Established in 1990 at Michigan State University, the Dart Center for Journalism and Trauma has been a resource for journalists who cover war, conflict, and disasters. On its website, the Dart Center presents its mission as an organization that:

> *Advocates* ethical and thorough reporting of trauma; compassionate, professional treatment of victims and survivors by journalists; and greater awareness by media organizations of the impact of trauma coverage on both news professionals and news consumers. *Educates* journalists and

journalism students about the science and psychology of trauma and the implications for news coverage. *Provides a professional forum* for journalists in all media to analyze issues, share knowledge and ideas, and advance strategies related to the craft of reporting on violence and tragedy. *Creates and sustains interdisciplinary collaboration* and communication among news professionals, clinicians, academic researchers and others concerned with violence, conflict and tragedy.[79]

The Executive Director of the Dart Center, Bruce Shapiro, said news organizations around the world should take steps to protect their reporters by instituting comprehensive training opportunities for their media workers. He said:

> I think that executives, owners, and news room managers need to take some responsibility both for advocating safety awareness and trauma awareness in the newsroom culture and for setting a standard and a tone as advocates for those issues. I think in news organizations where that's happened there's been very important culture change. I've seen that happen for example at the Globo TV network in Brazil which now provides some important training to its local correspondents in Rio and other dangerous places. They've seen a marked decline in the number of attacks, the number of injuries and deaths. Brazil used to be one of the most dangerous countries in the world of journalists. It's fallen down on the list now.[80]

Shapiro said he trusts in the mission of this organization because it promotes the safety of journalists in the most fundamental ways. He said, "It's also a way for journalists to remind themselves constantly of the stakes in our work and that we want to be here for the long haul...if you believe in the mission then you have to stay safe in order to accomplish it."[81]

Media professionals have been urged to be prepared and astutely aware of the risks while they ponder the worst-case scenarios when reporting from difficult and dangerous situations. Since the Crimean war, stories of conflict and war have been worth the risk to news operations because these are stories the audience expected and appreciated. However, the cost-benefit of reporting from war zones has recently come under investigation by news organizations and other journalism organizations. The new wars and the way they are waged have resulted in added dangers for the journalist and media worker. The results of these added risks have led many news organizations to provide specialized training and equipment for their reporters who cover danger assignments. Research about the psychological damage that war may inflict on journalists as well as soldiers has similarly prompted news operations to address this risk for their reporters and to find ways to mitigate these risks.

"There Must Be Another Way": Theoretical Prospects that Enlist Education and Alternative Reporting Approaches as Unique Tactics to Protect Journalists

If the ultimate goal is to protect journalists in all areas of conflict in perpetuity, the notion of comprehensive media education around the globe may be the most effective long-term tactic. It is commonplace to argue that media provide audiences with a great deal of social, cultural, and political information. Media influence on popular consciousness is easy to conceptualize through concepts like propaganda and advertising, which imply direct, intentional efforts to manipulate and persuade. Such efforts do exist, but such general notions ignore the complexity of media and its power to influence and change behavior. From this basic concept about the flow of media in a complex world, it can be argued that media wield some level of power on the world stage. Theories that relate to this notion of power offer a different way to think about the media's impact on public attitudes and behavior. These theories include media agenda setting theory, the spiral of silence, social learning theory, and cultivation theory.[82]

Media agenda setting theory suggests media focus public attention on some issues and away from others and cultivate a value judgment that influences public opinion of what is important and what is good and valuable and what is bad and threatening. These media inspired perceptions, like journalists who take sides when reporting from conflict, can in turn affect attitudes, especially when these perceptions reinforce longstanding predispositions.

The spiral of silence theory represents the opposite perception-creating theory, pioneered by social scientist Elisabeth Noelle-Neumann. This theory proposes that people who hold views which they feel represent a minority opinion, not often expressed in public, become silent and less inclined to express their opinions for fear of social isolation. Then, without personal and social reinforcement, the minority opinion dies. Thus, by tending to ignore certain minority opinions, media contribute to this erosion and silence.

Social learning theory proffers a proposition that people learn social norms from attending to the media. Children learn what constitutes polite behavior, how to act and react in a gendered fashion in each culture, and what constitutes other cultural norms. The media play a paramount role in telling these cultural and social stories to most of the children around the world. Cultivation theory represents social learning over the long term. Much attention to mediated information over a long period gradually leads to the adoption of beliefs and thus behaviors about how the social world works. This long-term cultivation leads to a stereotyped and selective view of reality. This theory, developed by social scientist, George Gerbner, holds that media often explain how a tiny picture of the world may lead to the population adopting this small vision of truth as universal.[83]

Thus media construct maps of the world which favor dominant values, institutions, elites or social relations, which may be contrary to the minority opinion of combatants or belligerents waging conflict and drawing maps on another battlefield. During times of conflict, the power the media storytellers possess shifts them from mere objective observers to sources of contrary stories for many combatants. Media also serve as sources of intelligence, weapons for each side, and ultimately the war of words battlefield itself. Media scholars suggest that media's power becomes increasingly effective on audiences with sparse knowledge of how media may ultimate affect them or with little motivation to critically examine the media content.[84] Thus, the contrary should also be true, that increased knowledge of media's effects and a value toward critical examination of the stories portrayed may have a mitigating effect on the media's power over their audiences.

The advent of new media production devices may have added voices and images to the vast array of media stories during conflict, but these new ways of communicating may not have diminished but rather enhanced the nature of media influence. Advances in technology may not have lead to a greater understanding of conflict but may have even contributed to mobilization or better organized violence. Robert Hackett, a Canadian media scholar, argued, "If both war and media are fundamental processes, then perhaps there are deep-rooted connections between the two."[85] Traditional practices of demonization of the enemy in the media may be so intertwined with conflict that even these traditional methods of reporting about conflict have been carried over into the new media. In some cases like the nationalistic conflicts of the 1990s in Bosnia, Rwanda, and Sierra Leone, new media operatives may have amplified the conflicts by disseminating hate speech and calling for killings using new forms of shouting from the mountain top.

While new technologies offer journalists, insurgents, and citizen observers new opportunities to share images and war stories, the new technologies can be a boon to repressive governments—allowing for surveillance and censorship on an unprecedented scale. The Committee to Protect Journalists reported that in 2009, half of all imprisoned journalists were targeted for the work they published online that was easily accessible by the authorities.[86] So while repressive governments and the combatants have determined the power of media, they have not yet uncovered the value of peace and the part media could play in that construction.

Human beings have an enormous need to find meaning and to understand where truth lies. Traditional and objective journalism has been historically enlisted as a technique in seeking truth during conflict. Since the turn of the last century the notion of objective journalism has dominated the way journalists are taught to pursue their profession. Objective reporting is associated with ways of gathering news (knowledge about places, people and events) and conveying them in a detached, impersonal way free of value judgments.[87] Objectivity is prized as a strategic ritual allowing for the profession to defend itself from criticism while constructing a wide distinction between facts and opinion.[88]

However, being objective should not be confused with not having a point of view. Journalists who claim they have no interest in the outcome of a conflict are disingenuous. For domestic or indigenous journalists who cover conflict within their own countries—journalism is personal. So as a practical matter, objectivity is an illusion: choices about what to cover, as well as how to cover, are not made in a moral vacuum. Objectivity may be simply a technique that has been an historical and cultural solution to this human need for truth. While traditional journalism has professed objectivity as the most effective means of presenting information, it has been, perhaps, an unattainable social construction.

Journalists do have a unique opportunity to impact a conflict—preemptively during the conflict, and restoratively following conflict. The extent of journalistic involvement is an old issue that takes on new significance in light of the changing tactics of new wars, expanded technological advancements, and the extent of political and military approaches to foreign conflicts. Balancing objectivity with social responsibility becomes paramount for today's storytellers. Philip Seib in his book, *The Global Journalist: News and Conscience in a World of Conflict,* reported that the press have dual responsibilities: "to call attention to situations in which governmental action—such as military intervention or non-military aid—may be appropriate, and to provide accurate descriptions of the results of policy, military or otherwise."[89] The knowledge of how journalists can accomplish both of these tasks should be part of every journalism education curriculum. Journalists themselves must recognize that the value of what they do can, and should, mitigate conflict. Rony Brauman, former head of Médecins sans Frontières wrote, "Although knowing about a crisis does not solve it, the knowledge does at least pave the way for the most basic act of justice. If the guilty cannot be punished, then at least the victims can be recognized."[90]

Media Education as a Strategy of Protection for Those Engaged in Journalism

The question again arises as to how to protect the journalist striving to tell the most accurate story of conflict. The short-term tactics like flak jackets and crisis training may offer initial protection, but combatants will find ways around these protections if they believe that journalism has little value and journalists are the enemy. As with many multifaceted and complex problems, the most effective long-term strategy may be through education. One of the primary reasons combatants are targeting journalists covering conflict stems from the perceived notion that journalists are not of value beyond the money they could fetch in a kidnapping scheme or the fear that the combatant could generate by targeting the journalist—because that fear would serve the combatant better than any other story. Thus the logical step in preventing these kinds of attacks would be to increase understanding of the role of journalists in society and to foster an appreciation for fair and accurate reporting about conflict and corruption. Basic media education about the benefits of free expression to all communities would serve to generate a greater respect for the journalists who tells these difficult stories.

The fundamental lessons of media literacy focus on learning to view conflict from all perspectives and critically examine underlying agendas of public communicators. These lessons could be universally disseminated, which would result in a nonviolent and less costly way to protect journalists in the long run. A number of steps toward this kind of long-term protection have been implemented by media literacy organizations around the world as well as some of the advocacy groups mentioned above. But prolonged efforts like this need constant attention.

Another way to approach the idea of media education to mitigate the targeting of journalists may be to retrain the journalists to tell their war stories differently. Once the public acquires the critical analysis tools to effectively evaluate the persuasive strategies of the media, they become hungry for reporting that addresses the origins of the conflict and not just the winners or losers. The public may also be interested in stories that focus on the solution of the conflict and not just the victory. Proponents of this type of reporting suggest that traditional war reporting may lead journalists to become so engrossed in the action of the conflict that they tend to ignore the stories about actual peace building. Advocates of Peace Journalism or conflict-sensitive reporting posit that in order to mitigate conflicts around the world journalists should be the first line of defense against the conflict—including its origins and nuances.

Conflict-Sensitive Reporting and Peace Journalism

Another means to approach the risks that journalists experience when telling war stories may be to develop an alternative or more sensitive way to tell those stories. The objective of this kind of alternative journalism would be to use the media to quell conflict rather than inflame it. Proponents of this kind of reporting suggest that journalism and journalists can be a force to mitigate conflict if their reporting is done with attention toward the fundamental theories of conflict negation, essentially how conflict develops and how it might end. In his handbook written in 2003 for the Danish organization International Media Support, Ross Howard, posited:

> For more than 50 years diplomats, negotiators and social scientists have studied conflict and developed a sophisticated understanding of it, just like medicine, business or music. But few journalists have any training in the theory of conflict. Most journalists merely report on the conflict as it happens. By comparison, medical reporters do not just report on a person's illness. They also report on what caused the illness and what may cure it. News reporters can have the same skill when it comes to reporting conflict.[91]

Howard's handbook outlines the basic concepts of how to practice conflict-sensitive reporting by first understanding the fundamental principles of what causes conflict and violence. He then introduces the part that journalism could play in enhancing communication between warring parties. This novel approach to reporting about conflict has been introduced through myriad seminars and journalism training sessions around the world. Highly designed training sessions developed by the International Media Support organization as well as Reporting for Peace for Internews, the Institute for War and Peace Reporting, the Center for War, Peace, and the News Media make full use of this handbook to rethink journalism as a tool for peace. Much of this training has taken place in Asian and African countries in recent years.

Howard, a Canadian expert on conflict-sensitive reporting, conducted a workshop that trained 20 journalists from various regions of Somalia in 2007.[92] The National Union of Somali Journalists and International Media Support sponsored the workshop. Howard said he was impressed by the courage of the Somali journalists. He added, "I was also pleased by their interest in learning new techniques of reporting which can make Somalia a better informed society, which can achieve conflict resolution and democracy. The fact is that a professional independent media is essential to Somalia's peaceful future."[93] At this workshop, Albert Sam, a veteran Ghanaian journalist who covered the conflict in Liberia and the country's 1997 elections, said the role of the media in conflict resolution or escalation cannot be overemphasized, "... the pen, used by journalists is mightier than any weapon of mass destruction," he said.[94]

In May 2010, the German government sponsored a program designed by its International Institute of Journalism whereby 15 West African journalists were trained in conflict-sensitive reporting.[95] The journalists were from Liberia, Nigeria, Sierra Leone, Togo, and Gambia. They were trained by German journalists who taught them about the theory of conflict, conflict mapping, conflict dynamics, and conflict resolution. The role of the media in conflict resolution, framing and angling of conflict sensitive stories, gender issues and the building of Africa's image, among others, were also part of the curriculum.[96]

Another term for this conflict-sensitive reporting technique is "Peace Journalism." In their book, *Peace Journalism*, Jake Lynch and Annabel McGoldrick[97] admitted that even the phrase "Peace Journalism" might not appeal to everyone. The term might be considered provocative because it promotes the notion that traditional or conventional journalism might be considered, conversely, as War Journalism. The idea that the phrase "Peace Journalism" may be loaded with preconceived impressions and suggest dichotomies that lead the reader to positive or negative connotations offers a precise analogy of what Peace Journalism is at its core: a way to break outdated conventions of war reporting. By approaching stories about war from a more critical, less binary, perspective, reporting about conflict may ostensibly become a much less dangerous occupation.

The emergence of Peace Journalism grew from the relatively new academic study of Conflict Analysis and Peace Research. The baseline normative theoretical assumptions of these research areas rest on the propositions that violence may not be its own cause, nonviolence may be considered an option, every conflict grew from more than two parties, and all parties in a conflict have a stake in the outcome.[98] One of the first lessons of Peace Journalism has been to recognize that language is subjective, and words have a powerful relationship with understanding, attitudes, and behaviors. But traditional journalism practice claims to avoid the traps of subjectivity. Those who have practiced journalism since the Enlightenment have taken great pains to obscure their personal viewpoints and replace that kind of reporting with the journalistic ethos of objectivity. Traditional journalism strives to get as close as it can to big "T" truth. But critical examinations of the current practice of war reporting using a Peace Journalism lens, question whether any journalism conducted during conflict can offer the fundamental conventions of objectivity and thus get closer to the truth about the conflicts. Lynch and McGoldrick claimed that under the conventions of objectivity, reporters who cover conflict tend to practice journalism that is biased in favor of official sources, focuses on events over processes, and perpetuates dualism in reporting conflicts.[99]

The creation of the border between them and us occurs often in sociopsychological literature and is reported to be found in all human relationships. Carl Schmitt in *The Concept of the Political* was one of the first to introduce the "we" versus "the other" in modern political thought.[100] Eventually, national governments and organized warring factions in conflict situations resort to defining the enemy as the other and creating scenarios and language that support the construction. Traditional journalists simply follow the lead.

Engaging in the practice of Peace Journalism, the journalists may include material on the background of the conflict, showing direct violence as an intelligible, if dysfunctional, response to identifiable conditions in social realism. The journalists will then likely highlight nonviolent actions as an alternative response that some people may be advocating, to the same situation. The journalist may strive to include a multiplicity of dividing lines as well as potential for common ground, among the conflicting parties. Most importantly, the journalists practicing

Peace Journalism will provide its audience with clues and cues to negotiate their own reading for propaganda from all sides.[101]

What Peace Journalism proffers is an approach to journalism that dissolves the veil of objectivity and replaces it with a conflict analysis tool. The practice essentially strives to provide an analytical model to predict, identify, and connect shortcomings in traditional war reporting. Thus, Peace Journalism proposes to be a set of journalistic tools, conceptual and practical, intended to equip journalists with the means to offer a better public service and perhaps create an inherent value in their discipline.

Lynch and McGoldrick posited that the original concept of Peace Journalism was presented in a table by Professor Johan Galtung who was a pioneer in the academic study of peace research.[102] In this template, Galtung suggested four main areas where Peace Journalism and traditional/conventional war reporting tended to be juxtaposed. He suggested that Peace Journalism was designed to explore the formation of the conflict, whereas traditional journalism focused on the area and events of the conflict and the goal to win. He added that Peace Journalism was truth-oriented, whereas War Journalism tended to be propaganda-oriented. The differences between the two practices were also found in the fundamental characteristics of the stories: Peace Journalism was designed to focus on the suffering of all people in the conflict; conversely, traditional journalism was historically developed to focus on the elite or official sources. The primary difference discussed between the two practices dealt with outcomes. Peace Journalism was reported to be focused on highlighting solutions to the conflict, while conventional journalism has tended to rally the readers to focus on the victory.[103]

Media in all its facets can be a profound tool to teach the world about the benefits of free expression. While it may seem self-serving and myopic, using the media to explain the vast potential of the media may be the best long-term tactic to address the dangers that face those who practice journalism today. Likewise, the media can adapt to help us become not only more aware of the values of free expression, but to equip us with the skills to challenge the message and to create new meaning and roles for ourselves as global citizens. Annabel McGoldrick posited that traditional war reporting implicates us in "a dysfunctional relationship with the world around us—dysfunctional because of the conventions of news, which have been developed in response to commercial and political interests."[104] It may be time to break those conventions and approach war stories from a critical and educational perspective. The media are not inherently good or evil, but how the audience is taught to appreciate the media can result in a world where people look upon the media as enemy or friend.

"Are We There Yet?": Measuring the Efficacy of Tactics and Strategies

Pragmatic strategies that appear to be most effective in protecting journalists in today's conflicts are ones that combine hostile environment training and language and culture seminars, along with physical protection like flak jackets. Although potentially the most effective, these strategies are also the most expensive, creating financial difficulty for many news organizations around the world. While nongovernmental organizations such as the International News Safety Institute and Reporters sans Frontières provide training at a reduced cost for journalists, this training does not ensure comprehensive coverage for journalists operating in conflict areas.

It is evident from the interviews surrounding the PEC strategy that significant disagreements exist about the best way to protect journalists in conflict. Many of the stakeholders suggested that mere physical identification may not be sufficient or may even be a detriment in protecting journalists in conflict situations. This divergence of opinions about the PEC most clearly demonstrates the need for increased collaboration and respect among members of the journalist community to come together to generate and promote a solution that will ultimately provide journalists the protection they deserve.

The rhetorical strategy of informing the public about this problem and engendering a foundational respect for the profession of journalism itself is fundamental to guarantee that journalists gathering information about war and conflict are protected. Increasing the understanding of the role journalists play in contributing to an open society will hopefully present an urgent appeal for the improvement of journalist protection under the auspices of international humanitarian law. This strategy can also be enhanced through increased responsibility of journalists to maintain high standards of integrity, accuracy, and fairness in their reporting.

"The role of journalists in society is a counterpart to power. They are the critical voice," said Freimut Duve, Organization for Security and Co-operation in Europe representative on Freedom of the Media.[105] Educating the public about the importance of journalists could lead to increased concern of community members, and result in supportive action for the protection of media.

While much work has been done by nonstate actors to generate strategies and tactics, both pragmatic and theoretical, to protect journalists in conflict, much work still needs to be done. Advocates, safety guides, and training strategies are designed to address the issue of journalists' protection today, while education strategies like media literacy and Peace Journalism were developed to generate a value in the cause of journalism and to promote a better way of telling the stories of conflict.

The next chapter highlights in some detail the traumatic events that journalists and media workers have suffered telling the stories of conflict and corruption. This text exists as a tribute to their lives and work.

Chapter 4

Don't Shoot the Messenger: Journalists Who Risk Everything to Tell Stories of Conflict

Far too many journalists pay a high price for practicing their craft in today's world. International frontline journalists, local media workers who support them, and local journalists telling stories of corruption in their own countries share similar dangers. They risk tear gas, rubber bullets, verbal abuse, kidnapping, beating, and death. During the past decade, more than 1,000 journalists and news support staff, including drivers, translators, and fixers, have paid with their lives for the right to report. Granted, some journalists and media workers have been killed accidentally or have died in situations unrelated to the conflict. But others have been directly targeted because of their profession as media storytellers.

The most disturbing aspect of this trend is that the majority of deliberate attacks on journalists around the world have occurred without the perpetrators being brought to justice. The Committee to Protect Journalists (CPJ) reported that of the 861 journalists killed since 1992, nearly 90 percent of those murderers have enjoyed complete impunity.[1] In 2008, CPJ developed an Impunity Index to help illustrate this problem. CPJ obtained the Impunity Index statistics by calculating the number of unsolved journalist murders as a percentage of the population in each country. According to CPJ, cases are considered unsolved if no convictions have been obtained.[2] The CPJ Impunity Index showed that:

> The countries with the worst records for impunity—Iraq, Sierra Leone, and Somalia—have been mired in conflict. But the majority of the 13 countries on CPJ's Impunity Index are established, peacetime democracies such as Mexico, pointing to alarming failures by those elected governments to protect journalists. CPJ Executive Director Joel Simon said:

"Every time a journalist is murdered and the killer is allowed to walk free it sends a terrible signal to the press and to others who would harm journalists." The governments on this list simply must do more to demonstrate a real commitment to a free press. Lip service won't help save journalists' lives. We are calling for action: thorough investigations and vigorous prosecutions in all journalist homicides.[3]

Another disturbing trend is the number of journalists who have been jailed for doing their jobs. In December 2010, CPJ issued a special report indicating that the number of journalists in prison has reached its highest level since 1996. It identified 145 reporters, editors, and photojournalists behind bars on December 1, 2010, an increase of nine from the 2009 tally.[4] CPJ reported that Iran and China were among the worst countries for imprisonment of journalists, but other nations like Eritrea, Burma/Myanmar, Uzbekistan, and Azerbaijan also find it easy to rely on vague, antistate charges to jail journalists.[5]

What the statistics from the CPJ and other organizations do not include are those journalists who are harassed or intimidated and who do not report these attacks to national or international advocacy groups. These statistics also do not reflect the damage these attacks may be having on self-censorship or editorial decisions, or the cumulative cost these attacks are having on free expression around the globe.

But statistics do not represent the whole story in another way—they are not personal. The following pages tell some of the individual stories of the brave journalists and media workers who have died, been harassed, or been jailed in this war on words. These stories represent the lives of international frontline journalists, local journalists, and media workers.

Daniel Pearl

Pakistan, 2002

None of us want to die; we don't do our work with a death wish. Increasingly, we are walking with targets on our backs. Danny's public execution marked a turning point in the modern day experience of journalists.[6]

Asra Q. Nomani, friend and former colleague of Daniel Pearl

Some suggest the turning point for the world's attention on the plight of journalists in conflict occurred when Daniel Pearl was murdered while covering a story in Pakistan in 2002. His murder brought worldwide attention to the issue of journalists being targeted in conflict.

Pearl began working for the *Wall Street Journal* in November 1990 as a reporter in Atlanta, before moving to the paper's Washington, D.C., bureau in 1993. Pearl assumed an important assignment in London in early 1996. He reported on the Middle East, and later, after transferring to Paris, covered the Balkan crisis. "If you were in the field, you wanted to be with Danny," said colleague A. Craig Copetas, a former *Journal* foreign correspondent who reported with him in Kosovo. "He was very prudent, very cautious."[7]

This opinion that Pearl was a journalist who did not take unnecessary risks was shared by many of his colleagues. They reported that Pearl did "not fit the stereotype of the pushy, swaggering cowboy correspondent." He was "regarded as self-effacing and sometimes absent-minded, though sly and funny in an offbeat way." During dinner in November 2002, Pearl said he was not interested in reporting from Afghanistan. "It's too dangerous," he explained. "I just got married, my wife is pregnant, and I'm just not going to do it." However, Pearl, a twelve-year veteran of the *Journal*, was also known for his tenacity and curiosity— "and for exasperating his editors on deadline by insisting on making just one more phone call."[8]

It was partially this persistence that led to his abduction on January 23, 2002, in Karachi, Pakistan.[9] Four days after Pearl's disappearance, a group called "The National Movement for the Restoration of Pakistani Sovereignty" sent an e-mail to several U.S. and Pakistani-based news organizations claiming responsibility for kidnapping Pearl and accusing him of being an American or an Israeli spy. In the e-mail, the kidnappers attached four photographs of Pearl, including one in which he was held at gunpoint.[10]

In the group's second e-mail, they threatened to kill Pearl if their demands were not met. Their demands were elaborate; with the captors calling for the release of Pakistani nationals being held in Guantanamo Bay, Cuba, and others detained in the United States as terrorism suspects. They called for the United States to give up the F-16 fighter jets purchased in the 1980s by Pakistan, (which were never delivered because of U.S. sanctions related to Pakistan's nuclear-weapons program[11]) and also called for the expulsion of all American journalists based in Pakistan. Although Pearl's family and colleagues along with U.S. and Pakistani officials immediately undertook an intensive effort to find his captors and negotiate Pearl's release, they were ultimately unsuccessful. Some time within the four weeks he was detained, his captors beheaded him and disseminated the video for the world to see.

In July 2002, a Pakistani judge convicted British-born Islamic militant Ahmed Omar Saeed Sheikh and three other men for Pearl's kidnapping and murder. Saeed was sentenced to death for plotting Pearl's abduction and murder, and the three accomplices were sentenced to life imprisonment, which in Pakistan typically means 25 years. All four have filed appeals. Seven other suspects remain at large, including some who allegedly helped to murder Pearl.[12] In 2007, at a hearing in Guantanamo Bay, the alleged mastermind of the September 11 attacks, Khalid Sheikh Mohammed confessed to killing Pearl. "I decapitated with my blessed right hand the head of the American Jew Daniel Pearl, in the city of Karachi, Pakistan," Mohammed said.[13] Mohammed is set to be tried in New York City, although the trial date is presently unknown. Pearl's family is reportedly furious that Mohammed will receive a public trial. Judea Pearl, Daniel Pearl's father, said he believed it would just give the terrorist exposure to espouse radical ideologies. In a statement released by the Daniel Pearl Foundation, Pearl's parents said, "We are respectful of the legal process, but believe that giving a confessed terrorist a worldwide platform to publicize their ideology sends the wrong message to potential terrorists."[14]

Pearl's family and friends report that they remain unsatisfied with the circumstances surrounding Pearl's death. As a result of this frustration, Pearl's *Wall Street Journal* colleague in Pakistan, Asra Q. Nomani, launched "The Pearl Project" with Barbara Feinman Todd, an associate dean at Georgetown University in Washington, D.C. in 2007. The goal of the Pearl Project, an investigative journalism class, is to figure out the exact details surrounding Pearl's death. "One of the goals of the Pearl Project is to establish whether there is any evidence linking ... Mohammed to the murder. Even if we establish conclusively that he did murder Danny, there were three murderers and we want to establish the identities of the other two."[15] Although the Project has conducted extensive investigative research into Pearl's death, it has yet to publish a final report detailing its findings.[16]

In a question and answer segment on the *Washington Post*'s website, Nomani described her colleague's extensive efforts to protect those who travel to dangerous assignments to cover conflicts. "As a reporter who had traveled in hot spots before, he had written a detailed memo to his boss, outlining precautions that should be taken to keep *Wall Street Journal* reporters safe—from bulletproof vests to defensive driving training. Sadly, one of the scenarios for which he made suggestions was a kidnapping. Most of his recommendations have been put in place not only at the *Wall Street Journal* but throughout our industry—alas, of course, too late to save Danny."[17]

Meanwhile, Pearl's wife, Mariane, resiliently carries on. "I knew too well the one thing that could defeat me and, by extension, my husband's memory and our son: helplessness. I decided that if those who killed my husband were determined to show the gruesome side of humanity, I would display its integrity, beauty and resilience. That would be my true revenge."[18]

Anna Politkovskaya

Russia, 2006

I thought that maybe I should not write about everything I see. Maybe I should spare you all . . . so that you can continue to enjoy your life thinking that the army and the new government are doing the right thing in Northern Caucasus. Maybe. But I know for sure that when we wake up it will be too late.[19]

Crisis mediator, human rights advocate, and award-winning investigative journalist, Anna Politkovskaya, fought for victims in Russia and Chechnya for more than twenty years as a special correspondent for one of Russia's last independent newspapers, *Novaya Gazeta*.[20] She believed she had a mission to report on the war in Chechnya that Russian President Vladimir Putin launched in the fall of 1999. She reported on mass executions, torture, and kidnapping by the Russian military and Chechen rebels.[21] Although other Russian journalists primarily avoided Chechnya, Politkovskaya took more than fifty trips to chronicle abuses on both sides of this conflict. She wrote about burned corpses, abductions of Chechen civilians by Russian forces, destroyed villages and savaged bodies.[22] Alexander Politkovsky, her ex-husband remarked in the film, *Letter to Anna: The Story of Journalist Politkovskaya's Death*, "Her sense of justice was the focal point of her life. Lying was forbidden. One must always tell the truth. This was the principle she always lived by. And it was precisely what took her to Chechnya."[23]

In retaliation for her work, Politkovskaya was repeatedly attacked and threatened by Russian authorities. In February 2001, security agents detained her in the Vedeno district in Chechnya, after accusing her of entering the country without accreditation. For three days, she was kept in a pit without food or water, while a military officer threatened to kill her.

Seven months later, the same military officer accused of crimes against civilians sent her death threats. She was forced to flee to Vienna after the officer sent an email to *Novaya Gazeta* promising that he would seek revenge.[24] The officer was detained but later released for lack of evidence.[25]

Then, in September 2004, Politkovskaya boarded a plane from Moscow to Beslan, North Ossetia after masked terrorists with explosives and guns took more than one thousand children, teachers, and parents hostage at an elementary school. Politkovskaya planned to meet with former Chechen President Aslan Maskhadov, whom she knew quite well, to urge his intervention in the crisis. While on the plane, however, Politkovskaya promptly became ill and fell into a coma after drinking a cup of tea offered to her.[26] The toxin was never identified but Politkovskaya assumed the FSB officers (the domestic successor to the KGB) she had seen on the plane had poisoned her because they did not want her interference in the Beslan crisis.[27]

Although despised by Russian authorities for her intrepid reporting, she was widely respected in Chechnya by its citizens, and even its rebels. Indeed, her influence was so great that on October 23, 2002, when Chechen rebels took more than 900 people hostage at Moscow's Dubrovka Theatre, the rebels requested through *Novaya Gazeta* that Politkovskaya serve as a mediator in the dispute.[28] Although her negotiation efforts proved futile, Politkovskaya was able to obtain water and juice for the hostages before she left the theatre. Later, Russian authorities released a potent gas into the room, killing 125 hostages along with many of the terrorists.[29]

On October 5, 2006 (Chechen President Ramzan Kadyrov's birthday), Politkovskaya was interviewed on Radio Liberty about her investigation of the young Chechen President who was installed by Putin and the FSB.[30] She told Radio Liberty: "Personally, I only have one dream for Kadyrov's birthday: I dream of him someday sitting in the dock, in a trial that meets the strictest legal standards, with all of his crimes listed and investigated."[31]

Two days later, on Putin's birthday, Politkovskaya was assassinated.

It was the afternoon of October 7, 2006. The forty-eight-year-old, soon-to-be grandmother was buying groceries and special items for her daughter Vera, who was expecting her first child. Meanwhile, a man in jeans and a white turtleneck and a light-haired woman in black were following her. At 3:30 p.m. Politkovskaya called her son, Ilya, to inform him she was on her way home. At approximately 4 p.m., in the lobby elevator, she was shot in post-Soviet fashion: three bullets to the chest and one control shot to the head. Her baseball-cap wearing killer then dumped his weapon, a pistol with a silencer, at the scene of the crime.[32]

Putin remained silent for three days as other world leaders expressed condolences. It was not until October 10 that he broke his silence by telling the German newspaper, *Süddeutsche Zeitung*, that his government would do everything to bring Politkovskaya's assassins to justice. He added that Politkovskaya's influence inside Russia was "negligible."[33] According to the *New York Times*, he said, "The level of her influence on political life in Russia was utterly insignificant."[34]

Many of those present at the funeral, however, seemed to disagree. "It was clearly a political murder," said one woman, who spoke to the BBC at Politkovskaya's funeral. "I think this was meant to show what happens if you speak out against the authorities. Unfortunately, we have very few journalists like her in Russia now."[35] "She was our hero," said Tatyana Karpova, who lost her son when Chechen rebels took over a Moscow theatre, and who was at Politkovskaya's funeral. "Nobody else could write with such courage and bravery against the wrongdoings and the crimes of Russian authorities.[36]

The Investigation

Politkovskaya's editor at *Novaya Gazeta*, Dmitri A. Muratov, said he believes Anna was killed because her investigations were threatening the financial interests of individuals in Russia.[37] Russian authorities vehemently disagree, saying the murder was ordered from abroad to discredit the Kremlin. At a press conference 10 months after her death, Prosecutor Yury Chaika said the killers hoped to "create a crisis situation and bring about a return to the old management system in which money and oligarchs decided everything."[38] It is widely believed he was referring to the exiled Russian billionaire Boris A. Berezovsky, now living in London, whom the Kremlin suspected in the deadly radiation poisoning of former KGB officer Alexander Litvinenko, just a month after Politkovskaya's death. At the same time, Chaika, whose office examines most major crimes, held a press conference where he announced 10 people—mainly Chechen thugs who were members of a Moscow criminal group that specialized in contract murders—had been arrested in connection with Politkovskaya's death.[39]

However, the investigation of those arrested was short lived. Chaika was no longer in charge of the case. Then in September 2007, Chaika's main investigator on the case was demoted, and new investigators were brought in. It was not until nine months later, in June 2008 that an investigative committee representative announced that the case was ready to go to court. But by this point only four men remained in custody. Three of the men were charged as accomplices to murder, while the fourth individual was being held on reduced charges of abuse of office and extortion. All four figures that were arrested were considered peripheral figures. Meanwhile, the person believed to have pulled the trigger had avoided capture, and the individual who ordered the killing has yet to be named or arrested.[40]

A conviction in the four original cases would have still been considered a partial victory. However, on February 19, 2009, a Moscow jury decided unanimously to acquit the three accused of murder.[41] But the next day the presiding judge ordered the Russian Investigative Committee to reopen the case. He also informed the Interfax news agency that he would give material evidence to the investigators.[42] Four months later, on June 25, 2009, Russia's Supreme Court overturned the acquittals of the four men accused and commanded that a new trial be held, thus agreeing with the prosecution that there had been procedural violations on the part of the judges and defense in the first trial.[43] However, many human rights defenders were not convinced of the Court's authenticity. "The Supreme Court has made a political decision, possibly on orders from higher structures," reported Nadezhda Prusenkova, press spokesperson for *Novaya Gazeta*. "The whole process was politicized, and we continue to believe that the people who should have found themselves accused are of a higher rank (than the four suspects who were eventually brought to trial, then acquitted)."[44]

In late September 2010, Chairman Alexander Bastrykin of the Investigative Committee, the Russian agency responsible for investigating serious crimes, told the Committee to Protect Journalists that his agency had "made a mistake" in "rushing" the previous case to trial against three suspected accomplices.[45] Then in early October 2010, detectives with the Committee said they were examining a number of suspects in possible connection with Politkovskaya's murder.[46] Meanwhile, the chief justice of Russia's Supreme Court, Vyacheslav M. Lebedev, said during an October 2010 meeting with the Committee to Protect Journalists, "The independence of journalists is just as important as the independence of judges," and he pointed to several recent decrees by the Supreme Court mandating public access to legal proceedings.[47]

Despite the Kremlin's pledge in early October 2010 that it would aggressively pursue investigations into 19 unsolved work-related murders of Russian journalists since Putin's rise to power a decade ago, many human rights activists are skeptical.[48] "We are used to these empty declarations that get pronounced from time to time," said Lev Ponomaryov, a veteran Russian human rights campaigner. "What happened here is that an international organization appealed to Medvedev, and our super-liberal president ordered his subordinates to tell them something. Why should we pay attention to this?"[49]

"Of course we're not satisfied," said Nina Ognianova, the Committee to Protect Journalist's Europe coordinator. "It's been four years, and both the killers and the mastermind who ordered her murder are still at large."[50]

As of November 2010, no new arrests in the murder of Politkovskaya have been made.

Massacre at Maguindanao

Philippines, 2009

Never in the history of journalism have the news media suffered such a heavy loss of life in one day.

Statement from Reporters sans Frontières

The deadliest mass murder of journalists on record occurred on November 2009 when 32 journalists and media workers were slain, along with more than 25 others in an ambush in the Philippines.[51] These media colleagues were not targeted because of their profession but because they were caught in the middle of a deadly political battle for leadership in Maguindanao province, on the island of Mindanao. The incident started when one of the political candidates, Buluan Vice Mayor Esmael "Toto" Mangudadatu, felt intimidated by his opponent so he asked several media professionals to bear witness to his candidacy. The journalists accompanied Mangudadatu's friends and family as they proceeded to a government office to file papers so Mangudadatu could run for governor of the province. A fellow journalist from a Mindanao newspaper, Aquiles Zonio, reported about Mangudadatu's trust in the media:

Believing in the power of the media, Mangudadatu, who felt helpless then, asked help from the media. He requested several journalists ... to cover the scheduled filing of his certificate of candidacy at the Commission on Elections provincial. "Maybe, they will not harm us if journalists are watching them," Mangudadatu said.[52]

Residents were surprised when just eight days after the murders, prosecutors charged Andal Ampatuan Jr., the mayor of a city in the Maguindanao Province, with the murders of the Mangudadatu supporters, relatives, and journalists. Investigators reported that the convoy of Mangudadatu supporters and journalists was hijacked by 100 gunmen at a checkpoint, and then escorted to a grassy hilltop not far from the highway. There, the victims were killed before being buried in mass graves by a backhoe belonging to the provincial government—a government whose governor is the defendant's father. Ampatuan surrendered to authorities but proclaimed his innocence.[53]

The international journalism community was outraged by this atrocity. They pursued the president at the time, Gloria Macapagal-Arroyo (who has since left office as a result of term limits), with statements pleading she take a direct stand against these murders. Macapagal-Arroyo was strongly urged to address this crime as more than a criminal act, and as an attack on free expression in her country. Organizations that pleaded with her included the United Nations, Amnesty International, and the International Federation of Journalists, among others.

UN Educational, Scientific and Cultural Organization (UNESCO) Director-General Irina Bokova condemned the barbaric killings in Maguindanao province as clearly an attack against democracy and democratic processes. She added that the killing of journalists violates the rights of the Philippine people to be freely and fairly informed of political developments.[54]

Aidan White, General-Secretary of the International Federation of Journalists, remarked that this mass murder was not the first case of attacks on the press in the Philippines. In his letter to the president, he said, "Journalists and the international media community are grieving and distraught at the failure of the Government of the Philippines to uphold its responsibility to protect our colleagues and to end the long-running culture of impunity for the murders of journalists in the Philippines."[55] The letter from the IFJ reminded the president that during her tenure 75 journalists had been killed in the Philippines with nearly all killed because of the relationship with their work. He added that only four of these killings had resulted in convictions.[56]

Donna Guest, Deputy Director of Amnesty International's Asia-Pacific program, said in her statement to the president:

> One of the major stumbling blocks to justice for human rights violations in the Philippines has been the intimidation of witnesses, at times accompanied by bribes or other inducements. This case, which has shocked the country and the world, cannot end in impunity as the vast majority of cases of political killings have in the past.[57]

The Committee to Protect Journalists has followed this case closely and reported that despite the quick arrest, a year later justice has yet to be served. While the main suspect is on trial in Manila, only a handful of the other suspects in the case have been arraigned. CPJ reported in November 2010 that another 130 suspects, including police officials and members of the Ampatuans' 3,000-strong militia, are still at large.[58]

Shortly after the murders in Maguindanao, an investigation was conducted by the Freedom Fund for Filipino Journalists, the National Union of Journalists of the Philippines, MindaNews, and the Philippine Center for Investigative Journalism. The report of the investigation indicated that the crime scene was badly secured and witnesses still feared for their lives.[59] The report concluded:

> The massacre claimed nearly an entire generation of journalists from the small print and broadcast communities of General Santos, Koronadal City, and nearby areas. At least 22 of the 31 fatalities were married and had children, indicating an enormous need for continuing humanitarian assistance.[60]

The complete list of journalists and media workers killed in the massacre as compiled by the National Union of Journalists of the Philippines in January 2010 included:

1. Adolfo, Benjie—Gold Star Daily, Koronadal City
2. Araneta, Henry—Radio DZRH, General Santos City
3. Arriola, Mark Gilbert "Mac-Mac"—UNTV, General Santos City
4. Bataluna, Rubello—Gold Star Daily, Koronadal City
5. Betia, Arturo—Periodico Ini, General Santos City
6. Cabillo, Romeo Jimmy—Midland Review, Tacurong City
7. Cablitas, Marites—News Focus, General Santos City
8. Cachuela, Hannibal—Punto News, Koronadal City

9. Cadagdagon, Jepon—Saksi News. General Santos City.
10. Caniban, John—Periodico Ini, General Santos City
11. Dalmacio, Lea—Socsargen News, General Santos City
12. Decina, Noel—Periodico Ini, General Santos City
13. Dela Cruz, Gina—Saksi News, General Santos City
14. Duhay, Jhoy—Gold Star Daily, Tacurong City
15. Evardo, Jolito—UNTV, General Santos City
16. Gatchalian, Santos—DXGO, Davao City
17. Legarte, Bienvenido, Jr.—Prontiera News, Koronadal City
18. Lupogan, Lindo—Mindanao Daily Gazette, Davao City
19. Maravilla, Ernesto "Bart"—Bombo Radyo, Koronadal City
20. Merisco, Rey—Periodico Ini, Koronadal City
21. Momay, Reynaldo "Bebot"—Midland Review, Tacurong City (still missing)
22. Montaño, Marife "Neneng"—Saksi News, General Santos City
23. Morales, Rosell—News Focus, General Santos City
24. Nuñez, Victor—UNTV, General Santos City
25. Perante, Ronnie—Gold Star Daily correspondent, Koronadal City
26. Parcon, Joel—Prontiera News, Koronadal City
27. Razon, Fernando "Rani"—Periodico Ini, General Santos City
28. Reblando, Alejandro "Bong"—Manila Bulletin, General Santos City
29. Salaysay, Napoleon—Mindanao Gazette, Cotabato City
30. Subang, Ian—Socsargen Today, General Santos City
31. Teodoro, Andres "Andy"—Central Mindanao Inquirer, Tacurong City
32. Tiamson, Daniel—UNTV, General Santos City[61]

Journalist Aquiles Zonio has not been deterred by the mass murder of colleagues in his country. He has pledged to continue the fight for a free press in the Philippines. His statement made the day after the massacre avowed:

> Once again, several working journalists shed their blood in the name of press freedom. This, however, will not deter us or discourage us from doing our job as journalists. Underpaid and under threat, be that as it may, we will continue answering the call of our beloved profession.[62]

Mahad Ahmed Elmi and Ali Iman Sharmarke

Somalia, 2007

All HornAfrik journalists were brave, but 30-year-old Elmi was exceptionally so. He not only reported on the grim street violence, but he challenged those responsible for it. Warlords walked away from interviews, Islamist leaders hung up on him, government officials were incensed, death threats were routine.

Michelle Shephard, *Toronto Star*, November 1, 2007

Within hours of each other, two Somali journalists were shot dead in separate attacks. Unknown gunmen shot Mahad Ahmed Elmi, 30, a popular radio personality for the prominent independent broadcaster HornAfrik Media in the head four times, as he headed toward his office on August 11.[63] A few hours later, as mourners left Elmi's funeral, Ali Iman Sharmarke, a Somali-Canadian, who was the founder and co-owner of HornAfrik Media, was killed when a landmine remotely detonated near the car in which he was traveling. The other 20-plus vehicles traveling in the funeral procession remained unscathed.[64]

Both Somali radio professionals had close ties to Canada. Sharmarke had fled Somalia and arrived in Canada as a refugee, but both returned to Somalia with two others to start HornAfrik. In 2002, the Canadian Journalists for Free Expression awarded the International Press Freedom Award to the three founders of HornAfrik—Sharmarke and his colleagues, Mohamed Elmi and Ahmed Abdisalam Adan. The award recognized HornAfrik as being the first independent radio network in Somalia and more specifically for its work in the face of intimidation and threats in a society where there is no protection for freedom of the press.[65]

Shortly after Elmi's death, Ross Howard, an award-winning Canadian journalist, international journalism trainer, and President of the Canadian nonprofit, Media&Democracy Group, reflected on meeting Elmi several years before at a journalism training seminar. Howard wrote:

> Mahad Ahmed Elmi showed up in a two-week workshop program for radio broadcasters in Bujumbura, Burundi, two years ago. How this skinny, slightly scruffy Somali reporter managed to get from the then utterly anarchic Mogadishu to a gathering of professionals across central Africa is a story in itself. But he was hungry to learn new techniques of reporting on conflict and the conciliatory effect of reliable media, and take them back to Mogadishu.[66]

Mogadishu residents regularly phoned in reports to Elmi's daily morning talk show about specific neighborhood news like crime or government security operations that affected their daily lives. As a result, Elmi's show challenged human-rights abuses, warlords and extremists–making it hugely popular among everyday citizens.[67] In April, Ethiopian troops backing Somalia's transitional government attacked suspected strongholds of Islamist fighters, destroying HornAfrik's studios.[68] The *Washington Post* reported that HornAfrik was considered the first independent radio station in Somalia as it often aired stories critical of Hawiye leaders, despite drawing most of its staff from Mogadishu's dominant Hawiye clan, which tends to oppose the government.[69] Howard added, "HornAfrik was willing to put Mahad on the air with a news and talk-radio show that consciously sought to explore reconciliation, instead of attracting and frightening listeners with screaming antagonists."[70]

According to Mogadishu's mayor, two men were arrested in connection with the killing of the Somali radio professionals three days after the murders occurred.[71] However, spokespersons for the Islamic Courts Union (in Eritrea), blamed the acting government for the murder of the journalists. Ahmed Abdisalam Adan, sole surviving member of the team that founded HornAfrik, believed either side could be responsible.[72] Adan said that the targeted violence was spreading beyond media: "Today it is Ali and Mahad, tomorrow it will be the heads of universities, anyone who tries to do something positive here," he said.[73] "Every minute, I am getting calls from civil society, angry at what is happening and saying we cannot allow this to go on. This cannot go on—they cannot wipe 10 million people off the map."[74]

A periodic review conducted by the National Union of Somali Journalists in 2010 reported that the Transitional Federal Government of Somalia has not convicted anyone of murdering journalists in the country despite 22 journalists being killed from 2007 until 2010.[75] The report added:

> All the 22 journalists killed in the period under review were targeted because of their journalistic work. They were defenders of freedom of expression or facilitators of exchange of information between the citizens of Somalia. As such, they were upholding the citizens' right to know.[76]

The periodic review also revealed that on September 19, 2010, Al-Shabaab and Hizbul Islam extremists forcibly took over HornAfrik radio in Mogadishu, stripping it of "its independence and professionalism."[77]

Eynulla Fatullayev

Azerbaijan, 2004 to today

As Secretary Clinton noted in Baku during her July 4 visit, when members of civil society are respected and allowed to work free of intimidation, democracies flourish and societies prosper. As a partner, the United States stands ready to assist the people and government of Azerbaijan in making the necessary reforms for democratic and economic progress. The conviction of Eynullah Fatullayev is not a step in the right direction.[78]

U.S. Department of State News Release, July 7, 2010.

Severe challenges exist for journalism in Azerbaijan. One newspaper editor, Eynulla Fatullayev, an outspoken critic and founder and editor-in-chief of two of Azerbaijan's largest independent newspapers, has personally experienced a number of these challenges; most prominently, he has been imprisoned since 2007. His story began in earnest in 2004 when he was beaten on the street after criticizing the government. In 2005, the newspaper where he worked was closed because the editor was killed. Two years later, after reporting that senior government officials had ordered the killing of that editor, he faced death threats. Then his father was kidnapped and released only when Fatullayev agreed to suspend publication of his newspaper, *Real Azerbaijan*. Shortly after that, he was sentenced to two-and-a-half years in prison for libel. After that conviction, he was sentenced to an additional eight-and-a-half years for an assortment of crimes: terrorism, incitement of ethnic hatred, and tax evasion.[79]

Fatullayev's initial conviction of libel in 2007 included both civil and criminal defamation in relation to a newspaper article and Internet posting about the 1992 Khojali massacre during the war between Azerbaijan and Armenia over the disputed territory of Nagorno-Karabakh. The article questioned the version of the Khojali events most commonly accepted in Azerbaijan.[80] Following that conviction, Fatullayev appealed to the European Court of Human Rights. On April 22, 2010, the European Court ruled that Fatullayev's imprisonment constituted a violation of his freedom of expression and right to a fair trial and ordered the Azerbaijani government to immediately release him and to pay him €27,822 for damages and legal expenses.[81] The Azerbaijani government appealed the case to the Grand Chamber of the European Court of Human Rights.[82] But that appeal was rejected on October 4, 2010; thus the European Court's decision in the case stands.

Curiously, in December 2009, after the European Court had heard arguments in Fatullayev's case, but before it had issued a judgment, the Azerbaijani authorities brought additional charges against Fatullayev for alleged possession of drugs. It seems guards at the prison, where he was being held allegedly found heroin in Fatullayev's shoes and coat sleeve during a search of his cell. As a result of these findings, on July 6,

2010, a Baku court convicted Fatullayev of illegal possession of narcotics for personal use and sentenced him to an additional two and a half years imprisonment for possession of drugs.[83]

The United States Department of State has also commented on Fatullayev's case:[84]

On July 6, Azerbaijani journalist Eynullah Fatullayev was convicted on criminal charges of drug possession and sentenced to two and a half years' imprisonment. The United States is concerned by the court ruling. We note that the OSCE Representative on Media Freedom characterized the drug charges on which Fatullayev was convicted as "highly improbable," and we join the OSCE Representative and others in calling for his release. We also note the recent judgment of the European Court of Human Rights that acquitted Fatullayev of charges raised against him in 2007.[85]

Human Rights Watch, an advocacy group in the United States focused on defending and protecting human rights, has observed abuses of free expression in Azerbaijan for several years. The organization published a 94-page document in October 2010, *Azerbaijan: Beaten, Blacklisted, and Behind Bars: The Vanishing Space for Freedom of Expression in Azerbaijan*, which highlights and explains many of the challenges for free expression in Azerbaijan today. The author of the publication, Giorgi Gogia, South Caucasus researcher at Human Rights Watch, said, "For this report, Human Rights Watch interviewed over 37 print and radio journalists and editors in June 2010."[86] This report included not only background information about arrests and harassment of journalists but it also explored the legal policies that have been instituted in Azerbaijan to suppress expression in this country. The report cited legislative amendments in 2009 that restricted journalists' ability to use video, photo, or sound recording without explicit consent of the individual being recorded or filmed, even at public events. The government has also banned all foreign radio broadcasting on FM frequencies. The report offered detailed information about state officials who have brought dozens of defamation charges against journalists, and in some cases, against human rights defenders who criticize the government or who otherwise work to secure accountability for human rights violations in Azerbaijan.[87]

In addition to the internationally prominent case of Eynullah Fatullayev, two young activists and bloggers have been imprisoned in Azerbaijan for seemingly unrelated criminal charges, which appear to be related to the young men's criticism of the government. Emin Milli and

Adnan Hajizade, were victims of a reportedly staged attack in a restaurant in July 2009, and subsequently convicted of "hooliganism" because of the episode. Milli and Hajizade are known for founding the youth movement "Be!" and an alumni network of former exchange students. They soon became better known for criticizing Azerbaijani government policies in blog postings on Facebook, Twitter, and in videos on YouTube, including one video which mocked the governments as donkeys which was released a week before their arrests.[88]

The two imprisoned bloggers have many supporters around the world, including U.S. President Barack Obama. When Obama met in September with Azerbaijani President Ilham Aliyev, he expressed hope that "Azerbaijan as a young democracy would implement democratic reforms and increase protections for human rights, by releasing the two jailed bloggers."[89] The two bloggers were released from prison in November 2010 and put on probation after serving 17 months in jail.[90]

Bladimir Antuna García

Mexico, 2009

They [people who run the state] know perfectly well who killed him. They don't need an investigation. They are either afraid of who did it or they are in business with them.

Victor Garza Ayala, owner of *El Tiempo de Durango*,
Antuna's principal employer

Bladimir Antuna García, father of two and reporter for *El Tiempo de Durango*, was ripped from his red Ford Explorer at 10:30 a.m. on November 2, 2009, by five men with assault rifles. He was found twelve hours later—tortured and strangled to death. A note next to his body said, "This happened to me because I gave information to the military and wrote things that I should not have written. Be careful when preparing stories. Sincerely, Bladimir."[91]

Considered to be the best crime reporter in the northwestern city of Durango, the thirty-nine-year-old Antuna often produced more than eight short articles per day. His extensive connections with the army and the police often meant front-page crime stories and exclusive interviews. He got his start in the 1980s, first with newspaper, and then radio. He worked his way up the ladder, honing his reputation as a veracious investigator and earning him the highest post on the police beat. Then, he spiraled into drugs and alcohol. He then turned his life around in 2006 and worked his way back up in the journalistic community. He soon went to work for a small but respectable newspaper *El Tiempo de Durango*. It was not long before Antuna's crime stories helped the paper become profitable. Despite his success there still was not enough money to pay his older son's way through university, so Antuna took an additional newspaper job, often working fourteen hours a day investigating stories or corruption. Then in 2008, he began receiving menacing phone calls, warning him to stop fishing for "delicate" information.[92] Numerous times the caller identified himself as a member of the criminal gang Los Zetas.[93] The Zetas are one of the most brutal drug gangs in Mexico. They were founded in the late 1990s by a group of Mexican special forces soldiers who defected to work for the Gulf Cartel. They served as the enforcers for the Gulf organization until recently when they broke loose on their own.[94]

The verbal threats were just the beginning, however. In April 2009, as Antuna was leaving his house for work, a gunman hopped out of a van driving by and started shooting at Antuna. Antuna swiftly fled into his house as a sheet of bullets hit the front of his home.[95] Later that day, Antuna's cell phone rang and a voice said, "We've found your home. It's over for you now."[96] Although Antuna filed complaints with the state attorney general's office, nothing came of it.[97]

The state's lack of investigation continued after Antuna's abduction and murder. When questioned by a delegation from the Committee to Protect Journalists about the lack of investigation into Antuna's case, Juan Lopez Ramirez, the state of Durango's top prosecutor for crimes against journalists, blamed his staff's ineffectiveness on the "grand chaos" of Mexico's changing court system and insisted his team should not be held accountable. He continued to deny responsibility even after CPJ pointed out that the court system had been changing for the past two years. According to CPJ's research, the prosecution failed to take basic steps to solve the case, such as not investigating Antuna's alleged affiliation with an army general in charge of military affairs of the state, because the military assured Ramirez there was no connection. After Antuna's death, his wife went into hiding for fear of assassination, and Antuna's eldest son dropped out of university after he could no longer afford tuition. He then took a newspaper job but was soon accosted on the street by men who threatened him unless he quit, which he did.

Antuna is only one of more than 30 journalists who have been murdered, abducted, or harassed in Mexico since December 2006, when

Mexican President Felipe Calderon came to power and declared war on the drug cartels. Since that time, at least eight journalists have been killed in direct reprisal for reporting on crime and corruption, while three media support workers have been killed and seven other journalists have gone missing. In addition, dozens of other journalists have been attacked, kidnapped, or forced into exile.[98]

Jason Beaubien, of National Public Radio, reported that every day reporters in this area of Mexico struggle with what to write and whether they should just give up their journalism career. In some parts of the country, reporters have stopped covering the drug trade entirely after their colleagues have been kidnapped, killed, or threatened. Some say they have limited reporting on crime to only what is in official government press releases, while others say they report whatever the local cartels order them to print.[99]

Gerardo Albarran, a journalist at the weekly national news magazine *Proceso* and a researcher for the Center for Journalism and Public Ethics, a media advocacy group in Mexico City, said: "Never have we seen threats at such an extreme level from organized crime as we've seen in the last 2 or 3 years."[100] He added that the cartels have grown to dominate the press completely in some areas of Mexico. When crime stories do appear, particularly in the north of the country, they tend to stick to just the facts lifted from police reports and are routinely published without bylines.[101]

The Committee to Protect Journalists reported that in Mexico more than 90 percent of press-related crimes are not prosecuted. As a result, Mexico is the ninth-worst country worldwide for journalists, according to CPJ's Impunity Index.[102]

Shi Tao

People's Republic of China, 2004

The story of the imprisonment of Shi Tao is closely related to a lawsuit by the World Organization for Human Rights against an Internet provider who gave the Chinese government information to find and arrest Shi Tao in 2007.

Shi Tao is a writer, poet, and journalist, who in April 2004 used his Yahoo! e-mail account to send a message to a pro-democracy website. In his e-mail, he summarized a government order directing media organizations in China to downplay the upcoming 15th anniversary of the 1989 crackdown on pro-democracy activists.[103] Police arrested him in November 2004, charging him with "illegally providing state secrets to foreign entities."[104] Authorities used e-mail account holder information supplied by Yahoo! to convict Shi Tao in April 2005 and sentence him to 10 years in prison.[105] In his unsuccessful appeal, Shi Tao claimed he was not aware at the time that the document that he had written about in his e-mail was classified as "top state secret," and disputed the validity of the manner in which the document had been declared classified.[106]

The arrest sparked controversy about the part that Yahoo! played in Shi Tao's arrest. In fact, the controversy surrounding the arrest and later conviction spurred Yahoo! to turn over its People's Republic of China operations to a Chinese company in 2005.[107]

Yahoo!'s cofounder, Jerry Yang, originally from Taiwan, said his company had no choice but to cooperate with the authorities:

> To be doing business in China, or anywhere else in the world, we have to comply with local law. We don't know what they want that information for, we're not told what they look for. If they give us the proper documentation and court orders, we give them things that satisfy both our privacy policy and the local rules. I do not like the outcome of what happens with these things. But we have to follow the law.[108]

The Shi case also highlighted vast differences in the Western and Chinese definitions of "state secrets." Beijing includes information on statistics, child labor laws, police behavior, strikes, and riots. "The content of state secrets in Chinese law goes far beyond ordinary definitions of national security to encompass, in fact, most information handled by the government," said Nicolas Becquelin, of Human Rights In China.[109]

In April 2007, in another case involving an engineer Wang Xiaoning, Wang's wife Yu Ling, filed a lawsuit in the United States against Yahoo! seeking reparations for the company's role in Wang's arrest and sentencing. Shi Tao's mother later joined the lawsuit. The *San Francisco Chronicle* quoted Yu as saying: "If Yahoo did not give out this information, then the Chinese government would not be able to sentence him."[110]

The U.S. Congress was brought into the discussion when a Congressional Hearing was convened in February 2006. U.S. Representative Tom Lantos delivered a scathing speech at this hearing directed at the founder of Yahoo! and his attorney:

> When Yahoo was asked to explain its actions, Yahoo said that it must adhere to local laws in all countries where it operates. But my response

to that is: if the secret police a half century ago asked where Anne Frank was hiding, would the correct answer be to hand over the information in order to comply with local laws? These are not victimless crimes. We must stand with the oppressed, not the oppressors.[111]

At the Congressional hearings, Jerry Yang bowed in apology to Shi Tao's mother three times. The mother of Shi Tao returned the bow, and then tried to wipe the tears from her eyes in front of the U.S. Congressional committee. Representative Lantos had just told the Yahoo! executives: "While technologically and financially you are giants, morally you are pygmies." The "pygmies" in question were Yang and his vice president and general counsel.[112]

Yahoo! settled the case with the family of Shi Tao and with Wang's wife in 2007. The terms of the settlement were not disclosed and Yahoo! refused to admit fault, an attorney for the families said.[113]

Despite the fact that Shi Tao remains in jail in China, Western Internet companies working in China have generally avoided the legal blunder made by Yahoo! in 2004. In January 2010, Google pulled out of China over a censorship disagreement. Other sites like eBay, Facebook, MySpace and Twitter have never managed to gain a significant foothold in China, partly because of government censorship and partly because most major Chinese Internet companies offer popular social networking features of their own. In fact, no major U.S. Internet company has gained dominance in China, which by some measures is the world's largest Internet market.[114]

Paul Kiggundu

Uganda, 2010

Journalists are not always murdered by well-organized operatives bent on limiting freedom of expression. In some parts of the world, people just have little respect for journalists or the work they do. Unfortunately, many local journalists pay the price for this lack of respect.

Paul Kiggundu was a correspondent for Top Radio and several television stations in Rakai District, Southern Buganda, Uganda. He was beaten to death in September 2010 when he was caught filming an angry mob of commercial motorcycle drivers destroying the home of another motorcyclist. The mob turned on Kiggundu, then attacked and killed him because they thought he was working for the police. Kiggundu repeatedly identified himself as a journalist, but that did not stop the mob that continued to brutalize him. He was later pronounced dead at a nearby hospital. Kiggundu was married and had two children aged three years and 18 months.[115]

The Eastern Africa Journalists Association (EAJA) condemned the killing as disturbing and barbaric. Omar Faruk Osman, EAJA Secretary General, said: "This is both sad and annoying given that the journalist had already identified himself, and meant no harm at all to the mob. His interest was just in getting a story and nothing more. This is yet another waste of a journalist's life in our region."[116]

A number of international journalism and human rights organizations pleaded with the local police to work quickly to find Kiggundu's murderers. "We call on the Ugandan Police to do their utmost to bring the perpetrators to justice. No journalist should be killed for simply carrying out their profession," said Tom Rhodes, the East Africa consultant for the Committee to Protect Journalists.[117] United Nations Educational, Scientific and Cultural Organization (UNESCO) Director-General Irina Bokova said in a statement:

> I deplore the death of Paul Kiggundu. He died in the exercise of his mission as a journalist, covering the news so that the public could be informed. His murder is a tragic illustration of the risks media professionals take every day in the name of freedom of expression. I call on the Ugandan authorities to make every effort to investigate this crime and bring the culprits to justice.[118]

Tragically, just three days after Kiggundu was murdered, another Ugandan journalist, Dickson Ssentongo, was beaten into a coma by iron-bar wielding thugs as he traveled to read the early morning news at Prime Radio in Mukono.[119]

Several days after the murders of the two media professionals, another journalist wrote an opinion piece for the local newspaper in Kampala, *The Monitor*, where he lamented the killings of his colleagues and the subsequent impunity that will probably exist as a result of these murders. Angelo Izama wrote:

> Like Kiggundu's death shows—we can also be double victims like other ordinary Ugandans, of the environment that this generalised lack of accountability breeds. The practices of those who manage society are

damaging thus twice—immediately as a single victim like Kiggundu suffered, and slowly as the society is infected with that act of cruelty, especially when no one is held accountable. Kiggundu's death is our collective death because it's another installment in the characterisation of our common morality.[120]

David Rohde

Afghanistan, 2009

"Tell them the truth," I told Tahir. "Tell them I'm American." Tahir relayed my answer and the burly driver beamed, raising his fist and shouting in Pashto. Tahir translated it for me: "They say they are going to send a blood message to Obama."[121]

David Rohde, 2009

A tattered rope and a prayer were all that *New York Times* journalist David Rohde and his Afghan journalist colleague, Tahir Ludin, had after the Taliban captured them in the fall of 2008. The two journalists and their driver, Asadullah Mangal, were abducted on November 10, as Rohde traveled to interview a Taliban commander in Afghanistan who was known for his involvement in fighting the Soviets in the 1980s.[122] Rohde was in Afghanistan to carry out book research on the history of U.S. involvement in Afghanistan.[123] However, as they were driving the 30 miles to Logar Province, gunmen swiftly surrounded them and forced their way into their car.

Over the next seven months, Rohde and his colleagues were transferred among numerous captors and were taunted with daily death threats and spurious claims of release. Their captors forced them to make embarrassing videos intended to pressure their families into wiring huge sums of money in exchange for their release. In an effort to save their lives, Rohde exaggerated the amount of money the Taliban could receive for them in ransom. In response, his captors made irrational demands, asking for $25 million and the release of Afghan prisoners from Guantanamo Bay, Cuba.[124] His captors insisted that Rohde would be their "golden hen."[125] Rohde reported that for months his value had been vastly exaggerated.[126]

Rohde had joined the *New York Times*, 12 years earlier after winning a Pulitzer Prize in international reporting in 1996 for documenting the massacre of Bosnian Muslims in Srebrenica. He was the first Western journalist to travel into Bosnian Serb territory to search for evidence of mass graves.[127] During the course of his investigation into these graves, he was detected by a plainclothes watchman, turned over to Bosnian Serb authorities, and imprisoned. He was held captive for 10 days, was interrogated relentlessly, and deprived of sleep. Family members and Rohde's editors traveled to Dayton, Ohio, where the Bosnian peace talks were being held to urge American diplomats to demand his release. He was freed shortly thereafter.[128]

In Afghanistan, his captors had made false claims about his release in Bosnia. Rohde said, "(They) falsely claimed that the American diplomat Richard C. Holbrooke had freed Serbian prisoners in 1995 to win my release in Bosnia."[129]

Back home, anguished colleagues and family members continued to work vigilantly with the FBI and private contracting firms to negotiate Rohde's release, while the *New York Times* appealed to other media outlets to black out coverage of Rohde's capture, to avoid an escalation in his captors' demands.[131] Yet, the negotiations failed to produce tangible results.

After seven months and 10 days in Taliban captivity, Rohde and his colleague Tahir had had enough.[131] "I stood in the bathroom of the Taliban compound and waited for my colleague to appear in the courtyard so we could make our escape. My heart pounded.... I feared that the guards who were holding us hostage might wake up and stop us. I feared even more that our captivity would drag on for years," Rohde recounted.[132]

Eventually his colleague appeared. They quickly tied a piece of purloined rope that Rohde had found a few weeks before to the wall surrounding the roof. It did not touch the ground, but it was close. "I got down on my hands and knees. Tahir stepped on my back and lifted himself over the wall. I heard his clothes scrape against the bricks, looked up and realized he was gone.... I ran after him. For the first time in seven months, I walked freely down a street."[133] Several torturous miles later, they reached a Pakistani military base, where, after some negotiation, they were let in and then transferred safely to U.S. authorities. They had escaped.

David Rohde's case was unique, not only because he escaped but also because the major news media operations decided to suppress the story of his capture. *New York Times* Executive Editor, Bill Keller said on the day Rohde escaped, "We agonized over it at the outset and, periodically, over the last seven months. Of all the subjects we discussed with the family that was the one we discussed more intensively than any other: Should we change strategy and go public?"[134] The decision was made early in the incident to keep the story out of the media. Keller was aided by silence from at least 40 major news organizations—including, after a personal appeal, Al Jazeera.[135] *Washington Post* Executive Editor, Marcus Brauchli, said, "We obviously would always err in favor of the safety of the reporter."[136] In the eyes of kidnappers, "someone may go from low-value capture to high-value capture by virtue of publicity.... I would hope we wouldn't treat anybody's life any differently if there was a safety issue involved."[137]

Sultan Munadi

Afghanistan, 2009

Being a journalist is not enough; it will not solve the problems of Afghanistan. I want to work for the education of the country, because the majority of people are illiterate. That is the main problem facing many Afghans. And if I leave this country, if other people like me leave, who will come to Afghanistan? I am really committed to come back and work for my country. That is why I want to come back, even if it means cleaning the streets of Kabul.

Sultan Munadi, 2009

It was over. Sultan was dead. He had died trying to help me, right up to the very last seconds of his life. It later emerged that one of the rescue party was also dead, mortally wounded during the raid. I thanked everyone who was still alive to thank. It wasn't, and never will be, enough.

Stephen Farrell, 2009

An unembedded British-born reporter working for the *New York Times*, Stephen Farrell, and his fellow Afghan journalist and former *New York Times* reporter, Sultan Munadi, were kidnapped on September 4, 2009. They were investigating a NATO air strike that had destroyed two fuel tankers hijacked by the Taliban when they were abducted. Farrell reported that during their four-day ordeal they were not treated badly, and Munadi even prayed with his abductors.[138] By the third night, they heard drones overhead and nearby explosions. They surmised that their rescue was imminent. When the Taliban left the compound where they were being held, they fled. Farrell described the ordeal from that point:

With him [Munadi] already in front we crouch-ran along a very narrow ledge of earth—less than a foot wide—along the outer wall of the compound. It was dark . . . We could see nothing more than a few feet in front of us. We had no idea who was where, and there were bullets flying through the air . . . We continued 20 yards along the wall until it suddenly reached the corner . . . He [Sultan] carried straight on beyond the corner of the wall, bringing him out into the open . . . He raised his hands and shouted, "Journaliste, journaliste," even as he stepped out. It was accented, in exactly the same way he had used 1,000 times in four days talking to the Taliban. In the dark I could not see around him to discover who he was trying to reassure: the troops that he wasn't Taliban, or the Taliban that he wasn't a soldier. There was a burst of gunfire and he went down immediately. In the dark, with firing all around . . . I did not know whether the bullets came from in front, to his right or to his left.[139]

The British had ordered a predawn commando raid in northern Afghanistan to rescue the British reporter and his Afghan interpreter and colleague after Afghan agents learned that the Taliban was planning to move the hostages into Pakistan, a senior Afghan official told the *New York Times*. The raid by British Special Forces and Afghan soldiers had freed the reporter, but Sultan Munadi and a British paratrooper were killed in a fierce firefight, as were two Afghan civilians, including a woman and child along with dozens of Taliban fighters.[140] Afghan President Hamid Karzai condemned the killing of the experienced Afghan journalist, according to a statement given to *Agence France-Presse*. The statement said Sultan Munadi "was killed mercilessly by the enemies of Afghanistan"—reportedly short-hand for Taliban insurgents.[141]

The tragedy became a controversy when questions arose as to whether Farrell had been warned not to go into this area to report and, more importantly, who exactly had shot and killed Sultan Munadi.

The British *Daily Telegraph* reported on September 11, 2009 that British army sources were concerned about the operation after it emerged that Farrell had ignored advice from Afghan police who told him not to travel in the area north of Kabul, a known Taliban stronghold. In his blog on the *New York Times* website, Farrell has defended his actions, saying that he and Munadi took the necessary precautions. Before leaving, he said his drivers verified that the roads were safe, and they waited to do reporting in the daytime when it would be safer. Before going to the bombing site, Farrell reported that he again verified with his local driver that the situation was safe.[142]

The *Daily Telegraph* also reported that Karban Mohammed, the father of Sultan Munadi, demanded to know why negotiations were abandoned in favor of a military rescue. He said he had heard from his son 90 minutes before he was shot. Sultan Munadi had told his father he was sure he and Farrell would soon be freed. Karban Mohammed said, "My son's words brought me so much happiness. He seemed so confident that things were working out. I feel sad and angry. Sultan was killed for no reason at all."[143] In the *Independent* the same day Mohammed was quoted as asking for his son's death to be explained, "We would just like an explanation, we deserve an explanation," he was quoted as saying.[144] On September 12, 2009, an Afghan journalist offered an explanation when it was reported in a local newspaper that based on information provided by the domestic media, Sultan Munadi had been killed on 9 September by the British forces during the rescue operation.[145]

This unfortunate rescue operation had come just eleven weeks after *New York Times* reporter David Rohde had escaped to safety after being held by his captors for seven months. Rohde knew Sultan Munadi and spoke fondly about him in a story on the *New York Times* website where Rohde described a note he had received from Munadi after his escape. Mr. Munadi sent a typically ebullient e-mail message. 'Oh my God!' he wrote. 'I'm really really happy for this great news. I'll thank billions of times the God for this freedom.'[146] Rohde went on to explain that the death of his colleague, Munadi, illustrated two truths about the war in Afghanistan: "Vastly more Afghans than foreigners have died battling the Taliban, and foreign journalists are only as good as the Afghan reporters who work with them."[147] Rohde lamented that Afghan journalists like Munadi are often called "interpreters," which greatly diminishes the role they play for the inserted journalists. These Afghan journalists work side-by-side with the foreign journalists as they interpret history and politics as well as language. The Afghan journalists take the same risks but do not enjoy nearly the same glory afforded the foreign correspondents.[148]

And among many Afghans, as reported by the British *Independent*, there is a feeling that Afghan lives do not count for as much as Western ones. They point out that while Farrell was whisked to safety in the British raid, Sultan Munadi's body was left abandoned on the ground, to be found later. Many Afghans thought not enough was done for Sultan Munadi even in death.

Epilogue: Journalists victimized by brutal attacks and murder, often leave behind family members who must carry on without them. Sultan

Munadi left a wife and two young boys behind when he was killed during a raid that freed his British colleague. The *New York Times* stepped up and established a fund where colleagues and friends could donate money to help the grieving Munadi family.

Michelle Lang

Afghanistan, 2009

The fallen Canwest journalist died representing something her killers don't understand—freedom. She was free to write what she saw and was gutsy enough to go right into the heart of the danger zone to get it. She knew that dying herself, or covering others who did, was part of the risk.

Joe Warmington, *Toronto Sun*

She was 34. She had plans to be married in the summer. She was on her first assignment in Afghanistan, and she had been on the job just three weeks. Then suddenly on the penultimate day of 2009, Michelle Lang was the first Canadian journalist to be killed while covering the war in Afghanistan.

It was the kind of accident that happens all too often along the road in Afghanistan. Lang was killed along with four Canadian soldiers, when their light-armored vehicle struck a powerful roadside bomb while on patrol on the outskirts of Kandahar city.[149] The explosion was so massive that the 23-ton armored vehicle that they were riding in was turned upside down and landed facing in the opposite direction. The crater created by the explosion may have been as much as 20 metres wide and several metres deep.[150]

Tobi Cohen at the *Canadian Press* realized how easily it could have been her photograph splashed posthumously in the Canadian newspapers. Two years ago, Cohen was in an armored vehicle that struck an explosive device in rural Afghanistan. She vividly recalled the terror she felt in the aftermath as soldiers combed the vicinity for insurgents and how she chattered incessantly while being driven to safety. Cohen said that field reporters are not driven by a morbid fascination with war or cheap thrills. She added, "I wanted to tell the story of why we're there, what our troops are doing there, the risks they're taking, and the sacrifices."[151]

Lang was described by coworkers as a consummate reporter who wanted to tell good stories well. A colleague called her tough as nails with obfuscating bureaucrats but also someone with a ready laugh, who loved "Buffy the Vampire Slayer" and was an avid ultimate Frisbee player, skier and hiker.[152] Patrick White was a *Globe and Mail* reporter who met Lang on the Canadian base in Afghanistan. He wrote that Lang could have stayed within the confines of Kandahar Air Field, the sprawling base which is the safest spot in that country. White added, "She was way too good a reporter for that."[153] She wanted to see with her own eyes what Canadian soldiers were doing. Columnist for the *Globe and Mail*, Christie Blatchford said: "Like them, Ms. Lang was a volunteer. Like them, she knew the risks. Like them, she was doing her job, and doing it right. The best definition of a reporter, in my view, is as witness. There is honour in that, and I hope there's some comfort there for her family and fiancé."[154]

Just three days before she was killed, Michelle Lang wrote that the leader of the Canadian troops had said it had been a rough year for Canadians in Afghanistan. But the general said he vowed, "to continue pursuing such strategies as having more soldiers leave fortified bases to live closer to the Afghan people."[155] Even though Michelle Lang cannot tell these stories of the soldiers living closer to the Afghan people, her former employer set up a fellowship in her honor to inspire Canadian journalism students to pursue stories just like that. The Michelle Lang Fellowship in Journalism, supported by Canwest Publishing, is a national program that will give a recent Canadian university graduate the chance to combine a passion for writing with an interest in current events. The trust will award up to $10,000 annually to fund a major news project that holds special significance for a Canadian audience. "Michelle Lang was passionate about her craft, which is why we are so delighted to be able to establish a permanent fellowship that promotes excellence in journalism and gives a young writer a head start in his or her career," said *Calgary Herald* publisher Malcolm Kirk.[156]

Tariq Ayoub, José Couso, and Taras Protsyuk

Iraq, 2003

The Americans said it was a war against terrorism. Who is doing the terrorism now? Didn't their radars tell them this is a press office and these are civilian houses? My message to you is that hatred grows more hatred. The Americans are asking why are there suicide bombers, which we do not consider as such, we consider them as martyrs. Let them ask Bush and Blair who targeted their families and friends.

Dima Tahboub, widow of Tariq Ayoub[157]

I went to Baghdad knowing that I was taking the risk of getting hit by an Iraqi bomb, or being kidnapped by Iraqis. I never expected to be fired upon—or that José would be killed—by American forces.

Olga Rodríguez, colleague of José Couso[158]

Within six hours on April 8, 2003, three foreign journalists died in Iraq. The U.S. military fired the shots that killed all of them. Tariq Ayoub, an Al Jazeera reporter, José Couso, a Spanish cameraman and Taras Protsyuk, a Ukrainian-born Reuters cameraman, all perished that single day in Baghdad. It continues to be debated whether this incident can be considered an accident of "friendly fire" or not.

What happened on that day in 2003 has been scrutinized by media and military critics around the world. Much of the debate focuses on military decisions in time of war as well as the difference in perspective and protection between embedded and unilateral journalists during the Iraq War. Peter Wilson, an Australian journalist, told the story of this day in his book, *A Long Drive through a Short War*, published in 2004. Wilson was staying at the Palestine Hotel in Baghdad with roughly 100 other unilateral journalists. He said the deadly incident began just before seven in the morning in Baghdad when a U.S. fighter jet made two passes over the Al Jazeera network's building and subsequently hit it with two air-to-surface missiles. The Arab network had supplied the Pentagon the coordinates of all its offices, but that precaution had not prevented an attack on the team in the Basra Sheraton, and now the Baghdad bureau had been hit. Reporter Tariq Ayyoub, a 35-year-old Jordanian with a one-year-old daughter, was killed on the roof just as he was about to go on air.[159]

Wilson then reported that several of the journalists in the hotel noticed U.S. tanks firing at buildings across the bridge. Then at 11:30 a.m. several of the journalists noticed that one of the tanks was swinging its turret around and pointing at the Palestine Hotel. Wilson then reported an enormous bang hit the hotel. He continued:

> We scrambled into our flak jackets and ran into the corridor to see a dozen stunned journalists coming out of other rooms.The lobby downstairs was chaotic. Children were crying, and confused reporters and scared hotel workers were pushing through the crowd as the last of the wounded were being bundled into cars at the front doors.[160]

In the end, two journalists had been killed. José Couso, a 37-year-old cameraman with the Spanish network Telecinco, was carried out of the hotel with a belt tied as a tourniquet to try to stop the blood spurting from one leg. He had been standing on the Reuters balcony and was hit by shrapnel in the leg, chest and jaw. He kept talking about his two sons as he was driven to hospital. He died soon after his leg was amputated. Taras Protsyuk, a Ukrainian-born Reuters cameraman, did not even last that long. He died on the way to the hospital.[161]

U.S. military officials at the time said that the attacks came in response to Iraqi gunfire at the locations. Repeating that initial explanation, General Colin Powell said a U.S. tank fired on the hotel in response to "hostile fire appearing to come from a location later identified as the Palestine Hotel." Journalists in the hotel at the time said that they did not hear gunshots coming from the hotel.[162]

Almost immediately the global journalistic community harshly criticized the U.S. forces, and the journalists demanded a full investigation into the incident. But the U.S. commander insisted that his soldiers had not deliberately targeted the hotel or the Al Jazeera headquarters. The U.S. Central Command said that his forces would not target journalists because they were protected civilians under international humanitarian law. "We regret the loss of life of correspondents and we extend our condolences to the family of your journalists and families of other journalists who have lost their lives," Brigadier-General Vince Brooks said at a Central Command briefing in Qatar the day after the incident.[163]

A former senior CNN reporter, Walter Rogers, was embedded with the U.S. military on the day the journalists died. He agreed that this was a tragic accident:

> I was in Iraq as an embedded reporter on April 8, 2003, when Couso was killed. I listened to the internal Army radio briefing on the incident. It was reported as an unfortunate consequence of someone being mistaken for an enemy combatant when rocket-propelled grenades, mortars, and small arms were pouring down on US troops.[164]

Others found the U.S. forces at fault. Editor of Al Jazeera, Samir Khader, said he believed the killing of his colleague at the Palestine Hotel was a deliberate attack by the U.S. forces on the Arab station. "They wanted to silence us. I can't prove it, of course, but my own feeling was that something was going on that day at the entrance of the Republican Palace and they didn't want any witness," he said.[165] Richard Sambrook, the director of BBC News, said the issue was not whether soldiers were justified in attacking what they believed to have been Iraqi fighters.

"What I think is extraordinary is that they had no idea that the Palestine [Hotel] was the media center," he said. "I think responsibility lies with certainly the Pentagon and the chain of command, which knew where the international media was based."[166]

On July 30, 2010, a Spanish judge reissued an international arrest warrant for three U.S. soldiers over the death of a Spanish television cameraman, José Couso. The Spanish Supreme Court had reopened an inquiry into Couso's death and called for this arrest. An inquiry into the incident conducted by the U.S. military in 2004 had cleared the soldiers of any wrongdoing.[167] The call for the arrest is the second time that the Spanish Supreme Court has said that the facts constitute a crime and break the norms of international human rights law. In the previous ruling in March 2006, the National Court ruled that the case should be closed, saying Couso's death was "an act of war, against an incorrectly identified enemy."[168]

Alan Johnston

Gaza, 2008

They handcuffed me and put the black hood back over my head, and led me slowly out into the cold of the night. There was no word of explanation, and as my mind searched for one in that terrifying moment of uncertainty, I feared, as I walked into the darkness, that I might be going to my death. That I was being taken somewhere to be shot.

Alan Johnston

Alan Johnston, a reporter for the BBC, was the last western journalist left in Gaza in March 2007. A 44-year-old Arabic speaker and veteran of other world trouble spots such as Afghanistan, Johnston was not just another visiting correspondent who made forays through the check-points from Israel on the other side of the border. He understood Gaza from the inside. Johnston was just 16 days from the end of a three-year posting when he was kidnapped at gunpoint by a group known as the Army of Islam. This marked the beginning of a 114-day ordeal where Johnston said he learned the meaning of freedom.[169]

In Gaza, kidnapping was an almost daily occurrence, and the targets of the kidnapping were often the dwindling population of Westerners. Typically, victims were kept for about a week until the kidnappers' demands were met, which they often were. The great majority of kidnappings was carried out by small militia groups or disgruntled gangs looking to use Westerners as bargaining chips to get someone out of prison. The situation changed, however, in August 2006, when jihadist groups began to emerge. Johnston said:

> I knew from then on it was dangerous. I was always frightened of being kidnapped even by the less serious groups. But I really worried after the jihadists emerged. I took all the steps I could to keep a lower profile. I used to think that because I had a low profile, living there was safer [for me] than for some of the visiting journalists who went to obvious places like the big hotel.[170]

Johnston reported that the first few days of his capture were the worst, an agony of uncertainty. On the first night the jihad leader came into the room and said in English that they knew his name and they knew everything. Johnston was told that he had been kidnapped to secure the release of Muslims jailed in Britain. When Johnston protested that Britain would not negotiate, he was told that Britain would be forced to listen.[171]

What became a blessing for Johnston was when he was given access to a radio. By listening Johnston knew he was not forgotten. He soon realized that the BBC was mobilizing, as only it can, an international campaign for his release. What touched him most profoundly was that ordinary Palestinians repeatedly took to the streets to protest, and friends and colleagues in the media in Gaza stormed the parliament and fought with police in a bid to get the legislature to focus on his case. [172]

Protests and campaigns on the streets in Gaza had been relentless since his capture. As Palestinian journalist Sami Abu Salem put it in an open letter after Johnston's abduction: "You were the journalist the Palestinian people are in need of—one who does not only cover bloodshed, violence and politics, but also knocks on all doors in Gaza: occupation, art, love, religion and all areas that show the entire world that we are human too."[173]

On July 4, 2007, Alan Johnston was delivered to Hamas and then to the BBC Arabic service. Johnston said when he was in captivity, he dreamt of being free. The first night he was freed he dreamt of being captured. He said he still dreams about Gaza. Over time, he said, the dreams are becoming less frightening.[174]

Atwar Bahjat

Iraq, 2006

Arab women as war reporters are looked at with great pride by the public, but looking at the professional part of the story, they were not offered training as war reporters, or equipped with protective gear, except bullet proof jackets worn by only two of them. None of them have been trained to report from conflict areas. Any of them could have ended up badly injured, kidnapped, or even dead. What leads them to such areas is their enthusiasm, and hopes to secure a better position in their careers in a male dominated society.

Iqbal Tamimi—(female) Arab journalist[175]

Considered a "daughter of Iraq," Atwar Bahjat, 30, was shot and killed after completing three live broadcasts from the edge of her native city on the day its golden-domed Shi'ite mosque was blown up, allegedly by Sunni terrorists. Atwar was born in Samarra to a Sunni father and a Shia mother from Karbala. She began her career as a reporter with the Iraqi Satellite Network, then joined Al Jazeera and then moved to Al Arabiya. She had previously worked for Iraqi TV under Saddam Hussein. She was a young Iraqi who found herself telling the story of her country under foreign occupation, on the brink of division and chaos. She quickly admitted she was not objective; she was biased in favor of Iraq.[176]

Uday al-Katib, a colleague at Al Jazeera said, "People saw this young Iraqi woman, reporting from hospitals, the scenes of explosions, deserted streets, the family homes of the deceased. People felt she belonged to them. They felt she represented them."[177] Some say Atwar was targeted by the Shia. Others contend she was targeted by the Sunni. The same arguments were made about the shrine.[178]

Mohammad Krieshan told the story of when he first met Bahjat:

We felt she possessed overwhelming passion for a profession she first started in the press and pursued later in Iraqi television. Very quickly, Atwar proved herself, especially in that she, as a woman, was not deterred by the risks of daily news coverage of bloodshed in Iraq. She was always the first to volunteer to go to the scene of the story when explosions or clashes took place. I remember very well when she came to me once during the first days of the siege of Fallujah in April 2004, upset and grumbling that the office director had not sent her to cover turbulent developments there, but rather preferred to dispatch other male colleagues of hers. I tried in vain to calm her down by telling her that it was out of fear for her life that she was not dispatched and not because of any doubts about her competence.[179]

Day by day, she began to obtain privileged information from Iraq's top officials as well as the militias they were fighting. Even when Al Jazeera was permanently banned from Iraq, Atwar managed to convince top Iraqi officials to give her exclusive interviews. Atwar laughed: "They knew if they didn't give me information, I would go to the streets of Najaf at 2am and get it in person. They would tell me, 'Please Atwar, we'll tell you everything, just don't go out and get hurt.' "[180]

João Silva

Afghanistan, 2010

The truth is that it's the photographers who usually end up taking the biggest risks of all. A reporter can get information from a distance, but a photographer or cameraman has to be right in the middle of the action.[181]

Nicholas Kristof

The kind of journalism, the photography we do—it's real lives; you know, people living, people dying.

João Silva

João Silva was a photojournalist who ran toward danger—but this time the danger found him. Silva, one of the two surviving members of the legendary "Bang Bang Club," was seriously injured after stepping on a landmine in Afghanistan in October 2010. Despite immediate help from medics, both his legs were lost below the knees and he suffered other severe, internal injuries. Silva, 44, was considered to be one of the leading combat photographers in the world, winning awards from World Press Photo, Pictures of the Year International, and other honors. He was a veteran of many conflicts including the Balkans, the Middle East, and various African countries.[182] He is the coauthor, with Greg Marinovich of, *The Bang-Bang Club*, a book about the work of photojournalists covering ethnic violence in South Africa before the country's first democratic elections in 1994.

The "Bang-Bang Club" was the name given to four young, white, middle-class South African photojournalists who built their careers shooting dramatic photographs during the final years of apartheid. The rest of the club included Ken Oosterbroek, who was accidently killed in

1994 by a volunteer peacekeeper; Kevin Carter, who committed suicide; and the other living member, Greg Marinovich.[183] The group was also the topic of a bio-pic feature film that debuted at the Toronto Film Festival in 2010. The film is based on the book written by Marinovich and Silva. In an interview in the *New York Times*, Silva explained how the club got its name:

> Basically, we were just a group of friends covering what was happening in the country at the time. We hung out together and we lived together. A magazine decided to do an article about us. *They* coined the term "Bang Bang Club." The Bang Bang Club never really existed; it was a figment of somebody else's imagination. But the name stuck. You know, it became a reality in later years, with the tragic events of Kevin's suicide and Ken Oosterbroek being killed in combat and Greg being injured.[184]

Silva was well respected among his peers. Many have posted memories of him and his talent and graciousness on the *New York Times* website. Among the kindest remarks is a statement from a fellow photographer, Stephanie Sinclair of the VII Photo Agency. She worked with João Silva in Lebanon and Iraq. She recalled an evening with Silva:

> We were at a Baghdad hospital in 2003, covering the aftermath of a bombing. Some of the younger photographers were very aggressive, stepping all over the place, being aggressive with the families. Joao went over and took pictures in a respectful way. He shot only when necessary so as not to upset the relatives. He got the picture, but he did it like a surgeon. He is the bravest amongst us, but he is also the most gracious, the most respectful of others.[185]

Silva's fellow Bang Bang Club member, Greg Marinovich, wrote about his friend and this incident in the *Cape Times* (South Africa). He praised his friend for his bravery and his photography talent. He reported:

> He [Silva] is, without doubt, the best war photographer in the world. Fearless, tactical, calm under stress and compassionate. He was also quite phlegmatic about the possibility that something might one day happen to him. Not that he was resigned to becoming a casualty, but with each return trip, the odds mounted. João being João, while they were working on him, he asked for his camera and a cigarette, telling them to get the Marlboros out of his trouser pocket. While the medics toiled on him, he took pictures. For me, that says everything about João.[186]

During the incident João Silva, was embedded with the U.S. Army and under contract with the *New York Times*. It is not known whether he will ever return to covering conflict. It has been reported that it may take as long as two years for him to recover. Friends have set up a website for donations to help Silva and his family: http://joaosilva.photoshelter.com/. At the site, funds are also raised through the purchase of Silva's photographs.

Kurt Schork

Sierra Leone, 2000

I was hitting 40 and knew if I didn't try it [being a war correspondent], it would be the unfulfilled dream of my life ... War reporting is a privilege. After three years, the grime and gore of combat, the dreadful logic of ethnic hatred are no longer abstractions for me. More important, every day I see the grace and dignity of ordinary people trying to survive under ordinary circumstances.

Kurt Schork

American-born Kurt Schork became a reporter late in his life and proved that following a passion for covering conflict was not just a job for young people. He died in a rebel ambush in Sierra Leone in May 2000, at 53, doing what he loved, reporting from conflict in Sierra Leone. Schork was killed alongside another journalist, Miguel Gil Moreno, 32, a Spanish cameraman with the news agency Associated Press Television News.

Schork first became a freelance reporter in Southeast Asia in the 1980s. He had studied at Oxford, but did not have professional journalism training.[187] He spent thousands traveling his way around Afghanistan and Sri Lanka, where he found little work, but amassed the experiences that would help him survive reporting about the fighting in Iraq, Bosnia, Chechnya, Kosovo, and East Timor.

After Iraq invaded Kuwait in 1990, Schork headed for the Middle East and started covering the Kurdish uprising against Saddam Hussein for Reuters. Assignments in Africa and Asia followed, but it was in Bosnia where Schork developed his most famous story about a poignant eyewitness account of a young couple shot on a bridge as they tried to escape Sarajevo. The boy was Serb; the girl was Muslim—the Romeo and Juliet of their time and place. Schork's account became the emblematic story of a city divided by ethnic and religious hatred.[188]

In his memoirs, General Sir Michael Rose, the UN commander in Bosnia, described Schork as one of the most courageous and honest reporters he had met. "Kurt was one of the most experienced journalists working in Sarajevo at that time and he had the cynical and inquiring mind of all members of his profession. His instincts were rarely wrong."[189] Richard Holbrooke, the U.S. Ambassador to the United Nations, called Schork "one of the bravest, smartest" journalists he ever knew in his 35 years as a diplomat. "He almost always knew more than any of the UN and government officials I would meet."[190]

Renowned journalist and author, Janine di Giovanni, wrote that she was horrified, saddened and shocked by the news of Schork's death in Sierra Leone:

> Kurt's death also stunned me because he was a symbol to all of us who do this job: of bravery and fearlessness. In a sense, he always seemed untouchable . . . Perhaps because, at 53, he was older than most war correspondents—he had lived many lives before becoming a journalist in his 40s—his reporting always had a finer-tuned analysis and sensitivity, along with a penetrating sense of humor.[191]

In 2001, Reuters, along with Kurt Schork's friends, launched the Kurt Schork Memorial Fund to help finance journalists who were most dear to Schork's heart: the freelancer. The Kurt Schork Fund offers two awards in International Journalism each year, created "to honor fearless freelance news reporting and those journalists who cannot leave their country when the story becomes secondary to survival."[192] Two annual prizes of $5,000 each are awarded, one to a freelance journalist covering foreign news, and the other to a local journalist in the developing world or countries in transition. For more information, see http://www.ksm fund.org/ksmfinfo.html.

Umar Cheema

Pakistan, 2010

No half-hearted police measures or words of consolation from the highest offices in the land will suffice in the aftermath of the brutal treatment meted out to journalist Umar Cheema of The News. This paper's stand is clear: the government and its intelligence agencies will be considered guilty until they can prove their innocence. Yes, Mr. Cheema wrote pieces that were highly critical of the government and in particular the presidency. Was it for that reason that he was kidnapped, stripped naked and filmed, hung upside down, had his hair and moustache shaved and beaten relentlessly for hours on end?

Editorial from *Dawn* (Pakistan), September 7, 2010[193]

The editorial comment above explains much of the story of Umar Cheema. The story is also visually demonstrated by the side-by-side photos of Cheema before and after his abduction where his head and eyebrows were shaved in an obvious effort to publicly humiliate him.

Cheema, 34, was an investigative reporter for a major Pakistani newspaper who had repeatedly not heeded the advice of authorities to stop writing critical stories. On September 4, 2010, he was on his way home from dinner when he was abducted and taken to a house outside of town. He was then beaten and videotaped in humiliating positions while his head and eyebrows were shaved. Six hours later, Cheema was dumped by the side of the road and told to not talk about the attack. But Cheema spoke out immediately about this assault. Cheema described in graphic detail to local and international news organizations what happened to him. This response is something rare in a country where victims who suspect that their brutal treatment was at the hands of government agents often choose, out of fear, to keep quiet. Cheema described his assailants as thugs of Pakistan's intelligence agency, the Inter-Services Intelligence agency (ISI). "I have suspicions and every journalist has suspicions that all fingers point to the ISI," Cheema told the *New York Times*.[194]

Earlier in 2010, Cheema said he was called to a coffee shop in Islamabad by an ISI officer and warned to fall into line. Cheema had written more than 50 articles this year that questioned various aspects of the conduct of the military and the government, including corruption accusations against the president, Asif Ali Zardari.[195]

Jane Perlez of the *New York Times* reported that Pakistan has developed a highly engaged news media spearheaded by 24-hour television news channels in the last decade. The military and the Inter-Services Intelligence agency are treated with respect by the powerful television anchors and by newspaper reporters who laud the ISI and rarely mention the organization by name. One reason for the deference, according to a Pakistani intelligence official who has worked with the media cell of the ISI, is that the agency keeps many journalists on its payroll.[196]

Despite the 2010 attack and numerous threats, Cheema continues to speak out to show his abductors that he cannot be intimidated. "Despite the risk, I will continue. I am trying to secure the future for the next generation," Cheema said.[197]

Marlene Garcia-Esperat

Philippines

I am not exactly new to this. Lumaki ako sa bala (I grew up on bullets). My father was a farmer who became the first chief of police of our town. After that he was a municipal councilor. There were threats on his life. He survived two assassination plots, but two of my uncles were not as lucky. They were felled by assassins' bullets.

Marlene Garcia-Esperat[198]

Originally, a chemist in the agriculture department on the southern island of Mindanao in the Philippines, Marlene Garcia-Esperat fell into journalism after realizing her unit was receiving only 40 percent of the funds entitled to it by the government. Angry, she quickly began her own investigation, and discovered government authorities were stealing millions from government contracts meant for destitute farmers to buy seeds, fertilizers, and pesticides. She filed complaints, provided testimony, and assisted as the ombudsman for her department.[199] But she did not stop there. Soon, she started hosting a program on a local radio station and writing a column, "Madame Witness."[200] Frustrated with continuing government apathy toward corruption, she jumped into journalism full time a couple years later, where her probing investigations garnered numerous enemies, resulting in three assassination attempts and the need for police bodyguards.

On Easter weekend in 2005, Garcia-Esperat sent her bodyguards home for the holidays. The decision resulted in tragedy. On March 24, a gunman casually walked into Garcia-Esperat's living room and shot her at point-blank range in front of her children. She did not survive. Garcia-Esperat had been pursuing high-profile investigations, including one that sought to link authorities friendly with President Gloria Macapagal-Arroyo to a multibillion-peso scam relating to government fertilizer purchases.

Fortunately, less than a month later, police arrested four individuals implicated in carrying out her murder.[201] Several months later, the Cebu Regional Trial Court successfully convicted three of the individuals with murder, sentencing them to a minimum of 30 years without parole. The military official involved in her murder, however, was acquitted and the two regional agricultural department officials who allegedly hired the hit on Garcia-Esperat were never convicted.[202]

The courageous personal stories here represent just a glimpse at the hundreds of journalists and media workers who have risked their lives, been threatened, kidnapped, or jailed for telling the important stories of our time. Unfortunately, there are many more stories than these pages could hold. The local journalists represented here have refused to be silent, and the international journalists have chosen not to remain in the hotel to file their stories. They have been killed and detained, tortured, and kidnapped, but they persevere to question authority and risk these dangers to promote the vestiges of free expression as well as democracy in the world. They are an inspiration.

The next chapter will present the opinions of journalists and advocates regarding who should be protecting journalists reporting from dangerous situations today.

ADDENDUM

The authors felt it important to include this addendum following the significant and unprecedentedly swift rise of unrest in the Middle East and the simultaneous increase in attacks against journalists, beginning in late December 2010 and continuing to present-day. According to CPJ, more than 450 attacks against journalists covering the unrest have occurred.[1] Twelve journalists have been killed in the region, whereas numerous others have been detained and/or assaulted.

Tunisia

The unrest currently spreading across several countries in the Middle East began with a seemingly innocuous event in relatively stable Tunisia in December 2010. A policewoman fined a street vendor for selling wares without a license, then reportedly slapped him in the face and confiscated his goods. In response, the vendor walked to the municipal building and demanded his goods be returned. Instead he was allegedly beaten again. He then walked to the governor's office, and demanded to speak with someone, but was refused. Around noon, he drenched himself in paint thinner and lit himself on fire. His self-immolation led to immediate protests, which were then filmed and posted on the Internet. These videos sparked outrage among the people in Tunisia and swiftly led to the uprising, (now known as the Jasmine Revolution) which disposed of Tunisian President Abidine Ben Ali, Tunisia's dictator for 23 years. Although, the end of Ben Ali's reign led to the unblocking of numerous news and human rights websites, journalists now worry about their safety amidst the current vacuum of power that has replaced Ben Ali. "The problem now is security. The gangs do not differentiate between journalists and others," said Soufiane Chourabi, a reporter for the weekly *Al-Tariq al-Jadid*, interviewed by CPJ.[2] One photographer died from head injuries incurred while covering the violence, and at least one other journalist, arrested in 2010, still languishes in prison in reprisal for his work.[3]

Egypt

Less than two weeks after the Tunisian riots toppled that country's president, protests erupted in Egypt against the 30-year, authoritarian rule of President Hosni Mubarak. In response to civilian-led street protests, pro-Mubarak supporters infiltrated the crowds and assaulted protesters and journalists. CPJ documented substantial evidence of more than 140 attacks against journalists during the 18-day uprising.[4] "The systematic and sustained attacks documented by CPJ leave no doubt that a government-orchestrated effort to target the media and suppress the news is well under way," said CPJ's Executive Director Joel Simon.[5] Within 24-hours, CPJ had recorded 30 detentions of journalists, 26 assaults, and eight instances of equipment being confiscated.[6] In addition, plainclothes and uniformed officials reportedly entered hotels used by international journalists to confiscate media equipment. Even prominent, internationally recognized journalists such as Anderson Cooper of CNN and Lara Logan of CBS News were directly affected by the crisis.[7] Cooper was punched ten times in the head, as he and his team tried to shield themselves from the violence. Logan was savagely beaten and sexually assaulted. She was rescued when a group of women and soldiers intervened and shielded her from further attack.

While these overt attacks against prominent international journalists in Egypt thrust the press protection debate into the public domain; some commentators' impromptu tweets on Twitter stirred a vitriolic debate in the mainstream press about the role of women journalists reporting from conflict environments.[8] One commentator stated that Lara Logan brought the attacks upon herself by trying to "outdo" Anderson Cooper. The commentator's remarks led to his immediate resignation; however, similar viewpoints in public discourse blaming a woman reporter for being sexually assaulted continued. On February 12, 2011, Mubarak was officially deposed, and the last of the remaining jailed journalists were freed.

Libya

Protests spread across Libya in mid-February. Libya's reckless and murderous leader of more than 40 years, Muammar al-Gaddafi, lashed out against the civil uprising with angry rhetoric and a barrage of bombs against his own civilians."It's alarming to see Libya, Bahrain, Yemen, and Iran take a page from Egypt and Tunisia to use violence and censorship to stop coverage of political unrest," said Mohamed Abdel Dayem, CPJ's Middle East and North Africa program coordinator.[9] As of March 27, 2011, CPJ had documented more than 60 attacks on the press since the unrest began in February, including: 36 detentions, nine assaults, two fatalities, a gunshot injury, two attacks on news facilities, and the jamming of Al Jazeera and Al Hurra's transmissions. In addition, at least seven journalists and media workers are currently missing.[10]

What follows is a glimpse at some of the attacks and harassments that have been inflicted on journalists while covering conflicts in other nations during the spring of 2011:

Bahrain

- Expulsion of a CNN reporter from Bahrain by authorities;[11]
- Yemeni authorities order the shutdown of Al Jazeera's offices and their journalists stripped of accreditation;
- Reduced Internet connection speed by the government in newspaper offices, hotels, and homes, but not in governmental institutions according to CPJ, which cited local journalists;
- Helicopter forces shot at the crowd and then at a *New York Times* reporter and videographer, as they attempted to film the helicopter;[12]
- 16 foreign journalists from BBC, CNN, McClatchy Newspapers, CBS, and other media outlets were detained at the airport and prevented from entering the country for hours;
- Foreign photographer injured;
- Independent journalists received threats by phone and SMS, warning them to stop reporting on the crackdown.[13]

Yemen

- Photojournalist Jamal Al-Sharaabi for the independent weekly *Al Masdar*, was killed along with 44 other individuals when security forces opened fire on a demonstration protesting the current president's rule;[14]
- Journalists were beaten after they were accused of working for Al Jazeera;
- A BBC correspondent and a BBC photographer were beaten by "men from the ruling party" while covering anti-government demonstrations in the country;[15]

- Al Arabiya's bureau chief in Yemen and one of Al Arabiya's cameramen were attacked;
- A Qatar TV cameraman, and an Iranian TV station correspondent were attacked and beaten;
- The *Guardian*'s correspondent in Sana'a was attacked and his equipment confiscated;
- Security forces attacked an unidentified cameraman working for an opposition TV channel.

Syria

- Responding to attacks on its staff, Al Jazeera suspended its activities inside Syria indefinitely;[16]
- At least five Reuters and two Associated Press journalists have been forced to leave the country in recent weeks;
- Numerous local journalist and bloggers have been detained;
- Freelance journalist working for France-Culture, a France public radio station, and *Le Monde*, was arrested with no justification given by the government;[17]
- The News website *Sawt Al-Kurd* was hacked by the ruling *Baath party*, deleting a substantial portion of archives and disorganizing the chronology of news articles;
- The Syrian government continues to disrupt phone service and Internet access in locales where protests have occurred;
- Security forces continue to block access to certain regions, preventing journalists from covering protests there.

Are We Doing Enough? What Stakeholders Suggest Should Be Done to Protect Journalists and Media Workers

It is safer to be a soldier these days than a war correspondent.[1]

Phillip Knightley, Author of *The First Casualty*

As journalists risk their lives in dangerous situations around the world, their colleagues struggle to find effective strategies to protect them. What follows are the opinions of more than 50 stakeholders and fellow journalists who are intimately engaged in this war on words. The respondents include local and international journalists—both embedded and unilateral journalists, freelance journalists, journalism educators and trainers, as well as press freedom and human rights advocates. These international actors were ostensibly asked how journalists who cover conflict could tell their stories under safer conditions. Opinions varied on what constituted a conflict as well as how the problems of local journalists and international journalists should be treated separately. The responses here also represent published accounts of personal opinions concerning the issue of journalists' protection. In a few cases, the names of the journalists have been excluded to protect the respondents from possible danger or retaliation. The passions and perspectives of these various constituents proffer a fundamental understanding of the need to protect journalists engaged in these difficult assignments today.

The individuals interviewed were first asked: what is meant by conflict situations? Mogens Schmidt, Deputy Assistant Director-General for Communication and Information and Director of the Division of

Freedom of Expression, Democracy and Peace at UNESCO offered clarity on this issue:

> Defining conflict environments is a very delicate and a very difficult issue. Take the one number that really pushed the overall numbers forward last year—the killing in the Philippines of the more than thirty journalists there—and do you define the Philippines as a conflict area or not? We normally define it as a non-conflict area, while we do know that in the southern islands, especially in Mindanao, there is a lot of conflict going on and there is very strong tension there. You can also take Mexico or Honduras, two countries with a relatively high number of journalists being killed over the last two years. Is Honduras a conflict area? Well, maybe you would define it as that after the throwing out of the former president and the whole unstable situation after that. And, Mexico—is that a conflict area? No, it's not, but it's an area marred by very, very strong banditry groups, the drug cartels and that of course creates a terrible situation for the journalists. So, my point is that there is a growing problem with the killing of journalists; the targeted killing of journalists.[2]

Likewise, Bruce Shapiro, Executive Director of the Dart Center for Journalism and Trauma, noted that today's danger spots for journalists may have developed as the result of a fundamental power shift:

> I think it [journalists being targeted] is a growing problem not only in formal conflict areas, but in a number of societies where power is in flux. I don't know if Russia would normally be considered a conflict area. I am not even sure if the US/Mexico border would normally be considered a conflict area and yet these are both increasingly dangerous places to do journalism and it's because of big disruptions in power arrangements in these societies.[3]

Brazilian journalist, Daniela Arbex, reiterated that journalists are not just being targeted in war zones:

> When it comes to conflict, we must remember the existing problems are not only those faced by the reporter when exposed to war coverage. In Latin America, and Brazil is an example, the existence of conflict is ongoing in news coverage. Although we do not live in a state of war, not even civil war, urban violence explodes day by day, making us the target of ongoing violations. We live under death threats and intimidation.[4]

Colombian journalist and filmmaker, Hollman Morris, remarked that even in the same nation, the experiences of journalists from large media outlets and independent news organizations might be different:

> Something you have to keep in mind with all of Latin America, is that a lot of times the interests of the major news outlets are not the same as the interest of the independent journalist. And in turn, the risk for journalists from the large media outlets is not the same type of risk as those from independent media sources. For example, in Colombia and Mexico, there have been great risks and death threats and threats towards the journalists that do not work in the large media outlets. So the journalists from the big outlets actually say "there is no problem at all—there is freedom and liberty of expression—we don't know what you are talking about."[5]

Whether journalists are telling stories of conflict from abroad or from their hometown; are from major media outlets or independent news operations; or are staff members or freelancers, all who were interviewed agreed that the targeting of journalists anywhere was a threat to journalism everywhere. But the vast differences in the conflict environment, individual framing, and journalism experience among these journalists and media workers demonstrated that no single strategy could possibly solve the issue of journalist protection. The vast range in responses from the interviewees underscored the complexity facing journalists across various conflict situations.

Who Is in Danger?

The question of who should protect journalists in conflict situations also necessitates clarification about the differences among those journalists and media workers who cover conflict situations. The five identities offered in preceding chapters included: (1) embedded foreign, frontline journalists; (2) non-embedded or unilateral journalists; (3) freelance journalists; (4) local or indigenous journalists; and (5) local media workers or fixers. The journalists interviewed were keen to discuss whom among them may be at risk or in danger when reporting about conflict and corruption. It was fundamentally clear to everyone that not all journalists who report from risky environments have the same constraints or dangers attached to them. The comments below clearly demonstrate the differing opinions about those dangers and the complexity of developing a method of protection for all journalists.

Several of the journalists interviewed said they believed the single greatest threat to freedom of expression in the world today was the intimidation and murder of local journalists practicing their trade in their own country. Data compiled by the Committee to Protect Journalists revealed that nearly 90 percent of the more than 861 journalists murdered since 1992 were local reporters.[6] The figure might be even higher if local media workers, fixers, translators, or drivers were included. And this figure also does not include the local journalists who are intimidated or harassed yet fail to report this harassment to an advocacy group like CPJ. This threat to free expression demands attention, and the journalists interviewed agreed. This was a serious concern for Tina Carr, Director of the Rory Peck Trust, who said:

> I think that indigenous journalists are more at risk because they can't really get the next plane out of town so they have to stay there and take whatever reprisals come to them for their work. What is more worrying is that their families are also targeted.[7]

One journalist from Iran, Omid Memarian, told of how journalists are pressured in his country:

> In countries like Iran, the government tries to control the communication channels. Journalists challenge the official narrative of the events and that's very problematic for the authorities who spend billions of dollars to create, perpetuate and spread their message. So we have witnessed an unprecedented wave of arbitrary arrests of journalists over the past two years. They are being monitored, threatened, intimidated and ultimately arrested. Just a few months ago, prominent journalist Jila Baniyaghoub, was sentenced to one year in prison and was forbidden to work as a journalist for 30 years. Basically it means that if she wants to stay in Iran she has to change her profession, even though according to the Iranian constitution everybody is free to choose his or her job. Since the 2009 elections, as the government experiences a substantial divide amongst the political elite and dissatisfaction amongst the people, we are witnessing more pressure on journalists. Now even criticizing the government's agriculture policies or publishing stupid things that ranking officials say might put journalists in danger.[8]

Some of the most dangerous places on earth for journalists can be found not in armed-conflict zones but in what journalists consider "hot" areas. Professor of International Journalism at City University in London,

John Owen, remarked that he was amazed that people in these hot areas keep telling stories. He said:

Look at Mexico, which is a perfect example where the journalists themselves were so frightened that they ran a front page editorial saying that you tell us what is acceptable and what is unacceptable. It's an extraordinarily dangerous place to be a journalist. Or take Russia, as another example, where one of the bravest journalists I have ever known, Anna Politkovskaya, was brutally murdered because she refused to stop writing and reporting about human rights violations.[9]

A journalist from Mexico, Dolia Estévez, explained how the dangers in her country have manifested for journalists:

Journalists in Mexico are being targeted primarily by organized crime. There is a war going on between the government and organized crime. And information is a very valuable asset in any war because it is through information that you control public opinion. The drug traffickers in Mexico want the news to reflect their position and their views so they target reporters and editors—particularly in the areas where there is more violence, which is the northern states and some of the southern states. They killed journalists, kidnapped them, threatened them, attacked them because the criminals want to make sure they are reporting in ways that serve their interests.[10]

Obviously, this burden of harassment and intimidation strikes the local or indigenous journalist personally, as recalled in the story of Brazilian journalist, Daniela Arbex, a reporter for the *Tribuna de Minas*:

Last year, due to a series of stories uncovering the wrongdoings of one of the most important politicians in my region, I was threatened directly by the Police Commissioner. He ordered me to stop writing, "for my safety." When this occurred, the newspaper I work for called me to tell me this would be my choice, because, due to the structure we have, there would be no means to ensure my safety. I decided to continue. The next day, when a new story was published, I received another phone call. "You did not stop," the military official said. I replied that if he could not protect me, then he shouldn't call me ever again. I never stopped signing my stories because, besides being my brand, it is, in some way, my safety and security. During the time we were publishing this series of articles, my editors and I would leave the newspaper [building] at dawn, with our cars in convoy, trying to protect one another. These were moments of great tension that affected me and my family.[11]

The dangers faced by local journalists are not just personal as they also affect the institution of journalism according to Ugandan radio reporter, Charles Odongtho. He said he is concerned that this intimidation and harassment may lead to significant issues of censorship:

> One of the biggest consequences is censorship at different levels. At the first level you fear going into and covering a violent situation. The second level of censorship is that you fear writing such a story. You think that if you write such a story about the ruling government and that it's violating people's rights to demonstrate by stopping them and eventually killing people in the process ... then you might be victimized by the government in power or by a certain group of politicians ... but the other consequence is, of course, your life ... you could die in the process.[12]

In addition to myriad dangers faced by local reporters, freelance journalists who cover conflict situations were also mentioned by the people interviewed as being reporters who may be in exceptional danger. The respondents said they were concerned because freelance journalists were being called on more often to cover dangerous assignments in this world of shrinking news budgets. Judith Matloff teaches conflict reporting at the Columbia Graduate School of Journalism and was a foreign correspondent for 20 years. She said:

> Freelancers are particularly vulnerable because they don't have the protections offered to staff correspondents, such as hostile environment training, body armor, chase cars, security guards, etc. Freelancers are more likely to take silly risks, in order to sell stories, as opposed to a staff reporter who will get a salary regardless and whose boss insists on caution. Besides, increasing numbers of freelancers are filling the gap as established news organizations close down foreign bureaus.[13]

One freelance photo journalist, Holly Picket, who has worked in conflict areas around the world as an embedded and non-embedded photographer, explained her experiences with filming stories without the protection of a large media organization:

> If you're freelancing, it doesn't matter who you're working for, you are working more cheaply than you would as a staffer and it's easier for publications to not look out for you ... I'm not saying that anybody that I've worked for has been that way ... the publications I've worked for have

been great but as far as paying for insurance and things like that, I think media outlets could do better.[14]

Director of the Rory Peck Trust, Tina Carr, is especially concerned with the plight of freelance journalists because that is the primary focus of her organization:

I am coming from a specific point of view . . . my community and my area is freelancers. Organizations on the whole protect their staff. The problem we have is that we fight for them to equally protect the freelancers who they commission to go into these places, because more and more these are "no-go" areas for these major news gathering organizations. They can't get into Gaza, they can't get into Burma, what do they do? They can't get into Mexico at the moment, actually, they can get in there but they don't want to go in there. But when there is an actual lock-down like there was in Gaza a couple of years ago and nobody was let in, the international media community . . . what do they do? They rely on several things. They rely on the local journalists . . . and they rely on the odd adventurer coming in from outside who will risk their life to do this story. I still don't think there is enough being done. It's actually a shared responsibility. I don't buy it when the broadcaster or the newspaper or someone like that says to me, "but we don't use freelancers" . . . of course they do. They use their footage, they use what comes through Reuters, they use the Associated Press. They use free-lance material all the time to tell their stories . . . sometimes without a sense of responsibility.[15]

Global Editor for Multimedia at Reuters News and Honorary President of the International News Safety Institute, Chris Cramer, noted that it is incumbent on all media outlets to offer some protection for their freelance reporters:

It's still unbelievable that there are some media institutions; some of them quite distinguished, who believe that . . . "well if staff people can't be sent to war zones any longer we can actually send freelancers and somehow get away with it." . . . Well that's just bordering on the criminal. The mature, respect-able and responsible part of the industry has a responsibility towards all peo-ple who work in our name whether they be staff people or freelancers.[16]

It is obvious that managers of news staffs around the world struggle with how to maintain this responsibility toward freelancers. Manager of Staff Development at the Australian Broadcasting Corporation, ABC News, Heather Forbes, told the story of freelance camera operator, Paul

Moran, who was killed by a suicide bomb in March of 2003 and was the first media person to die in the Iraq war, and the first Australian casualty. Forbes said ABC News was disturbed by Moran's killing and made changes about the network's use of freelancers in war zones in the future as the result of this tragic event. She said that ABC News would be unlikely to use a freelance camera operator in a war zone again.[17]

But several of the journalists interviewed thought that because media operations today are generating stories of conflict around the clock and budgets are tight, the news organizations may not be paying attention to the journalists at risk in the field. Former South Asia bureau chief for the *Chicago Tribune*, Kim Barker, voiced her opinion of the dangerous situation for local and freelance journalists:

> I think that everybody tries to do this on the cheap. And journalists' organizations don't necessarily want to know what it takes to do a story. And they don't necessarily know if you are doing something that isn't safe ... especially with freelancers ... They say "do what you want and if we like the story, we'll pay you for it" which just sort of encourages journalists to take a lot more risks. I know plenty of young folks over there who don't have a flak jacket ... they don't have a helmet and anytime they want to go on an embed they have to call around and try to beg, borrow or steal one. Well, the thing about a flak jacket and a helmet, you don't want to use somebody else's. You want it to be fitted to you and you want to know what's in that flak vest, what sort of level of protection it has, whether this helmet is a good helmet or not ... everybody is trying to do this on the cheap and trying to do drivers on the cheap. They're trying to do fixers on the cheap ... You need to pay good money to get a good fixer in a war zone ... someone who will tell you, "that's not really a good decision" or "that's a dangerous thing to do." And then you need to listen. I just had too many of my Afghan friends put in danger or even killed in these sorts of situations with journalists.[18]

Cali Bagby, from the Pacific Northwest, has worked as a freelance reporter and photojournalist in Iraq and Afghanistan. As an embedded freelancer, she received protection from the U.S. military, but not from a news organization. She said fewer news organizations are using freelancers because of the liability they may face if the freelancer is hurt or killed. As a result, fewer journalists are getting to the field, leading to a worrisome decrease in the flow of information:

> What I have seen trying to get people to pay me to go over there as an employee or even to sign paperwork that I am a freelancer working for

them is that they don't want to assume the liability because of the state of how things are going. I have been turned down by two different media organizations I was freelancing for because they said their lawyers could not approve the paperwork saying I worked as a freelancer for them. I am not even an employee. I am just a freelancer, but they don't want to be affiliated with you because of the potential financial obligation if something goes wrong. I don't know—I don't see how that is going to increase the flow of information and then on top of it our nation is fatigued with information on the war. So it is not necessarily selling more media to have people there . . . there is not that incentive. The incentive has to be "this is the right thing to do," which is hard to do when you are trying to keep your business afloat.[19]

Several people interviewed mentioned they thought that freelancers and local people who put themselves in danger to assist the network-funded frontline reporters should be rewarded with some kind of extra protection or fund if dangers arise. Journalist and author of *Seeds of Terror*, Gretchen Peters, was particularly interested in generating interest in such a fund:

I think it would be nice if there was a fund for freelancers . . . a foundation along the lines of the Rory Peck Award . . . It would be nice if there were funds available for journalists who have been injured or who have had to flee their home country, but who are not receiving financial support from their employer. I can think of about five or six journalists off the top of my head from Pakistan and Afghanistan who had to leave the region, and who are now living in the U.S. and are struggling to make ends meet. And I think we need to help protect the reporters who are our eyes and ears there. They are reporting from places that are extremely dangerous, and that most foreigners can't get into and they are bringing out information at a critical time in our nation's history in regard to that part of the world. And I think we owe it to them to develop resources to put displaced reporters through vocational training programs to get them resettled in a new country. I wish there were more organizations that provided that type of support to the journalists who have to flee.[20]

Are the Assignments More Dangerous for Women?

It has been reported that an additional vulnerability exists for women who choose to cover dangerous journalism assignments. To address this issue, the International News Safety Institute researched the extent of these added dangers in a survey conducted in 2010 that asked whether women reporters found the assignment of reporting from a conflict situation especially difficult. The women surveyed included freelancers and staff members, traveling reporters, women based in foreign bureaus and line producers and managers. While the survey did not include local women reporters, INSI encouraged further research to include these respondents. The research was sponsored by the Swedish International Development Cooperation Agency.[21] The INSI survey data suggested that more than 80 percent of respondents reported physical attack or intimidation while covering conflict. However, the majority of the responses indicated that many women journalists working in conflict areas do not believe they should be treated differently from their male colleagues.[22] This conclusion held true with regard to most of the journalists interviewed for this project.

Conversely, several of the women interviewed thought that their job as journalists in conflict zones was not more difficult because of their sex. Gretchen Peters, who covered Pakistan and Afghanistan for more than a decade for the Associated Press and later as an award-winning reporter for ABC News in the U.S., said she never found it more difficult to be a woman journalist in these places. She added:

> I don't think about it much nor let it bother me. I think in many ways that being a female reporter in Afghanistan or Pakistan is a great advantage. We are able to interact with 50 percent of the population that foreign male journalists can not interview and that allows us to provide a more complete picture of what's going on. I could probably count on one hand the number of times that being a woman has limited my activities there. In general, I get the best seat in the car, I get the best room to sleep in . . . in general, I am treated like a queen wherever I go. And there have only been a few occasions that somebody has objected to my presence because I'm female. What tends to happen more often is that a local colleague may not want me to travel to a particular location because I'm a foreigner. It has less to do with being a female, than being foreign because just being a foreigner makes the entire operation more dangerous. When you travel to places where there are few women out in public, you tend to get followed around like the Pied Piper, and this can make it hard to report, but my general experience is that people are curious, and not in a hostile way.[23]

Kim Barker, remarked that women actually have an advantage as reporters in Afghanistan and Pakistan:

> I think it's great being a woman over there. There have been a couple of women kidnapped but those were random situations and again those were people who didn't know the environment and they didn't know, "Hey,

I shouldn't be out here all by myself without my fixer." But I think that it's easier to be a woman at least in Pakistan and Afghanistan because you're not really seen as a local woman and you are not really seen as a foreign man. You are the in-between. You're the third sex. So you get access to absolutely everyone. I get access to the Afghan women who aren't going to talk to a foreign man or a foreign male journalist and I get access to the Afghan men, to these leaders who are charmed by the idea of some foreign woman running around the countryside. If you look at the very successful journalists in Pakistan many of them are women. Carlotta Gall from the *New York Times*, Aryn Baker from *Time*, Pamela Constable from the *Washington Post*, Soraya Sarhaddi Nelson from NPR . . . A lot of organizations send women over there and women do very well. There is this aspect of the culture, most definitely in Afghanistan, where women are not seen as part of the conflict.[24]

Anne Nivat, an independent French war correspondent and author of books about Iraq, Afghanistan and Chechnya including, *Chienne de Guerre: A Woman Reporter Behind the Lines of the War in Chechnya,* 2001, also found it easier for a woman than a man to report, particularly in recent conflicts in Muslim countries. She added this was true because:

In Muslim countries nobody pays attention to women and in a way, that plays in our favor—that is a plus for us—for non-local, Western women covering conflicts in the Muslim world, because as a woman you can go everywhere and see and watch without being seen— without being noticed. No one would pay attention to you . . . I was of course dressed like a local woman, that is the condition of the job. If I am not dressed like a local woman, I am risking being potentially targeted, but if you are dressed like a local woman—if you behave like a local woman, then you can see without being seen . . . that has happened for me. I remember I was walking through the streets of Baghdad during the peak of the civil war in 2006 and 2007 . . . walking through the streets without any problem and I could tell the story. You can't invent it. You have to go and feel it and go through it yourself. Also, as a woman the second thing is you have access to women. So you do have the other side—the feminine side of the story, because who is actually doing the war? Of course men. Men are warriors. After you talk to the man, you get the woman's story. And the woman's story is completely the other side of the male story. It is very interesting to have both sides and that is something that the male reporter definitely doesn't have access to.[25]

But not all women agree. Caroline Vuillemin, Chief Operations Officer for Fondation Hirondelle, a Swiss NGO founded by journalists that creates independent media in conflict and post-conflict zones, said she does not believe the assignment of covering conflict is easier for women:

> I think it's more difficult for women . . . it's more difficult right at the beginning from the news gathering perspective. Nine times out of ten an editor and chief will not send a woman to these situations. So even within the profession, within the journalistic family, it's difficult. Then once the woman is on the ground it's difficult for any human being to be put in such a situation. But I think that the first difficulty comes from the lack of trust and also the lack of access for women to these positions of being a war reporter or being sent to dangerous missions.[26]

Radio station manager from northern Uganda, Evelyn Abbo agreed. She thought the assignment of covering conflict tends to be more difficult for women because of a few factors:

> First the social attitude towards women is still not favorable. Many people still believe mediating conflict or handling serious issues should be spearheaded by men. The woman involved in this kind of work is treated as stubborn and disrespectful.[27]

But another woman interviewed who works as a reporter for Al Jazeera English, Juliana Ruhfus, explained several reasons why she felt safer as a foreign journalist working alongside women journalists. She added that she thought the difficulties women face when covering conflict may be as much in the office as in the field. She commented:

> I'd have to say, I do love working with other women; on the whole I feel safer with women. We are less of a threat to men and even though there may be reason to be afraid of rape this is not something I have ever heard of. Generally, male sources are far less intimidated by women and with women you don't get into that macho bravado thing at a road block, sort of looking at each other and saying, "you're not going through," "yes I am" . . . When you're a woman at a road block you can be nice, polite and smile and you are far more likely to get through. There is still a certain surprise element when we turn up and I think that on the whole, people are generally more polite with women including crooks or warlords. So

I am a great fan of working with women and some years I've done 70 percent of my work with women. I don't think it is more difficult, I can't see why it would be. But I do think it is far more difficult in the office for a woman and that's where you get a lot of problems, not on location.[28]

Other women may tell a different story. Senior Advisor and Spokesperson for Reporters without Borders in Washington, DC, Tala Dowlatshahi, spoke about historical cultural pressures and said her experiences are unique as an Iranian woman traveling in Afghanistan with Americans.

For me personally, being a Middle Eastern Iranian woman traveling into Afghanistan, I find I am under certain customary rules that are invisible, that colleagues don't even think about. So traveling with male journalists who are working for Reuters, for example, they are treated as American, where all of a sudden I become an Iranian woman with the added requirement to cover my hair, which I don't have a problem doing—I don't judge it . . . just like most of the women who travel to Afghanistan, whether they are American, Danish, German or any other nationality they are required to wear something over their head, like a scarf, when going into ministerial meetings or interviewing government officials. That puts a layer of cultural pressure on women. And that's something women experience all over the world. It's also in African countries, mostly Muslim African countries, where you see that same dynamic. So yes, in some ways women do have cultural standards that are placed on them. I believe as a woman it's always going to be there and it's always going to be a cultural pressure.[29]

Hedayat Abdel Nabi, President of the Press Emblem Campaign (PEC), said she felt there was no difference between men and women when working in the field of journalism these days. She added:

. . . in fact you have women who have risen to the tip top of TV journalism and the opportunity was provided to them when satellite TV transmission was created with CNN and then followed by others. However, in situations of military conflict, extreme duress and torture applies to both men and women. But in the case of women it can go one horrible step further which is that of rape, and this has happened to women journalists in Africa. Truly this is not the norm but the exception and if and when it happens, war zones become more dangerous for women journalists in this sense.[30]

Several of the men interviewed also mentioned the dangers of sexual violence which they thought made womens' jobs more risky in conflict situations. Ross Howard, a Canadian journalism educator who teaches in Africa, voiced his concerns about this kind of danger for women reporting from conflict:

> It's widely known that gender-based violence that ends in sexual assault are intimidation weapons in a number of places, so female journalists both indigenous and inserted journalists face many risks that way . . . They are functioning in a number of countries that have much less respect for women . . . Many of those countries simply don't accord women the same rights and opportunities. But if it's a foreign journalist—an inserted journalist—these Westerners may be granted a higher degree of tolerance if they are female journalists. But consider the challenge for indigenous journalists who are women functioning in what are already misogynist countries. There is no doubt that it's a pretty tough road for them.[31]

John Owen, Professor of International Journalism at City University who also conducts journalism training for Al Jazeera, remarked about what he had learned from other journalists—that women are equally strong and resilient as men when covering conflict situations. He added:

> I had the outstanding Al Jazeera English channel documentary correspondent Juliana Ruhfus speak to my City class. She was asked about whether women are more at risk than men in conflict zones. She argued that in many respects it was easier for women, especially in macho cultures where women can work under the radar more easily than men. Certainly women are every bit as tough as men and have proven time and again their mettle. Correspondents such as Elizabeth Palmer of CBS News or Lindsey Hilsum from Channel 4 News in Britain or Orla Guerin from BBC or Janine di Giovanni from the *Times*. Bravest of all is perhaps Marie Colvin, an American journalist who has worked for decades for the *Sunday Times*. I heard her speak recently at a moving ceremony paying tribute to all the journalists who have lost their lives this century bearing witness. Marie was blinded in one eye and wears an eye patch. She survived what she feels was a deliberate targeting by the Sri Lankan government when she was reporting on the Tamil Tigers. This near blinding hasn't stopped her from returning to war zones. She's just been in Afghanistan where she was embedded and once again was under fire.[32]

But journalism trainer and freelance journalist from Nepal, Binod Bhattarai, thought that cultural constraints might make the job more difficult for women:

> Again this has to do with the roles different cultures "assign" to the different sexes. For example, in some countries like Nepal—which is still patriarchal,

in practical terms—women face difficulties because of the social norms that expect them to act/behave in certain ways. This I also believe influences opportunities for all to train and learn the skills equally, which then reflects on their overall capacities. This argument is generally heard from employers who say that women are not as qualified as men for higher level journalism jobs.[33]

New York Times investigative reporter and former kidnap victim, David Rohde, remarked that there may be advantages and disadvantages to being a female correspondent:

Being a female foreign correspondent can be a double-edged sword. It's a disadvantage in some ways and an advantage in others. Overall they do an extraordinary job. The number of women covering conflicts from Bosnia to Kosovo to Afghanistan to Iraq has been steadily growing. The disadvantage is a lot of attention female reporters will get from male government officials abroad or male military commanders. It's inappropriate at times. I've seen women who very effectively push back and say what's unacceptable and they're able to do their jobs. And sometimes commanders are so amazed to see women that it will lead them to talk to them more readily. They're impressed that they're out there.[34]

Why Are Journalists Being Targeted?

In order to understand the basic question of who should protect journalists, it is important to try to uncover why journalists may be increasingly in danger while reporting from conflict arenas. The journalists interviewed offered myriad reasons why they believed journalists may be increasingly targeted. Often respondents, local and international, cited the dramatic change in the way wars are fought as one of the primary reasons journalists find themselves in danger. One respondent, however, put a positive spin on the issue. Caroline Vuillemin, the Chief Operations Officer of Fondation Hirondelle, a Swiss nongovernmental organization that supports indigenous media in conflict areas, suggested the issue may be related to increased democratization:

... Because maybe there is more awareness about the importance of reporting and also more ways of informing the rest of the world about the threats and the problems. But if you consider the evolution of democratizations and opening societies and the government efforts in the last

30 years, there is more progress in the rights of journalists to work and the rights of the citizens to be informed.[35]

While journalism may be gaining prominence in today's society, there are those who believe that this growing presence may contribute to global fatigue toward journalism and lack of trust. Juliana Ruhfus, a reporter for Al Jazeera English, said that this lack of trust may be undermining the relationship between journalists and their constituency and lead to more journalists finding themselves in more danger. She said:

> There is a breakdown of trust. The breakdown of trust is not just caused by the war on terror. The breakdown of trust is also an increasing polarity in terms of rich and poor. Poor people in the world, for example in places like Haiti, have been promised so much for so long-we have promised development and democracy and all these big words that we like to export so much. But in spite of these promises to places like Haiti and others, or the Niger Delta where I go quite a lot . . . there has just not been any change and I think there's disillusionment with what telling the story might achieve. Quite often I am embarrassed now. I was embarrassed when I was in Haiti two weeks ago thinking gosh, I'm back, I'm asking the same stupid old questions and people just look at me and their willingness to talk is gone because they just don't know what's the point of it. I feel that in places that are reaching an absolute poverty and disillusionment and nihilism . . . probably a lot of young men will just grab what they can grab because they no longer believe in long term benefits and change. So [I would] imagine that could involve the kidnapping a journalist . . . with all these broken promises and dreams the loyalties and niceness have all gone.[36]

In addition to the loss of trust, the general loss of neutrality that journalists experienced in the past as a protection was posited as a reason why journalists may be targeted today. Some journalists interviewed focused on this reduced neutrality primarily from the perspective of the international journalist. Hugh Lunn, an Australian correspondent in Vietnam and author of *Vietnam: A Reporter's War*, explained how his experiences reporting in Vietnam were different from reporting in today's conflicts:

> Although the Vietnam War was dangerous for reporters, and three of the five in my office were shot and killed by the Vietcong, it was not generally in the communists' interest to deliberately target journalists. The

communists wanted the Americans to leave their country; therefore they saw themselves as also waging a PR [public relations] war to get the American public to call for troop withdrawal. So they wanted Western reporters to look at them relatively positively. Whereas in Iraq and Afghanistan and Pakistan, it seems insurgents are not interested in changing public opinion in the west: they know that is not going to happen post 9/11. Perhaps this is because this is not seen as a political war but a religious one. They want the Americans to leave, but they don't feel the need for the press to tell the insurgents' side of the story. So they appear happy to target journalists.[37]

Terry Anderson, Honorary Co-Chairman of the Committee to Protect Journalists, was swept up in a violent conflict in the Middle East in 1985 when he was held captive at the mercy of Shiite captors for seven years. He described how things have changed regarding the perception of international journalists since that time:

As a civilian journalist I never wore anything that looked like a uniform and I never carried a gun .... In other words I did not want to look like a combatant. The only protection that I had was the perception that people had that journalists were more or less neutral. And it worked for a long time ... up until 1985 when new players entered the game and again they didn't care if we were journalists. The only thing they cared about was that we were Americans or westerners. The rules changed and they have since changed beyond that. They changed beyond that not caring that you were a journalist to targeting journalists.[38]

As more international journalists descended on the world's conflict areas, their shield of neutrality faded and they became more vulnerable. But other aspects of the international journalists' environment contributed to their increased susceptibility to attack. Kim Barker, former South Asia bureau chief for the *Chicago Tribune* suggested that attacks on journalists became prevalent because many foreign journalists were easy, high-profile targets in the hot conflict areas:

I guess you could say that the first incident was in Pakistan in 2002 when Daniel Pearl was kidnapped and eventually killed. I think it just started becoming more of a tactic to be used because here you've got these people who want to talk to the insurgents who present themselves as a very easy target to pick up and then their kidnapping becomes guaranteed press coverage.[39]

So what was happening at this time was also a growing understanding of the power of the word and image. Press coverage was becoming a weapon of war. But the Western idea of press coverage did not correspond to this same idea where these conflicts were taking place. John Daniszewski, Senior Managing Editor for International News and Photography for the Associated Press, addressed why journalists are increasingly in danger:

> I think it's partly the nature of the kinds of conflicts that exist today. Again reporters represent a culture of openness to some extent. So in many countries like Afghanistan or Pakistan, Iraq or Somalia where the journalist might say "I'm only here to record events or to write about what's happening and to give all sides a fair say," the extremists in those areas or the political and irregular forces fighting would tend to see the journalists as being on one side—because what the journalists represent is accurate information and facts and discussion . . . those are the things that are a threat to their world view.[40]

And Joel Simon, Executive Director of the Committee to Protect Journalists, reinforced this notion that journalists were not being seen as the neutral forces they had been in the past. He offered two reasons why foreign journalists may be in greater danger:

> As a journalist myself who has worked in conflict zones, the fact that you were a journalist gave you a sort of get out of jail free card no matter who was hostile. I mean if there were two competing interests and you were the journalist, you could mediate them. Or you could navigate between them by making clear that your primary role was to report what both sides were saying. But that is not necessarily going to be compelling to many militants, even governments because of (1) alternate means of communication and because (2) the message they might want to send is one of fear and terror. The most effective way to send that is not to give you an interview, but to kill you.[41]

It would seem that the relationship between the foreign journalists and their sources on the ground during conflict situations has become strained and thus dangerous for the reporter. Journalist and author, Gretchen Peters, explained this phenomenon from her experiences:

> I think American journalists in Afghanistan and Pakistan are often seen as an extension of the U.S. government, as stakeholders in the conflict and

not independent observers. Therefore they may be perceived as legitimate targets for insurgents and terror groups. This is a change. I first worked in Pakistan and Afghanistan in the 1990s and we were able to interview the Taliban on a regular basis in Afghanistan. And in Pakistan we were able to go interview many of the militant groups that are now on the U.S. terrorist list. They had offices and they gave press conferences. There were a number of Western journalists who even interviewed Osama Bin Laden prior to 2001. Now the relationship between the media and these groups is a one-way street. Al Qaeda, the Taliban and other extremist organizations put out statements and videos and they will call some members of the media to make statements, but interviews with members of the insurgency are much more rare. They happen, but in general the media is on the receiving end and unable to question the insurgents and militant groups.[42]

While these challenges continue to grow for international correspondents due to various vulnerabilities and perceptions, the job of the local journalists has also become more dangerous. These journalists have honed their journalistic skills to become forces of democratic free expression in many of their countries. They have incorporated Western notions of investigative reporting and used these skills to uncover corruption. These advanced skills may have served the discipline of journalism but may have increased the dangers for local journalists. Ross Howard, journalism educator and president of the Media&Democracy Group with headquarters in Canada explained this issue:

We are getting better journalism even in the most repressive environments and better journalism equals greater exposure equals greater risks of retaliation for journalists. There are more people doing better work perhaps because of international training efforts which teach journalists to look underneath rocks and uncover fairly lethal critics who don't want that kind of information out there.[43]

This thesis was further expanded by Bruce Shapiro, who commented that perhaps the reason local journalists have been targeted has to do with the expanded role of journalism in the developing world:

Over the last decade or so there's been a lot of training of journalists in the developing world . . . a lot of raising of the standards for local reporting. There's a much wider culture of journalism training and a much wider culture of investigative reporting in countries that never had it before. That is good for journalism but it also puts journalists in the line of fire.[44]

Impunity

One of the other serious concerns for those interviewed is the growing trend toward impunity for those who target journalists. The majority of the people interviewed considered impunity as one of the primary reasons journalists are in danger around the world. Terry Anderson, Honorary Co-Chairman of the Committee to Protect Journalists and the longest held American hostage during the Lebanese Civil War, said he was disturbed that an increasing number of journalists are being targeted by their own governments or people working on behalf of their own governments. "That means that those attacks are never investigated or punished and that's very dangerous. Not just for the journalists but for the world."[45]

Journalism educator and president of the Media&Democracy Group, Ross Howard, trains journalists in remote parts of the world. He suggested that the high-level of impunity is related to increasingly corrupt environments:

> The widespread failure of the rule of law is what's leading to a culture of impunity concerning journalists' deaths. Journalism previously had a certain degree of respect and immunity. This respect existed for both domestic journalists and international ones. A lot has eroded predominantly not because of journalists but because of the environments in which they're working . . . which have become increasingly corrupt and lawless.[46]

This issue of impunity was described as a problem in nations where governments are not only corrupt but also fail to recognize the importance of a free press to democratic progress. Independent journalist and Senior Advisor to the Woodrow Wilson Center's U.S.–Mexico Journalism Initiative, Dolia Estévez, described the issue of impunity in her country:

> In the case of Mexico, one of the biggest problems we have is impunity. This year [2010] there have already been 10 assassinations of reporters, which is a number higher than Iraq, where six reporters have been killed. And since 2006, the year President Calderon took office and declared his war on drugs, 33 reporters have been killed or have gone missing, who

are essentially considered dead, although their bodies have not been found. None of these crimes have been prosecuted. There have not been arrests or prosecutions much less punishment. So impunity in Mexico is an invitation for the criminals and corrupt officials at all levels of government, to continue killing or harassing or targeting reporters. To the extent that the government doesn't protect freedom of the press and the physical integrity of reporters—which it doesn't in Mexico—violence against reporters will continue.[47]

This issue of impunity emerges in countries around the world. In Azerbaijan, Chairman of the Baku-based Institute for Reporters' Freedom and Safety, Emin Huseynov, was particularly concerned with the issue of impunity for those who perpetrated criminal acts against journalists in his nation:

> Today, journalists in Azerbaijan face harassment, threats, imprisonment, and violence for conducting their professional activities. There can be no press freedom where journalists exist in conditions of corruption, poverty or fear. The murderers of Elmar Huseynov, the Editor-in-Chief for *Monitor* weekly, who was shot dead on the second of March 2005, are still running free. The problem cannot be solved until this criminal case is opened.[48]

The issue of impunity was further explained by Frank Smyth, from the Committee to Protect Journalists. Smyth reported in his article for the *Harvard International Review*, that the trend toward impunity for crimes against journalists was disturbing:

> When it comes to journalists, the killers get away with the murders in nearly nine out of ten cases. In no less than 89 percent of journalist murders worldwide, there has been little or no prosecution whatsoever. Moreover, only in four percent of journalist murder cases has full prosecution occurred, which in most cases means that both the assassins and the masterminds who ordered or hired them, have been brought to justice.[49]

This growing trend suggests it is the prevailing view of many belligerents and insurgents as well as corrupt government officials that it is all right to kill a journalist because you are likely never going to be put on trial. More importantly, if you kill the journalists you may also kill the story.

However, not all of the respondents agreed that there was a growing problem of journalists being targeted. Professor Dan Morrison, from the University of Oregon School of Journalism and Communication, reported that he was not convinced the targeting of journalists was a problem in conflict:

> First, I do not believe journalists being targeted is a growing problem. Journalists are seldom targeted, with perhaps the notable exception of the Bosnian conflict in which the Serbs did indeed target journalists. Journalists get killed in wars because most of the violence in war does not discriminate between combat troops and journalists who travel with them.[50]

Whether journalists are increasingly targeted may be contested, but the majority of the journalists questioned agreed that the targeting of journalists increasingly goes unpunished, and is a growing problem for journalists individually and for free expression generally. They did not all agree on why journalists may be under attack, but they all had suggestions on how to mitigate this growing problem.

What Strategies Could Be Used to Protect Journalists?

Nearly all the journalists interviewed felt that bringing this problem of journalists being targeted to the public's attention was a worthwhile objective. They agreed that it was the responsibility of the journalism community to take charge of this issue and address it head on, even though, as Bruce Shapiro of the Dart Center, explained, "I think as journalists we sometimes have a tendency to understate and under-dramatize the importance of attacks on us. Our instincts as journalists are that the journalist is not the story the people are the story." But the growing attacks on journalists have become an important story all journalists seem willing to tackle.

The respondents offered strong suggestions for strategies of protection that generally fell into the broad categories of advocate, mitigate, and educate. Some variance appeared when the interview subject was primarily concerned with the protection of international correspondents, local journalists, or freelancers. Most of the people interviewed admitted that no one strategy or entity could possibly be responsible for protecting all journalists in all situations all the time. In fact, this section also includes strategies to protect journalists that were controversial or lacked consensus among this nonscientific group of journalists.

Advocate

Advocacy in this context was seen not only in the traditional sense of collecting data about the number of journalists attacked and killed around the world and disseminating those figures to the public. But advocacy in this situation also refers to putting pressure on local governments and international bodies to seriously address the issue of journalists being targeted in overt and subversive conflicts. The journalists' responses that focused on advocacy as an effective measure to protect journalists contained a host of suggestions. A senior advisor and spokesperson for Reporters sans Frontières, Tala Dowlatshahi, said her organization has worked to offer protection for journalists in a number places in the world. She offered some specific advocacy suggestions and a success story:

> Specific strategies could involve journalists getting involved with local journalism associations and groups that work to defend freedom of information and freedom of the press within their own countries as well as reaching out to international advocacy groups like our own Reporters without Borders or Amnesty International . . . groups that work to ensure human rights and groups that have lobbying powers with other governments that may be working with that particular country . . . be it Mexico, be it Zambia, be it Iraq, these groups can put pressure on a particular government to release the journalist or to refrain from abusing the journalist in any way. That helps. That's one particular strategy. Often times, journalists don't want to come out and share their cases for fear of reprisals against their families or against their colleagues or against their own lives. At Reporters without Borders we addressed that issue in China during the Olympic campaign. Chinese journalists were being detained and harassed and told not to cover human rights issues when the Olympic Games were there in 2008. So they worked as unnamed sources, interlocutors, who provided information to our group and other international advocacy groups about particular government stances against journalists. But these Chinese sources remained unnamed so we could protect their lives and the lives of their families.[51]

Another official for a prominent advocacy organization suggested media owners as well as local and regional governments needed to be pressured to address the issue of impunity. Executive Director and cofounder of International Media Support, Jesper Højberg, suggested that his organization finds ways to work with various stakeholders and governments to address the issue of impunity:

> Some argue 0% of journalists killers have been brought to justice. Impunity is almost at 100% of killing journalists which is not helping anyone. So there you need to put more effort into getting media owners seriously involved. Media organizations in Mexico are trying their best to do something about it. And they try to get the government involved to address it. Last week, the government said that now they are going to try and do something about it [protecting journalists].[52]

Joel Simon, the Executive Director of the Committee to Protect Journalists said that this problem of impunity cannot be solved without the cooperation of the local governments so pressure should be focused there:

> You can't say, the government is part of the problem so we're not going to talk to them. You have to talk to them. You have to confront them. Who else is going to prosecute these cases? It's not like you're saying you guys should do more of this because we ask. Governments do things because it's in their interest. You have to make it in their interest. Even the meetings … you make it in their interest to meet with you. They are not doing it because they want to be nice. What you need is a high-level commitment. You have greater public awareness, but does that translate to prosecutions or convictions? I think we've had some success in every place we've focused our efforts. Russia, Philippines, Mexico … those are the three best examples. In all three countries we've gotten high-level engagement. In Mexico the level of the president and in the Philippines we've had high-level engagement.[53]

Nicaraguan journalist Carlos Fernando Chamorro is also in favor of pressure on local governments from international and regional organizations to address the issue of impunity. President of the board of CINCO—a nonprofit journalism organization in Latin America—Chamorro's journalist father was assassinated, and Chamorro has been harassed by the government. He said the international community should continue putting pressure on the states regarding the issue of impunity:

> What is closest to my own reality, what I've seen in Mexico and Honduras is something dramatic in terms of the increase in numbers and

aggressions and assassinations of journalists. Most of these cases occur with impunity. So I think it is an issue that should gain higher attention internationally.

One important thing is to establish some kind of precedent on impunity. Those journalists who are already killed or attacked should not be forgotten. There should be international pressure and local pressure on governments to play particular importance to the issue of impunity. There should also be journalistic organizations—which must be much more responsible in establishing conditions for the protection of journalists when they go into situations of risk and crisis and conflict. But the most important pressure I think should be put on the state, on the governments.[54]

Brazilian journalist, Daniela Arbex, explained that the best way to address the issue of impunity would be to create a network of protection supported by the international journalism community. She said journalists would be best protected:

> ... By putting an end to impunity and creating an international effort so that crimes against journalists are investigated and the perpetrators are held accountable. The discussion of a specific law for this type of crime could also be analyzed. The continuing qualification of journalists and the creation of a worldwide network of protection, led by journalists and supported by international agencies would be another option.[55]

One international body that has forged efforts to address the issue of impunity for criminal acts against journalists is UNESCO. Deputy Assistant Director-General for Communication and Information Mogens Schmidt described what his organization was doing to protect journalists:

> At UNESCO what we have done, is that our Director-General is issuing a condemnation every time a journalist is being killed in the line of duty or in any way related to her work. What we do is that we are now following up on these condemnations by writing to the different countries where journalists have been killed and we are asking them to provide an overview of the legal action that has been taken in order to bring the perpetrators to the court. That is a very uphill kind of work, and sometimes countries do react, quite frankly, but some do not. We've approached all those countries where we had condemnations and let's say that 35% have reacted in a satisfactory way. That is where the attention paid to this issue by the international community is really important, because without that

attention and that bit of noise, I think that impunity will just go on and on and on. The UN has to demand accountability from the various countries where this is happening.[56]

But one Palestinian photojournalist (anonymous) contended that in his opinion, issuing statements may not be strong enough pressure to protect journalists in harm's way. He said:

Most of the specialized institutions designed for protection of journalists are unable to protect them. They just issue statements. This is not what journalists need. What we need is a law to protect journalists. The most important strategy can be a strong union to protect journalists. This comes only when applied with international law for the protection of journalists during the war.[57]

Another journalist, Charles Odongtho from the Uganda Radio Network, said he appreciates the work of the United Nations and their undeniable ability to provide protocols and pressure on nation members. Odongtho also recognized the part international journalism advocacy groups can play to secure protection for local journalists:

... probably journalists at the international level should put pressure on the international community through the UN systems so there are protocols designed to protect journalists throughout the world at all levels of society. We know that there are protocols against the use of certain kinds of ammunitions or arms, warring factions usually respect them. So if they can respect the rules of war why can't they respect minimum protocols to protect journalists? I think that international organizations, embassies, donor agencies should put pressure on governments like ours (Uganda) to stop looking at journalists as enemies and as people who are spying on their excesses. It's our job to expose the excess and to make sure that there is a human rights observance in the country and to bring people to account. And international journalist associations can play a part through advocacy and publicizing some of these things and making comparisons and also by documenting some of the excesses in the whole world.[58]

Odongtho mentioned pressure from donor agencies should be put on governments, thus referring to the strategy of putting economic pressure on nations to recognize the importance of free expression. He was not the only interview subject to mention tying freedom of the press and protection of journalists to issues of aid from donor nations. The Director of the

International News Safety Institute, Rodney Pinder, also recommended economic pressure as a possible strategy of protection. He remarked:

> One thing is that international aid should not be given to countries where journalists have been murdered with impunity: Democracies should not support with their taxpayers' money countries where there is no freedom of expression. There has been no take up of that ... firmer action by the international community to bring pressure is quite obvious.[59]

Pinder's call for firmer fiscal action was echoed by Chairman of the Baku-based Institute for Reporters' Freedom and Safety, Emin Huseynov. Huseynov reported that the media operations in Azerbaijan are in dire need of financial support from outside funding agencies. He added that this support would strengthen the media environment in his nation. He said:

> Without long-term financial support from international donors this struggle is mission impossible. There is an undeniable need for institutional long-term support from international donors. This will enable local media NGOs to watchdog media rights, influence the law, change legislation, in other words to conduct activities aiming at protection of journalists. The funds from global organizations would help create new media outlets that should be totally independent from the government.[60]

Professor of International Journalism at City University in London, John Owen, has been a leader in international journalism for more than 30 years as a senior supervisor at the Canadian Broadcasting Corporation and founding director of the European Center for the Freedom Forum in London. Owen was also the founding executive producer of News Xchange and founding chairman of the Frontline Club in London. Owen repeated the sentiments that international funding organizations should be the ones exerting the pressure on countries to step up their protection of journalists:

> I also feel that we need to press international funding groups such as the IMF to demand that countries who seek financial assistance must demonstrate that they not only support a free and independent press but they will prosecute the killers of journalists. If they refuse to or have not done so, they ought to be denied IMF funding. That may seem simplistic but how else to pressure what the Paris-based journalists' rights group calls the "Predator" countries that have terrible records regarding press freedom and fail to pursue killers of journalists.[61]

Caroline Vuillemin, Chief Operations Officer for Fondation Hirondelle, also recognized the strategy of putting money where journalists' protection should be by designating free expression as a cornerstone to development. She said:

> There should be a real political will internationally and I think there should be very strong commitment from some of the donors and international institutions that do contribute to reconstruction or development of many countries to say that investing in media, investing in the right of people to be informed as a right, as a sector of activity is an integrated part of the strategy. You can't just finance roads or finance schools or hospitals and not give the people the right to be informed. So I would integrate media as a sector as one of the terms of reconstruction and building society.[62]

These journalists and advocacy leaders recognized that through financial pressures, countries may be inclined to address the issue of impunity for criminals that target journalists and use donor funds to build the institution of journalism throughout the world. Many of these organizations have also begun a strategy of working in collaboration in the form of partnerships, to advocate for the protection of journalists in conflict. One of the leaders in this partnership effort has been the International Media Support organization. Jesper Højberg, Executive Director and cofounder of IMS, said that his organization has devised various strategies centered on these unique partnerships:

> IMS has devised strategies around partnerships. With the Mexico approach—we had 11 organizations going in at the same time. IMS is facilitating a lot of these partnerships, [to build a] comprehensive approach to protection and advocacy, media and development. This is one area where media organizations have really suffered. Hardcore and competitive—not good at getting together to say we have a collective problem here.[63]

Tala Dowlatshahi, Senior Advisor and Spokesperson for Reporters Without Borders, represents one of the organizations working as a partner in this collaboration. She said she thinks what is being done with the international partnership group is very important:

> ... because journalist advocacy groups and various aid organizations tend to work in a vertical fashion and develop their own operations when they get into a country. So, in Haiti or other parts of the world, you see

organizations with their own mandates ... so the groups don't collaborate and work in a multi-dimensional fashion. So what this partnership is doing is suggesting that all groups use their resources and efforts to minimize duplication and to work with what they have ... to determine who's doing what and communicate among all the groups. Knowledge is power and organizations often want to get money from donors which tends to create competition ... but this partnership is something that is eliminating the competition and saying, "look we've got to work on principle ... journalists are dying and we need to work together and maximize our resources and work more efficiently and effectively to tackle and combat these problems in these conflict zones."[64]

Executive Director of the Committee to Protect Journalists, Joel Simon, also represents an organization involved in the partnership operations. He said that cooperation of advocacy groups is essential. He added:

I am not skeptical about it [the collaboration effort]. I think that there is a proper level of collaboration and I don't think we've achieved it yet. On the other hand, I believe movements especially in a network era are more effective when they are networked, when they are not hierarchical and they are not dependent on regional consensus on every point. Generally it is positive that there are many groups operating at different perspectives reaching the same conclusions about many of these issues. So I want to preserve that autonomy, preserve that independence .... There probably could be fewer groups with more collaboration, but I don't think it's an enormous problem; it's a manageable one. The problem is if you collaborate your position of consensus is the lowest common denominator. It's a recipe for inaction. You are all negotiating and the point at which you agree on is a less strong position because of one person ... I think coordination is essential and collaboration is optional. Decisions to collaborate should be strategic and they should be strategic around the issues, not around any interest of an organization.[65]

One of the most distinctive advocacy strategies to address protection of journalists came from Umar Cheema, an investigative reporter for a major Pakistani newspaper, *The News*. As described in Chapter Four, Cheema was kidnapped, beaten, and humiliated in 2010 by members of Pakistan's secretive intelligence agencies.[66] The *New York Times* reported that Umar Cheema had previously written articles that had questioned the conduct and performance of the army and the intelligence services and detailed accusations of corruption against President

Asif Ali Zardari.[67] Cheema had bravely spoken out about this ordeal despite being told by his captures not to tell anyone about this attack. He described in graphic detail what happened during his captivity and why he believes he was targeted. Responding in this way to the violence perpetrated against him is something rare in a country where victims who suspect that their brutal treatment was at the hands of government officials often choose, out of fear, not to speak up.

Cheema responded by e-mail to an interview request by the authors, that he was considering starting a unique advocacy group to pressure those responsible for these kinds of journalists attacks. "I sometimes think about the option of forming an International Alliance of the Victim Journalists. The presence of such a forum will send a strong message to the hostile parties," he remarked.[68]

Mitigate

In addition to advocating for the cause of journalists' protection, interview subjects offered various strategies that fell into the category of pragmatic efforts that could be used to mitigate the problem of dangerous situations faced by journalists today. These strategies took the form of hostile environment training as well as other practical suggestions. Special efforts that journalists could do to prepare for potentially dangerous assignments were also discussed. including trauma and psychological training.

International Security Consultant and Chief Hostile Environment Trainer for Dynamiq in Australia, Shaun Filer, said journalists need to think twice about arming themselves. He believed that it was important for journalists to recognize that training for hostile environments does not mean arming:

> I think Hollywood has done this all a big disservice where we think one person with a gun is going to increase our personal safety ... we'll just duck behind a car door or all these other things ... It's really an issue where you have to break down those impressions. All of my American friends who participate in this training say things like ... "we put locks on the doors and we have a guard out front and a shotgun under my bed. It's a very quick progression to actually arming yourself. I think this compromises you. It then raises questions in the minds of the militia that you may face at a random vehicle check point in these environments or the local officials .... as to who are you and why does a journalist ...

why do these people need arms. Perhaps there is something off about their story and it increases your profile and it raises more suspicion. There are instances of other security firms rolling down the window in an armored or unarmored vehicle and shooting weapons out the window towards a suburb or into an apartment building. And that only needs to happen once before all journalists become targets . . . because the expectation is that they are going to shoot.[69]

Another hostile environment trainer, Robert Klamser, cofounder and Executive Director of Crisis Consulting International, said journalists need more than just training; they need updated information intelligence about the environment:

Training is really important and it gives you a set a skills in different situations. But you've got to be able to assess the situation. But fundamental to good training is having good information and really knowing the risk, understanding the decision you are making, being informed . . . Don't get into trouble by default or ignorance . . . that just happens too much.[70]

As mentioned earlier, most large media operations provide this kind of systematic training for their employees who engage in assignments in conflict areas. But many of the people interviewed were seriously concerned about whether all of the journalists who work in conflict zones have access to this kind of training. Ross Howard, who conducts journalism training in Africa, discussed why technology seems to be bypassing issues of safety in the field of journalism and how his African students train themselves:

The necessity for hostile environment training for all international journalists who are sent abroad . . . it's still not there. . . . I think there has been a technologically enhanced capacity to get to the firefight or to the front of the conflict quickly but it hasn't been followed up with respect for journalists' safety and for their lives. . . . Hostile environment training surely it doesn't even exist for most journalists in conflict-stressed countries which are repressive to begin with. Most of the journalists whom I have ever worked with have absolutely nothing but street smarts and of course, they have very little protection by their employer or by law. I once trained a group of journalists from Somalia . . . we had to do it in Djibouti because you couldn't go into Somalia at that time. Several of them were exceptional journalists. Some were veterans for more than ten years in that country working as journalists. They had a good understanding, at least according to my expectations, of their role and their obligations and their responsibilities. They knew what they were trying to do it in the most horrendous and life threatening environments. I had nothing but enormous respect for them. But no sense of protection other than what they themselves had adopted as a kind of survival technique. They had no concept of the rule of law protecting them.[71]

The Rory Peck Trust has taken seriously the charge of financially assisting freelance journalists with safety training. Tina Carr, Director of the Rory Peck Trust, works to raise funds for these journalists who might not otherwise have access to safety training. She explained:

I set up a fund in 2000, it was like Robin Hood, to rob from the rich and give to the poor. I robbed, if you want, from all the news gathering organizations and got them to put money into this fund so that I could hand out money to freelancers, so we give them bursaries so that they can do safety training. We work with partners literally all around the world. And we were involved in setting up the first ever safety training courses for journalists in Mexico ... the first safety training course there was a joint project undertaken by ARTICLE 19 and The Rory Peck Trust with funds from the Dutch and British Embassies and the Open Society Institute.[72]

Safety training does cost money. But Heather Forbes, Manager of Staff Development for ABC News (Australia), agreed with Tina Carr, that the news organizations in the West should pay for this safety training:

I think media organization in the first world ... so we are talking European countries, the United States, Canada and Australia—we've got the money. If we have the money to send somebody to a war zone we have the money to train them properly. And I think we have to be responsible for our own people. I know that the bean counters in every news organization start jumping up and down saying it costs too much money. But news gathering is an expensive business. There is no way around it, it costs money, so you either do it or you don't.[73]

In addition to the necessity of hostile environment or physical training, many of the people interviewed also recommended the idea of psychological training—to pragmatically prepare the journalists for these dangerous assignments and to ensure they are taken care of after.

Daniela Arbex, special reporter at the *Tribuna de Minas*, suggested that in order to report from a conflict zone there should be:

> ... preparation of the reporter, increased support in areas of conflict and systematic follow-up after the end of the work, as many journalists subjected to permanent situations of tension develop trauma that compromise their professional future and family relations.[74]

Dr. Feinstein, who has worked closely with journalists returning from conflict zone assignments, said he thinks journalists need to understand the psychological risks of doing very dangerous work:

> Because I think that education is very important here. So that should a journalist develop symptoms of emotional distress in response to the danger that they confront they are able to recognize what is going on and have an appreciation of what needs to be done. And certainly news organizations need to know how to deal with this.

What freelance journalist Holly Picket recommended was the practical tactic of basic communication. She suggested a forum where journalists keep each other informed, despite issues of competition, about what's happening on the ground:

> I think it's also important for journalists when they are going to conflict areas ... to talk to other journalists and look out for each other as well and if there are areas that are more dangerous or if people have had problems, I think it would be helpful to have some kind of forum where journalists could talk to each other about problems they are having or if they received threats as well as keeping in touch with their editors and people that they're working for and keeping them very aware of problems they are having. I think all of that is really important ... maintaining a collegial atmosphere where people can look out for each other because these areas are dangerous and we are all competing with each other but at the same time if it comes down to somebody getting injured or hurt or targeted we just need to be there for each other.[75]

A journalist from northern Uganda, a 27-year-old radio station manager, Evelyn Abbo, spoke of the basic strategy of sticking to the fundamentals of good journalism while adhering to tenants of conflict-sensitive reporting. She said:

The journalist should exercise the highest level of professionalism in conflict sensitive reporting but it is also important for the parties involved in the conflict to begin to appreciate, and not interfere with the work of the journalist.[76]

Yet again, it is not only the international journalist who needs protection strategies when reporting from conflict or corrupt areas. Omid Memarian, an Iranian journalist, offered a practical suggestion to secure safety for journalists in his country. His fellow journalists are dealing with incidents where major online companies have lax security operations, so government officials have access to the names and identities of journalists who are using the Internet to disseminate stories of corruption. Memarian suggested:

Major companies like Yahoo!, Google, Facebook, Twitter, Skype and so on, should be sensitive about securing the communication means they provide. They should empower their human rights divisions, in case they have such divisions like Yahoo!, and if not they should develop such a division and try to secure their networks. Some of the journalists have been arrested by being tracked via their e-mail boxes. It's a shared responsibility.[77]

Educate

Many of the respondents introduced the importance of attending to a difficult yet perhaps highly effective long-term strategy that would involve comprehensive media education. In this context, education was mentioned as a prospect to enlighten everyone about the value of journalism in a democratic society. Education was also referred to in the most specific context of journalism training and education.

One journalist, who asked not to be named for security reasons, described a journalism education program that would be directed to all the world's citizens:

I think the most important thing is to have a very aggressive campaign of awareness that explains the job of the journalist so that everyone is aware as to what our job is and what our limitations are ... People should know that everyone on the ground, for example, does not make decisions as to what should go out.... You've got editorial producers; you've got an editorial board and so on ... The job of the journalists needs to be better understood by everyone ... so I think an aggressive campaign for everyone . . . a warlord, or militia or a government official . . . all the organizations that we deal with . . . they need to know what the actual job of the journalist is . . . it is not to report from any person's side—it's just impartial reporting. So the strategy would be an aggressive campaign to better understand the role of journalists and reporters in covering situations. But how does one do that? That's a debatable issue.[78]

Freelance journalist and trainer, Binod Bhattarai, from Nepal agreed that a greater understanding of the "role" of journalism might be an effective strategy. He said this kind of education might be needed:

> . . . because different societies still do not seem to be in a common understanding of the role of journalism and journalists—for example, some states still believe that journalism is something it uses for buttressing its position and communications (or propaganda), while in others it could be influenced by their own cultural norms. That said it might be an opportunity to work towards creating common minimum values on the role of journalists and journalism.[79]

A journalism educator in Uganda, John K. Matovu, suggested that teaching the value of journalism to society should begin with the military. Matovu also suggested that journalists could be instrumental in mitigating conflict through their role in society:

> There is a need to educate the armies as part of their training about the nature of work and roles of the media so they don't look at journalists as enemies. Ugandan society generally requires civic education in primary school and secondary school so that people grow up with knowledge about their rights, responsibilities and obligations. This kind of education should be reminded to the military as well. But also journalists can play a major role in resolving the conflict itself because they have this unique opportunity to engage the different parties to a conflict. They can be a very useful avenue to identify strategies that would lead to peaceful resolution of such conflicts.[80]

Michelle Betz, of Betz International Media Consulting, has been participating in journalism education projects in Africa for more than fifteen years. She has found that journalism training and media education across various constituencies has been successful in her experience:

> I think ultimately we need to try to take a holistic approach and I think we need to target and educate all the stakeholders involved in a conflict

situation and a couple of examples come to mind. One is we need to educate journalists who are working in conflict zones. Whether it's some kind
of hostile regions training and education that involves just what the conflict is about and understanding of the history of the conflict as well as
the context. I think it also may be useful to try to educate those who may
be targeting journalists. I was involved in this kind of training this year
in southern Sudan where we got together some journalists and security
forces and essentially put them together hoping they would learn more
about the roles and responsibilities of one another and thereby mitigate
the possibility that the journalists would be a target at the hands of the
security forces. It was quite successful. So successful in fact that these dia-
logues between these two parties are continuing today in southern Sudan
and have even gone on to include the police.[81]

Charles Odongtho, a radio journalist in Uganda, explained a similar
experience whereby the journalists got together with governmental officials to explain how journalism should work with the leaders to ensure
democracy:

As a journalist, I know that there also are cases where journalists have
been detained by police during riots in our country. Then we [journalists]
met with the police. We got the attention of leaders in the country and the
attention of the police commanders to tell them that as journalists we are
not supposed to be enemies but rather we are supposed to be viewed as
partners in promoting democracy.[82]

Another African journalist, Martin Wanjala Ocholi, a media and communication consultant from Nairobi, described a similar program in
Kenya sponsored by an international advocacy organization whereby
journalists are to be valued as much as medical and rescue workers:

One of the organizations was started by the IFJ . . . The International News
Safety Institute has designed programs for the protection of journalists.
The idea was to provide education for journalists and conduct seminars
training journalists how to behave in conflict situations. Of course, there
have been attempts to have governments trained and especially to teach
military personnel to recognize and respect journalists . . . The idea is to
demonstrate that journalists have a legitimate reason to be there when
conflict is taking place. Often belligerents and combatants don't really
see what the journalists are doing there. So training has targeted the
belligerents to accept that journalists are just like medical and rescue

workers . . . they have an important role and a legitimate reason to be present in conflict zones.[83]

Award-winning journalist, educator, and president of Media&Democracy Group, Ross Howard, recommended that journalism training across the world should include some kind of course work on conflict theories. He said:

> It's absolutely fascinating that for a business that dwells on and depends on conflict how little journalists know about conflict as a social process. There are almost no journalism schools where it is mandatory for students to take at least one half-term course in conflict analysis . . . basic kind of conflict theory. And it ought to be mandatory because it doesn't only apply to war zone reporting; it applies to covering a neighborhood gun fight between two gangs in south Vancouver. It's been a real short coming in the profession of journalism and journalism education that we haven't embraced this more significantly. Conflict analysis enables reporters to get beyond symptoms and body counts and to include root causes and potential solutions as part of accurate, fair-balanced and responsible reporting.[84]

The Director of the International News Safety Institute, Rodney Pinder, also mentioned the need to address safety training in journalism schools around the world:

> And we [INSI] are also working on a plan to get safety training more deeply embedded in journalism schools, to get safety more implemented in the curriculum of all major journalism schools, which introduces students to the issues and helps them prepare for the world they are going to encounter when they get out there.[85]

International Security Consultant and Chief Hostile Environment Trainer, Dynamiq, Shaun Filer, said he was disappointed that training for hostile environments is not addressed in journalism programs:

> I think it's very unfortunate in training or at universities there is not a real focus on what the job actually entails. You spend 20 or 40 thousand dollars per semester and you come out and you're a journalist and you get a job and you're traveling the world if you want to and you are going to all these wonderful places and that's it. There needs to be some reality put into the preparation and understanding for the younger journalists before they make their way out into these environments.[86]

A unique educational initiative was described by Senior Vice President of Exhibits, Programs & Media Relations at the Newseum in Washington, DC, Susan Bennett. She explained the educational program at the Newseum whereby people from around the world are informed about the dangers faced by journalists through a comprehensive exhibit. She said:

> We were looking for the most effective way of acquainting the largest number of people with the importance of a free press in a free society. We knew that we could do this by explaining how and why journalists do their jobs and how, in some cases, reporters risk their lives to do their jobs. We came to the conclusion that the way to reach the most people was through one dramatic program and that program is the Newseum. We now have more than 700,000 people come here each year—many of them from overseas. At the Newseum, they hear the stories of the journalists. They see the *Time* truck, which is pockmarked with bullets and shrapnel when journalists were covering the Balkan Conflict. They see the laptop computer and passport of Daniel Pearl who was beheaded by extremists in Pakistan. They see the Journalists Memorial, which has more than 2,000 names of journalists from around the world killed while on assignment. So, we think the contribution we can make is to raise awareness and hopefully that has a ripple effect when our visitors go back to their homes—be it in Chicago or Paris or Baghdad—and they tell other people about the importance of a free press.[87]

Controversial Strategies

Obviously, not all of the respondents agreed that all current or proposed strategies used to protect journalists around the world were useful or effective. In fact, some of those interviewed were vehemently opposed to various ways journalists' protection has been attended to in the past or how current efforts have been conducted. Below are some of the primary areas where the journalists interviewed never reach consensus.

Strength of law

One of the areas where interview subjects did not agree was whether the law in its current form was sufficient enough to be an effective strategy to protect journalists. Executive Director of the Committee to Protect Journalists, Joel Simon, said he was not convinced that reforming law would be an effective strategy:

I'm not a big proponent, which I'm sure you know, of reforming international humanitarian law to address this issue. I think it is absolutely the wrong political environment to do that. I think the legal issues were sorted out once before in an environment in which the outcome was probably the best that we could have hoped for at that moment. When I look at why journalists are killed, I don't think that the reason is because of the lack of familiarity with international humanitarian law. That's just not the main reason. IHL is not even relevant in most of these cases, because most journalists are killed by criminal or militant organizations in their own country, that's the leading cause of death. Of course in theory ... there might be ways to strengthen it ... but I don't think there is a great opportunity to push for meaningful reform in this at this moment and I am not sure that any of the proposed reforms would make any significant difference in terms of the actual causes of journalists being murdered.[88]

John Matovu, journalism educator from Uganda, said he thought there were already laws in effect to protect journalists but questioned whether there was enough awareness of those laws. He described an incident where knowledge of the law was an issue:

The most important drive now should be creating awareness about these existing laws and rights because in many cases journalists themselves and other stakeholders aren't aware about them. Implementation therefore becomes a problem. In Uganda, journalists are prohibited by law from photographing military installations but I was confronted by a guard at a bank when I was shooting footage for a documentary. He even wanted to confiscate my camera and it took me over four hours to clarify this to him and the bank officials. To me this is lack of awareness.[89]

Blaise Lempen, United Nations Correspondent in Geneva for the Swiss News Agency (ATS), Secretary-General of the Press Emblem Campaign (PEC), and author of "Massacres sans témoins" (Xenia, 2007) said he believes current IHL protection for journalists is not strong enough:

They are protected by the Geneva Conventions as civilians. But this protection appears to be insufficient because they face more dangers than other civilians if they want to be testimony of the violations of IHL and HR [human rights] in conflict zones. There must be better mechanisms of enquiry and prosecutions of the criminals. The rules must be clarified in order to facilitate the access of media to conflict zones. There is a need for a specific Convention or a draft protocol on the protection of

journalists in conflict zones to clarify and enhance the rules. All these mat-
ters must be discussed with all concerned parties.[90]

But Deputy Assistant Director-General for Communication and Information at UNESCO, Mogens Schmidt said the problem is not that
international humanitarian law is not good enough. He said the problem
is that it is not applied. He added:

> It's honestly not a matter of changing the law. I think it's really a matter of
> making it clear to member states that they should apply the already well-
> established international humanitarian law, but it is not always
> respected.[91]

Press Emblem Campaign

One of the most controversial strategies discussed by the respondents
was the Press Emblem Campaign, begun in Geneva in 2004. President
of the PEC, Hedayat Abdel Nabi, said she thought the journalism community had a golden opportunity several years ago to strengthen the
protection of journalists who report from conflict:

> The PEC since its beginning, which is about seven years ago, has called
> upon the community of actors in the journalistic business to unite behind
> us in getting something like a legal instrument . . . a convention to protect
> journalists in conflict zones. I said it in the Human Rights Council when
> we were discussing this issue, we now have a golden opportunity for states
> and journalists to agree on guidelines or legal instruments because we
> both are facing terrorism from non-state actors. So states if they give us
> a hand, they will be protecting the media work and protecting themselves
> at the same moment. How far will this go? I don't know and I think this is
> a very difficult process. I think the golden opportunity came to the com-
> munity of journalists and journalism in 2004 when the PEC launched that
> idea in a meeting in Geneva. It was September 2004. We hoped at the time
> that the whole community would rally around with us, there were differ-
> ences and a sort of division between those who supported the idea and
> those who opposed the idea. And now with the second golden opportu-
> nity, if we miss it . . . I don't know where we'll go.[92]

But not everyone agreed that the PEC would result in an effective
strategy. Ronald Koven, European Representative for the World Press
Freedom Committee, suggested that this campaign would be contrary

to the autonomy journalists experience around the world. He was opposed to this idea because he said it is connected with the notion of licensing journalists. He added:

> Schemes to create a uniform, universal international emblem are nothing but the thin edge of the wedge for reviving efforts to introduce international licensing of journalists. Such schemes reintroduce the vexed debate over determining "who is a journalist" that was central to the controversy over a New World Information and Communication Order that nearly sank UNESCO.[93]

But the founder of Ethiopia's *Awramba Times* newspaper, Dawit Kebede, who spent two years in a crowded prison for his independent reporting on Ethiopia's 2005 election violence, said he thinks the PEC would be an effective rhetorical strategy. "Yes, that would give the individual journalist a feeling that there is a world-wide brotherhood of journalists, and a measure of pride and protections. That is a good idea," Kebede said.[94]

Embed Program

A strategy of protection for journalists devised by the U.S. military for the Afghanistan and 2003 Iraq war was the embed program. This program met with mixed reviews among the journalists interviewed. Phillip Knightley, author of *The First Casualty*, said the embed program was not ideal:

> The military has come up with what they consider to be the solution— embedding. If you agree to be embedded with an army unit, at least you have some protection from being fired upon, or shot at, or killed. It's probably not good for journalism, but it does offer a little, slightly more protection than normal.[95]

One journalist interviewed who had been an embedded journalist, Holly Picket, said that being an embedded reporter makes it harder to work independently, but the program does have significant advantages. She said:

> I think you see this a lot in certain areas of Afghanistan where journalists can't move about freely at all or at least foreign journalists can't and even local journalists in some cases because it's so dangerous that they have to

embed with the military. It's great that that option is there . . . I'm thankful for it but at the same time it provides a very different picture of what you would see otherwise. Because the military is a target itself so it just shows a different side that you wouldn't necessarily see if you went in and talked to people and photographed people as they were.[96]

New York Times journalist, David Rohde, is not convinced that the military has as much control as many people perceive them to have over the embedded journalist. He remarked:

I think many embeds have led to many embarrassing stories for the U.S. military and it's not as controlled as critics contend. Journalists are aggressively reporting what they see on embeds. And it's not as sanitized as people suspect. [97]

Photojournalist for Time, Robert Nickelsberg, said he believed the embedded journalist was much safer than any independent or unilateral journalist during the early days of the conflict in Iraq. He added:

It depends on what you think you can do. And the independents in Iraq for instance, going in not having any language facility, no gasoline, no food . . . the only vehicles on the road then were Iraqis trying to flee and journalists coming in the other direction were certainly under threat. How are you going to get to Baghdad? Well some did and some came along with the military and certainly you are only going to get part of the story by being with the military but that is certainly 50 percent of the story. If you were an independent I don't think you were going to get close to 50 percent unless you spoke Arabic. And it's nice to go out there and be sort of an impressionist but I felt we needed to be with the military and I would do the best I could to photograph as much as possible given the restrictions we had to work under. That was not revealing current or future operations; not revealing our position; or casualties . . . waiting 24 hours, 36 hours if someone was wounded or was killed so their families could be notified. These were not difficult rules. But I noticed the 10 or 15 journalists who were with us on the way to Baghdad in 2003, they sat there and waited just to get anything at all. And they had to trade for food and they had to trade for power. I really didn't want to do that. I've done it so many times and the military then had opened up its doors . . . particularly the Marines. And that is true to this day. The Marines are very forthcoming and straight ahead with the journalists and as long as you are accurate you can say whatever is out there but you must be accurate. If they did something wrong and you can back it up, [they would let you] go with it. [98]

ABC news reporter, Robert Woodruff, said there have always been arguments as to whether it's a good or bad thing to report as an embedded journalist. He discussed the idea of physical proximity to the action, for journalists both at home and abroad:

Certainly when you are embedded you are closer and you get closer to a particular story . . . in the sense that you get closer personally to the people you are covering. I am not sure it's that different than when you are a reporter embedded in the White House and you are covering the White House which is what reporters do there. People are embedded in the justice department when they are working out of the justice department. Perhaps the one difference is that once you are embedding and it's in a war you can't get far away from it physically. You can't go off to get another side and you can't wander over the line and interview an insurgent that just attacked or that we attacked to try to get their side of the story. It is true that you're generally getting that side of the story except when the stories create a side that exists within the company or the platoon or whatever you might be with . . . may be different. Some different opinions exist within a group like that. Literally, within Afghanistan, less so now in Iraq . . . but there are not many places you can go and report unless you are going in with the protection of the military. Even with private protection, it is not nearly as effective as it is being with the U.S. or British Army that is there. Without them to protect you it is very hard to go into those places. It is kind of a Catch-22 in a sense. The perfect thing would be to not be buried in a military team but if you don't do that you probably can't see much of the countryside of these nations to cover them.[99]

Anne Nivat, an independent French war correspondent and author of books about Iraq, Afghanistan, and Chechnya, disagreed. She remarked that despite being well-organized for the journalist, the embed program is not always safe and may not be an effective strategy to help tell the story of conflicts. She added:

Everybody thinks it is easier to go with them [the military] and everything will be organized for you. I disagree with the fact that it is safer to be with them. Absolutely not . . . because we have plenty of examples of journalists who died because they were with the army. So the danger of dying while covering a war is the same being embedded or not being embedded—a war is a war and of course the main danger is to lose your life—that is something we should not forget. It is not a video game to cover a war. This tendency of treating this new war and the way we cover them more and more like video games is very shocking to me because we completely lost the contact with the reality. And reality of war is the most striking element that you have to convey back to your readers or listeners.[100]

Why is this Journalistic Endeavor so Important?

At least one of the journalists interviewed thought this area of questioning was a bit obvious and responded, "The answer can be found in Journalism 101, take the class." But once the journalists reflected on this question, the responses were rich and profound and offer a glimpse at the passion for this field that transcends the identity, geography, or gender of the respondents.

When Chief Operations Officer of Fondation Hirondelle, Caroline Vuillemin, was asked why journalists should bother with such difficult stories like the dangerous stories of conflict she responded:

That's a commentary from people in the north who don't have many problems. If you are a citizen from an area where there is a conflict . . . if you are a citizen suffering everyday from corruption you want to be heard, you want your story to be told and you want to try to understand what's going on. It is first of all for the victims or for people affected by these situations that the journalists should work. It's not only to inform the north or people sitting in their dining rooms in Washington or Paris. It's really for the people who are concerned for the problem.[101]

Journalist for Uganda Radio Network, Charles Odongtho, spoke of his personal passion to work as a journalist in his country:

Journalism is a job I love. It's a profession I admire so much. The coverage of these elections should be my last because I covered the last two elections in Uganda which have all been very violent where I was hit by tear gas, by rubber bullets and ran together with rioters and fell and was bruised and lost my phone and recorder. This is another one that is probably going to be very violent again because the signs are all there . . . I was telling friends on Facebook that this should be my last election that I cover as a journalist. But you know you finish that and then you look up at the next year and then two years and three years come and five years again and you find yourself covering it. Journalism is a job of passion for me and I think that unless I am not able I will continue doing it to bring out the opposition voices and the people who are suffering.[102]

Nicaraguan Carlos Fernando Chamorro, TV Director of "Esta Semana" and "Esta Noche" and Director of the weekly newsletter, *Confidencial* (print and online) told the story of how he began his career in journalism:

> I went into journalism in 1978 after my father's assassination. I never thought about being a journalist; I wanted to be an economist. And then I worked at *La Prensa*. My first motivation was more political and then after the victory of the revolution in Nicaragua, I was part of it ... Journalism and journalists are important because society requires transparency; society requires accountability and public debate and pluralism. And we are instrumental [in promoting] to those necessities in society. We are not unique—we are not the only ones doing that. I think we are necessary, but not sufficient. You need the press, but you need much more. If you don't have the press, you know, we are dead. If we don't have the press we are less protected. I think there is some kind of inseparable matrimony or marriage between journalists and democracy. We have different roles, we have contradictions, we have permanent conflict, but without free press you cannot have strong democracy.[103]

Special reporter at the *Tribuna de Minas* newspaper in Brazil, Daniela Arbex, also has a personal story as to why this kind of journalism is important to her:

> This year, I was threatened with death by the owner of a clinic provider of medical services ... Rather than allow her to intimidate me, I registered a formal complaint at the police station against her. She was sued and she had to pay a fine. . . . What we cannot do is to let ourselves be intimidated. When I look back, I think it was worth it. And though I feel gratified by the changes I was able to provoke, I have a permanent concern. Every day, I wonder what I can do to improve people's lives. Every time I achieve a positive result, I remind myself: that's why I'm a journalist.[104]

Executive Director and cofounder of International Media Support, Jesper Højberg, said that we all know that information is important during conflict. He added:

> Providing information to the public is one of the first things that suffers because it will often be controlled by warring factions. So you have to get in there and provide alternative information. It has been proven in

so many countries—Zimbabwe, Darfur, Pakistan, Iraq, Afghanistan—that society and democracy will suffer [without journalists], if there is a democracy. If there is no democracy, society and the public will suffer. And then corruption, of course . . . with conflicts you have corruption. This is when things become really dangerous—both in conflicts and humanitarian disasters. Corruption is a huge problem in a lot of countries [and journalists help expose this]. It is important to support journalists for being authentic journalists, not for being public relation officers or part of humanitarian organizations, or the military.[105]

Anne Nivat, an independent French war correspondent and author offered some profound insights into the work she does:

I do agree it is a huge responsibility and sometimes I even ask myself if I am capable of the challenge. I am going to Afghanistan five days from now and to be there on the ground—I know what I will decide to write about will by strict definition mean that I will not write about something else. I mean, this very choice of the very source of the information is very difficult. It is very complex. And sometimes it is illogical. And maybe because of all that it will become more and more difficult and fewer journalists will be ready to confront this challenge. But if we do give up—we the so-called war journalists—then that is the end. We won't have information any more. We will live in total fiction. And then the population, the people who vote—they will be surprised to have September 11ths and to have other dramas in this world. But no wonder. If we, the people from the West, do not pay attention to what happens outside the Western bubble, no wonder then we don't understand the world we live in.[106]

Whom Do You Admire?

The journalists had little trouble recalling the people they most admire who are or have been engaged in dangerous journalism work. Among the responders was Senior Advisor and Spokesperson for Reporters without Borders, Tala Dowlatshahi who said:

My heroes right now are all of the reporters who are on the Mexico/US border. The Mexican-American reporters, be they female or male, they are the ones who, every day, have to go to Ciudad Juárez and cover these gang wars. I find that amazing and the bravery that they show . . . here they are living in Texas one day, and the next day they are driving over to a gang zone. It's not like they are in Iraq and that's all they see every day for weeks and weeks. It must be such culture shock. They have an amazing adaptability that I really, really admire and honor.[107]

New York Times reporter, David Rohde, said his first response would be Sultan Mundai, the Afghan interpreter who was killed when a *New York Times* reporter, Stephen Farrell, was freed in a military commando raid in 2009. "[Sultan] faced the greatest danger and was most heroic," he said.[108]

Emin Huseynov, chairman of the Baku-based Institute for Reporters' Freedom and Safety, was himself attacked by police while covering a protest of the opposition during presidential elections. In 2008, he was severely beaten by the police while monitoring an event of the oppositional youth, and in spite of medical treatment he never completely recovered. Huseynov, a hero to many journalists in Azerbaijan, reported that he most admired Elmar Huseynov:

> ... and his courageous reporting is what a professional and honest journalist should be. He was one of those journalists who dared to publish criticism against top officials and close associates of the President [in Azerbaijan.][109]

Professor of International Journalism at City University in London, John Owen, reported that he admired many of the local journalists he had known:

> I have an impressive young Iranian student journalist who is in my international journalism class at City University. He is in exile because of his fearless reporting inside Iran. He was the only Iranian journalist who agreed to take all the risks to get to the family of the young woman, Neda, whose bloody death during the Iranian street protests was captured on mobile phone video and seen all over the world. He recorded an interview with the family. The documentary about Neda aired on HBO and has won many awards. But my young Iranian journalist was shown in the film and is now at risk should he try and return home.[110]

Author of *Seeds of Terror*, Gretchen Peters, would like local colleagues to be honored and remembered:

> I would say that my heroes in this field in all of the countries that I have worked in have been my local colleagues who in the face of great danger

have taken it upon themselves to report what is going on in their country to the rest of the world. I worked with a group of journalists in Cambodia who became journalists at a time when it was a communist government and it was illegal to learn English and some of them learned English by hiding their notebooks in their underwear for more than a year and they were relatively fearless in what they were willing to report about their country at a time when there were elections taking place. Similarly in Afghanistan and Pakistan I have worked with reporters who have taken great risk to document a world that is virtually closed off to the rest of us at the border areas and they have done this with incredible grace and courage and persistence so I would say these people are definitely my heroes.[111]

The diversity of opinions found in the comments from these stakeholders demonstrates the complexity of this issue of journalists' protection. The stakeholders interviewed agreed that journalists face different risks in different situations but no journalist seeks to be the story. When journalists' safety is threatened, however, the story becomes significant beyond the participants and situations. Significant not just to the individual journalists, but to all who long to uphold the universal value of freedom. Thus, protection for journalists in turn provides protection for those who risk their lives for fair governance or fairness in all fights.

It may be time for the global community to recognize that not providing significant universal protection for journalists represents a global risk for those who seek democratic justice and human rights. Strategies of protection that include advocacy, mitigation and education may be effective initial tactics—but the work must continue. The time has come for a ceasefire on the war on words.

Appendices

Appendix A. Human Rights Council 13th Session Resolution *Protection of journalists in situations of armed conflict*

Resolution adopted by the Human Rights Council[*] 13/24
Protection of journalists in situations of armed conflict

The Human Rights Council,
Reaffirming the vital role played by the press in situations of armed conflict,
Alarmed at the large and increasing number of deaths and injuries among members of the press in armed conflict,

1. *Decides* to convene, within existing resources, a panel discussion at its fourteenth session on the issue of protection of journalists in armed conflict;
2. *Requests* the Office of the United Nations High Commissioner for Human Rights to liaise with the Special Rapporteur on the right to freedom of opinion and expression, the International Committee of the Red Cross and all concerned parties and stakeholders, including relevant press organizations and associations and United Nations bodies and agencies, with a view to ensuring their participation in the panel discussion;
3. *Also requests* the Office of the High Commissioner to prepare a report on the outcome of the panel discussion in the form of a summary.

44th meeting
26 March 2010
[Adopted without a vote]
Source: General Assembly Human Rights Council Resolution A/HRC/ 13/24. (c) United Nations, 2010. Reproduced with permission.

---

[*]The resolutions and decisions of the Human Rights Council will be contained in the report of the Council on its thirteenth session (A/HRC/13/56), Chap. 1.

Appendix B. United Nations Security Council Resolution 1738

Security Council
Resolution 1738 (2006)
Adopted by the Security Council at its 5613th meeting, on 23 December 2006

The Security Council,
Bearing in mind its primary responsibility under the Charter of the United Nations for the maintenance of international peace and security, and underlining the importance of taking measures aimed at conflict prevention and resolution;

Reaffirming its resolutions 1265 (1999), 1296 (2000) and 1674 (2006) on the protection of civilians in armed conflict and its resolution 1502 (2003) on protection of United Nations personnel, associated personnel and humanitarian personnel in conflict zones, as well as other relevant resolutions and presidential statements,

Reaffirming its commitment to the Purposes of the Charter of the United Nations as set out in Article 1 (1–4) of the Charter, and to the Principles of the Charter as set out in Article 2 (1–7) of the Charter, including its commitment to the principles of the political independence, sovereign equality and territorial integrity of all States, and respect for the sovereignty of all States,

Reaffirming that parties to an armed conflict bear the primary responsibility to take all feasible steps to ensure the protection of affected civilians,

Recalling the Geneva Conventions of 12 August 1949, in particular the Third Geneva Convention of 12 August 1949 on the treatment of prisoners of war, and the Additional Protocols of 8 June 1977, in particular article 79 of the Additional Protocol I regarding the protection of journalists engaged in dangerous professional missions in areas of armed conflict,

Emphasizing that there are existing prohibitions under international humanitarian law against attacks intentionally directed against civilians, as such, which in situations of armed conflict constitute war crimes, and *recalling* the need for States to end impunity for such criminal acts,

Recalling that the States Parties to the Geneva Conventions have an obligation to search for persons alleged to have committed, or to have ordered to be committed a grave breach of these Conventions, and an obligation to try them before their own courts, regardless of their nationality, or may hand them over for trial to another concerned State provided this State has made out a prima facie case against the said persons,

Drawing the attention of all States to the full range of justice and reconciliation mechanisms, including national, international and "mixed" criminal courts and tribunals and truth and reconciliation commissions, and *noting* that such mechanisms can promote not only individual responsibility for serious crimes, but also peace, truth, reconciliation and the rights of the victims,

Recognizing the importance of a comprehensive, coherent and action-oriented approach, including in early planning, of protection of civilians in situations of armed conflict.

Stressing, in this regard, the need to adopt a broad strategy of conflict prevention, which addresses the root causes of armed conflict in a comprehensive manner in order to enhance the protection of civilians on a long-term basis, including by promoting sustainable development, poverty eradication, national reconciliation, good governance, democracy, the rule of law and respect for and protection of human rights,

Deeply concerned at the frequency of acts of violence in many parts of the world against journalists, media professionals and associated personnel in armed conflict, in particular deliberate attacks in violation of international humanitarian law,

Recognizing that the consideration of the issue of protection of journalists in armed conflict by the Security Council is based on the urgency and importance of this issue, and recognizing the valuable role that the Secretary-General can play in providing more information on this issue,

1. *Condemns* intentional attacks against journalists, media professionals and associated personnel, as such, in situations of armed conflict, and calls upon all parties to put an end to such practices;

2. *Recalls* in this regard that journalists, media professionals and associated personnel engaged in dangerous professional missions in areas of armed conflict shall be considered as civilians and shall be respected and protected as such, provided that they take no action adversely affecting their status as civilians. This is without prejudice to the right of war correspondents accredited to the armed forces to the status of prisoners of war provided for in article 4.A.4 of the Third Geneva Convention;

3. *Recalls also* that media equipment and installations constitute civilian objects, and in this respect shall not be the object of attack or of reprisals, unless they are military objectives;

4. *Reaffirms* its condemnation of all incitements to violence against civilians in situations of armed conflict, further reaffirms the need to bring to justice, in accordance with applicable international law, individuals who incite such violence, and indicates its willingness, when authorizing

missions, to consider, where appropriate, steps in response to media broadcast inciting genocide, crimes against humanity and serious violations of international humanitarian law;

5. *Recalls its demand* that all parties to an armed conflict comply fully with the obligations applicable to them under international law related to the protection of civilians in armed conflict, including journalists, media professionals and associated personnel;

6. *Urges* States and all other parties to an armed conflict to do their utmost to prevent violations of international humanitarian law against civilians, including journalists, media professionals and associated personnel;

7. *Emphasizes* the responsibility of States to comply with the relevant obligations under international law to end impunity and to prosecute those responsible for serious violations of international humanitarian law;

8. *Urges* all parties involved in situations of armed conflict to respect the professional independence and rights of journalists, media professionals and associated personnel as civilians;

9. *Recalls* that the deliberate targeting of civilians and other protected persons, and the commission of systematic, flagrant and widespread violations of international humanitarian and human rights law in situations of armed conflict may constitute a threat to international peace and security, and *reaffirms in this regard its readiness* to consider such situations and, where necessary, to adopt appropriate steps;

10. *Invites* States which have not yet done so to consider becoming parties to the Additional Protocols I and II of 1977 to the Geneva Conventions at the earliest possible date;

11. *Affirms* that it will address the issue of protection of journalists in armed conflict strictly under the agenda item "protection of civilians in armed conflict;"

12. *Requests* the Secretary-General to include as a sub-item in his next reports on the protection of civilians in armed conflict the issue of the safety and security of journalists, media professionals and associated personnel.

Source: Security Council Resolution 1738. (c) United Nations, 2006. Reproduced with permission.

Appendix C. United Nations Universal Declaration of Human Rights

PREAMBLE

Whereas recognition of the inherent dignity and of the equal and inalienable rights of all members of the human family is the foundation of freedom, justice and peace in the world,

Whereas disregard and contempt for human rights have resulted in barbarous acts which have outraged the conscience of mankind, and the advent of a world in which human beings shall enjoy freedom of speech and belief and freedom from fear and want has been proclaimed as the highest aspiration of the common people,

Whereas it is essential, if man is not to be compelled to have recourse, as a last resort, to rebellion against tyranny and oppression, that human rights should be protected by the rule of law,

Whereas it is essential to promote the development of friendly relations between nations,

Whereas the peoples of the United Nations have in the Charter reaffirmed their faith in fundamental human rights, in the dignity and worth of the human person and in the equal rights of men and women and have determined to promote social progress and better standards of life in larger freedom,

Whereas Member States have pledged themselves to achieve, in co-operation with the United Nations, the promotion of universal respect for and observance of human rights and fundamental freedoms,

Whereas a common understanding of these rights and freedoms is of the greatest importance for the full realization of this pledge,

Now, Therefore THE GENERAL ASSEMBLY proclaims THIS UNIVERSAL DECLARATION OF HUMAN RIGHTS as a common standard of achievement for all peoples and all nations, to the end that every individual and every organ of society, keeping this Declaration constantly in mind, shall strive by teaching and education to promote respect for these rights and freedoms and by progressive measures, national and international, to secure their universal and effective recognition and observance, both among the peoples of Member States themselves and among the peoples of territories under their jurisdiction.

Article 1.

All human beings are born free and equal in dignity and rights. They are endowed with reason and conscience and should act towards one another in a spirit of brotherhood.

Article 2.

Everyone is entitled to all the rights and freedoms set forth in this Declaration, without distinction of any kind, such as race, colour, sex, language, religion, political or other opinion, national or social origin, property, birth or other status. Furthermore, no distinction shall be made on the basis of the political, jurisdictional or international status of the country or territory to which a person belongs, whether it be independent, trust, non-self-governing or under any other limitation of sovereignty.

Article 3.

Everyone has the right to life, liberty and security of person.

Article 4.

No one shall be held in slavery or servitude; slavery and the slave trade shall be prohibited in all their forms.

Article 5.

No one shall be subjected to torture or to cruel, inhuman or degrading treatment or punishment.

Article 6.

Everyone has the right to recognition everywhere as a person before the law.

Article 7.

All are equal before the law and are entitled without any discrimination to equal protection of the law. All are entitled to equal protection against any discrimination in violation of this Declaration and against any incitement to such discrimination.

Article 8.

Everyone has the right to an effective remedy by the competent national tribunals for acts violating the fundamental rights granted him by the constitution or by law.

Article 9.

No one shall be subjected to arbitrary arrest, detention or exile.

Article 10.

Everyone is entitled in full equality to a fair and public hearing by an independent and impartial tribunal, in the determination of his rights and obligations and of any criminal charge against him.

Article 11.

(1) Everyone charged with a penal offence has the right to be presumed innocent until proved guilty according to law in a public trial at which he has had all the guarantees necessary for his defence.
(2) No one shall be held guilty of any penal offence on account of any act or omission which did not constitute a penal offence, under national or

international law, at the time when it was committed. Nor shall a heavier penalty be imposed than the one that was applicable at the time the penal offence was committed.

Article 12.

No one shall be subjected to arbitrary interference with his privacy, family, home or correspondence, nor to attacks upon his honour and reputation. Everyone has the right to the protection of the law against such interference or attacks.

Article 13.

(1) Everyone has the right to freedom of movement and residence within the borders of each state.
(2) Everyone has the right to leave any country, including his own, and to return to his country.

Article 14.

(3) Everyone has the right to seek and to enjoy in other countries asylum from persecution.
(4) This right may not be invoked in the case of prosecutions genuinely arising from non-political crimes or from acts contrary to the purposes and principles of the United Nations.

Article 15.

(5) Everyone has the right to a nationality.
(6) No one shall be arbitrarily deprived of his nationality nor denied the right to change his nationality.

Article 16.

(7) Men and women of full age, without any limitation due to race, nationality or religion, have the right to marry and to found a family. They are entitled to equal rights as to marriage, during marriage and at its dissolution.
(8) Marriage shall be entered into only with the free and full consent of the intending spouses.
(9) The family is the natural and fundamental group unit of society and is entitled to protection by society and the State.

Article 17.

(10) Everyone has the right to own property alone as well as in association with others.
(11) No one shall be arbitrarily deprived of his property.

Article 18.

Everyone has the right to freedom of thought, conscience and religion; this right includes freedom to change his religion or belief, and freedom, either alone or in community with others and in public or private, to manifest his religion or belief in teaching, practice, worship and observance.

Article 19.

Everyone has the right to freedom of opinion and expression; this right includes freedom to hold opinions without interference and to seek, receive and impart information and ideas through any media and regardless of frontiers.

Article 20.

(12) Everyone has the right to freedom of peaceful assembly and association.
(13) No one may be compelled to belong to an association.

Article 21.

(14) Everyone has the right to take part in the government of his country, directly or through freely chosen representatives.
(15) Everyone has the right of equal access to public service in his country.
(16) The will of the people shall be the basis of the authority of government; this will shall be expressed in periodic and genuine elections which shall be by universal and equal suffrage and shall be held by secret vote or by equivalent free voting procedures.

Article 22.

Everyone, as a member of society, has the right to social security and is entitled to realization, through national effort and international co-operation and in accordance with the organization and resources of each State, of the economic, social and cultural rights indispensable for his dignity and the free development of his personality.

Article 23.

(17) Everyone has the right to work, to free choice of employment, to just and favourable conditions of work and to protection against unemployment.
(18) Everyone, without any discrimination, has the right to equal pay for equal work.
(19) Everyone who works has the right to just and favourable remuneration ensuring for himself and his family an existence worthy of human dignity, and supplemented, if necessary, by other means of social protection.
(20) Everyone has the right to form and to join trade unions for the protection of his interests.

Article 24.

Everyone has the right to rest and leisure, including reasonable limitation of working hours and periodic holidays with pay.

Article 25.

(21) Everyone has the right to a standard of living adequate for the health and well-being of himself and of his family, including food, clothing, housing and medical care and necessary social services, and the right to security in the event of unemployment, sickness, disability, widowhood, old age or other lack of livelihood in circumstances beyond his control.

(22) Motherhood and childhood are entitled to special care and assistance. All children, whether born in or out of wedlock, shall enjoy the same social protection.

Article 26.

(23) Everyone has the right to education. Education shall be free, at least in the elementary and fundamental stages. Elementary education shall be compulsory. Technical and professional education shall be made generally available and higher education shall be equally accessible to all on the basis of merit.

(24) Education shall be directed to the full development of the human personality and to the strengthening of respect for human rights and fundamental freedoms. It shall promote understanding, tolerance and friendship among all nations, racial or religious groups, and shall further the activities of the United Nations for the maintenance of peace.

(25) Parents have a prior right to choose the kind of education that shall be given to their children.

Article 27.

(26) Everyone has the right freely to participate in the cultural life of the community, to enjoy the arts and to share in scientific advancement and its benefits.

(27) Everyone has the right to the protection of the moral and material interests resulting from any scientific, literary or artistic production of which he is the author.

Article 28.

Everyone is entitled to a social and international order in which the rights and freedoms set forth in this Declaration can be fully realized.

Article 29.

(28) Everyone has duties to the community in which alone the free and full development of his personality is possible.

(29) In the exercise of his rights and freedoms, everyone shall be subject only to such limitations as are determined by law solely for the purpose of securing due recognition and respect for the rights and freedoms of others and of meeting the just requirements of morality, public order and the general welfare in a democratic society.

(30) These rights and freedoms may in no case be exercised contrary to the purposes and principles of the United Nations.

Article 30.

Nothing in this Declaration may be interpreted as implying for any State, group or person any right to engage in any activity or to perform any act aimed at the destruction of any of the rights and freedoms set forth herein.

Source: The Universal Declaration of Human Rights. (c) United Nations, 1948. Reproduced with permission.

Appendix D. Medellin Declaration: Securing the Safety of Journalists and Combating Impunity

UNESCO

Medellin Declaration
Securing the Safety of Journalists and Combating Impunity

We, the participants at the UNESCO conference on Press Freedom, Safety of Journalists and Impunity, meeting in Medellin, Colombia, on World Press Freedom Day, 3–4 May 2007,

Deeply concerned by attacks on the freedom of expression of the press including murder, deliberate attacks, abductions, hostage-taking, harassment, intimidation, illegal arrest and detention against journalists, media professionals and associated personnel because of their professional activity,

Believing that press freedom can only be enjoyed when media professionals are free from intimidation, pressure and coercion, whether from political, social, economic forces,

Recalling Article 19 of the Universal Declaration of Human Rights that guarantees freedom of expression as a fundamental right, and *confirming* that freedom of expression is essential to the realization of other rights set forth in international human rights instruments,

Recalling 29 C/Resolution 29 entitled "Condemnation of violence against journalists", adopted by the General Conference of UNESCO on 12 November 1997, which condemns violence against journalists and call on Member States to uphold their obligations to prevent, investigate and punish crimes against journalists,

Underscoring the provisions of the Colombo Declaration of 3 May 2006 on Media and Poverty Eradication, and Dakar Declaration of 3 May 2005 on Media and Good Governance, and of the Belgrade Declaration of 3 May 2004 on Media in Violent Conflict and Countries in Transition,

Welcoming the adoption by the Security Council of the United Nations of Resolution 1738 on 23 December 2006 calling on all parties to an armed conflict to fulfil their obligations towards journalists under international law, including the need to prevent impunity for crimes against them and *further requesting* the Secretary-General to include as a sub-item in his next reports on the protection of civilians in armed conflict the issue of the safety and security of journalists, media professionals and associated personnel,

Noting the potential contribution of a free, independent and pluralistic press to sustainable development, poverty eradication, good governance, peace and reconciliation, and respect for human rights,

Urging all the parties concerned to ensure the safety of journalists, media professionals and associated personnel, and respect for their media equipment and installations,

Considering that most murders of media professionals occur outside of conflict zones and that the safety of media professionals is an urgent problem that is not limited to situations of armed conflict.

Reaffirming our condemnation of all incitement to violence against media professionals.

Call on Member States

To investigate all acts of violence of which journalists, media professionals and associated personnel are victim which have occurred in their territory or abroad when their armed or security forces may have been involved in them;

To search for persons alleged to have committed, or to have ordered to be committed, a crime against journalists, media professionals or associated personnel, to bring such persons, regardless of their nationality, before their own courts or to hand them over for trial to another concerned State, provided this State has made out a credible case against the said persons;

To fulfill the duty incumbent upon them to prevent crimes against journalists, media professionals and associated personnel, to investigate them, to sanction them, to provide witness protection for those testifying against them and to repair the consequences so that such crimes do not go unpunished;

To adopt the principle that there should be no statute of limitations for crimes against persons when these are perpetrated to prevent the exercise of freedom of information and expression or when their purpose is the obstruction of justice;

To release immediately journalists detained to this day for having freely exercised their profession;

To promote awareness and train their armed forces and police forces to respect and promote the safety of journalists in situations of risk, and to ensure that journalists are able to work in full security and independence in their territory;

To recommend to multilateral and bilateral institutions of international cooperation and financial assistance that they require from recipient countries as a specific condition of eligibility respect for freedom of expression and effective protection of the exercise of press freedom, also to recommend to these institutions that a state's failure to comply with its obligation to investigate and punish killers of journalists could be cause for revision, suspension or revocation of such cooperation;

To sign and ratify the Additional Protocols I and II to the Geneva Conventions, the Rome Statute of the International Criminal Court and other relevant international instruments of international humanitarian law and international human rights law, and to take the appropriate legislative, judicial and administrative measures to ensure application of the aforementioned instruments nationally, in so far as they provide protection for civilians, in particular those working in journalism;

To comply with the commitments of UNESCO Resolution 29 to promote legislation with the intention of investigating and prosecuting the killers of journalists and to combat impunity;

Call on International Community and Professional Associations:

To take resolute action for the safety of journalists in situations of risk and to ensure respect for their professional independence;

To sensitize news organizations, editors and managers about the dangers surrounding their staff when covering hazardous stories, particularly the dangers present to local journalists;

To urge news associations to develop and sustain safety provisions that work regardless of whether their staff are covering domestic stories such as crime and corruption, disasters and demonstrations or health issues or international armed conflict;

To promote actions that secure the safety of journalists, including, but not limited to, safety training for journalists, safety codes, healthcare and life insurance, and equal access to social protection for free-lance employees and full-time staff;

To coordinate widespread publicity campaigns on unpunished crimes against journalists and other acts of violence to bring about news coverage of all violations of press freedom;

To encourage journalism schools and mass communication departments to include in their curricula studies on the impact that crimes against journalists—and subsequent impunity—have on democratic societies. In addition to promote the inclusion in the curricula of subjects or specific courses on press freedom and to coordinate activities, including safety training, among press freedom associations, news media and journalism schools;

To further encourage collaboration amongst journalists, media owners, educators, press freedom groups and appropriate development agencies, at national and global level, to ensure the inclusion of media development activities in social and economic development programmes;

Call on UNESCO

To invite the Director General of UNESCO to study, in consultation with the relevant international organizations and non-governmental organizations:

a) To act in favour of measures to better ensure application of the rules and principles of a humanitarian nature safeguarding journalists, media professionals and associated personnel in situations of armed conflict, and to promote the security of the persons concerned;

b) To work against the emergence of new threats to journalists and media staff, including hostage-taking and kidnapping;

c) To encourage mechanisms for including media development in programmes aimed at improving the social, economic and political life of societies in the process of development, political transition or emerging from the crisis of social conflict.

To require that data be submitted to the General Conference in a report on crimes against journalists and the number of cases that continue with impunity; To sensitize governments regarding the importance of freedom of expression and threat that impunity for crimes against media professionals represents to this freedom;

To invite the Director General of UNESCO to recall to member states at the General Conference their legal and moral obligations to comply with Resolution 29 and prevent crimes against journalists.

Source: Medellin Declaration: Securing the Safety of Journalists and Combating Impunity. (c) UNESCO, 2007. Reproduced with permission.

Appendix E. General Assembly Resolution: Protection of Journalists Engaged in Dangerous Missions in Areas of Armed Conflict, United Nations, 1971

Having considered the observations submitted by some Member States in accordance with Commission on Human Rights resolution 17 (XXVII) and the observations of the Conference of Government Experts as well as the discussions on the item and the alternate draft convention submitted during the debate at the twenty-sixth session of the General Assembly,

1. Believes that it is necessary to adopt a convention providing for the protection of journalists engaged in dangerous missions in areas of armed conflict;

2. Invites the Economic and Social Council to request the Commission on Human Rights to consider as a matter of priority at its twenty-eight session the preliminary draft convention contained in Council resolution 1597 (L), taking into consideration the draft conventions submitted by Australia and by the United States of America, and the observations of Governments, as well as all subsequent documents including the draft protocol prepared by the Working Group in accordance with resolution 15 (XXVII) of the Commission;

3. Further requests the Commission on Human Rights to transmit its report on its twenty-eighth session to the Conference of Government Experts on the Reaffirmation and Development of International Humanitarian Law Applicable in Armed Conflicts at its second session to be convened in 1972 by the International Committee of the Red Cross, in order that the International Committee may submit its observations to the General Assembly at its twenty-seventh session;

4. Invites Governments to transmit their observations on that part of the report of the Commission on Human Rights on its twenty-eight session relating to this question;

5. Requests the Secretary-General to submit the replies received and an analytic report on those replies to the General Assembly at its twenty-seventh session;

6. Decides to examine this question as a matter of the highest priority at its twenty-seventh session, taking into consideration the recommendations transmitted to the General Assembly by the Economic and Social Council.

2027th plenary meeting,
20 December 1971.

Source: General Assembly Resolution: Protection of Journalists Engaged in Dangerous Missions in Areas of Armed Conflict. (c) United Nations, 1971. Reproduced with permission.

Notes

Introduction

1. Speech of the Assistant Director for Communication and Information, UNESCO, Belgrade, 2–3, 2004. http://tinyurl.com/6ybdrxw (accessed June 10, 2010).
2. Frank Smyth, "Murdering with Impunity: The Rise in Terror Tactics Against News Reporters," *Harvard International Review*, http://hir.harvard.edu/pressing-change/murdering-with-impunity (accessed November 20, 2010).
3. Committee to Protect Journalists, https://cpj.org/killed/ (accessed November 20, 2010).
4. Kyung-wha Kang, Deputy High Commissioner for Human Rights at the Panel Discussion on the Protection of Journalists in Armed Conflict, 14th session of the Human Rights Council Geneva, June 4, 2010. http://tinyurl.com/6e94xpx (accessed July 27, 2010).
5. Frank LaRue, Special Rapporteur on the promotion and protection of the right to freedom of opinion and expression, at the Panel on the Protection of Journalists in Armed Conflict, 14th session of the Human Rights Council Geneva, June 4, 2010. http://tinyurl.com/6zwc4j5 (accessed July 27, 2010).
6. Reporters sans Frontières George Gordon-Lennox, June 4, 2010. http://tinyurl.com/63pvnfj (accessed April 29, 2011).

Chapter 1: Risks and Rewards: Reporting from Armed and Non-Armed Conflict Situations

1. Samuel B. Huntington, *The Third Wave: Democratization in the Late Twentieth Century* (Norman: University of Oklahoma Press, 1993).
2. Ronald Inglehart, "How Solid Is Mass Support for Democracy: And How Can We Measure It?" *Political Science and Politics*, 36, (January 2003): 51–57.
3. Thomas I. Emerson, *The System of Freedom of Expression* (New York: Random House, 1970).
4. Juha Mustonen, ed. *World's First Freedom of Information Act: Anders Chydenius' Legacy Today*, 2006. http://www.scribd.com/doc/5885744/The-Worlds-First-Freedom-of-Information-Act-SwedenFinland-1766 (accessed November 29, 2010).

5. J. Herbert Altschull, *Agents of Power: The Media and Public Policy*, 2nd ed. (New York: Longman, 1995), 8.

6. Human Constitutional Rights Documents, http://www.hrcr.org/docs/Banjul/afrhr.html (accessed October 10, 2010).

7. Robert L. Stevenson, "Freedom of Press Around the World," *Global Journalism: Topical Issues and Media Systems,* 4th ed., Arnold S. de Beer and John C. Merrill, eds. 2004, 66–83.

8. United Nations homepage. UN Resolutions adopted during its first session, http://daccess-dds-ny.un.org/doc/RESOLUTION/GEN/NR0/033/10/IMG/NR003310.pdf?OpenElement (accessed August 11, 2010).

9. United Nations Development Programme Bureau for Development Policy. *Right to Information Practical Guidance Note,* http://tinyurl.com/6k5ntmh (accessed November 10, 2010).

10. The Universal Declaration of Human Rights. http://www.un.org/en/documents/udhr/index.shtml (accessed August 6, 2010).

11. Toby Mendel, "Freedom of Information as an Internationally Protected Human Right" http://www.article19.org/pdfs/publications/foi-as-an-international-right.pdf (accessed November 10, 2010).

12. *New York Times*, "U.S. to Promote Press Freedom." May 17, 2010. http://www.nytimes.com/2010/05/18/world/18press.html (accessed November 10, 2010).

13. Robert L. Stevenson, "Freedom of Press around the World," in *Global Journalism: Topical Issues and Media Systems* 4th ed., Arnold S. de Beer and John C. Merrill, eds. 2004, 66–83.

14. Freedom House, Freedom of the Press Survey Release, http://freedomhouse.org/template.cfm?page=533 (accessed August 6, 2010).

15. Ibid.

16. Karin Deutsch Karlekar, "Press Freedom in 2009, Broad Setbacks to Global Media Freedom," Freedom House, http://freedomhouse.org/images/File/fop/2010/OverviewEssayFOTP2010finallaid-out.pdf (accessed August 7, 2010).

17. Michael A. Weatherson and Hal W. Bochin, *Hiram Johnson: Political Revivalist*, Lanham, Maryland: University Press of America, 1995. [Note: Authors contend although this quotation appears in several texts, it is unverified. 213.].

18. John Hohenberg, *Foreign Correspondence: The Great Reporters and Their Times*, New York and London: Columbia University Press, 1964, 1.

19. Miles Hudson and John Stanier, *War and the Media: A Random Searchlight*, (New York: New York University Press, 1998), 1–20.

20. Phillip Knightley, *The First Casualty*, (Baltimore and London: The Johns Hopkins University Press, 2004), 2.

21. Rollo Odgen, ed. *The Life and Letters of Edwin Lawrence Godkin*.Vol. I, New York Macmillan 1907, 102–103.

22. George W. Ochs, *Annals of the American Academy of Political and Social Science*, Vol. 28, Business Professions July, 1906, 38–57.

23. Harold D. Lasswell, *Propaganda Technique in the World War*, (New York: MIT Press, 1971), 47.

24. Ibid.

25. Ibid.

26. Ibid., 220.

27. Mitchel Roth, *Historical Dictionary of War Journalism* (Westport, CT: Greenwood Press, 1997), 352.

28. Lee Miller, *The Story of Ernie Pyle* (New York: Monarch Books 1950), 252.

29. Michelle Ferrari, comp., with commentary by James Tobin. *Reporting America at War: An Oral History*. New York: Hyperion, 2003.

30. Ibid., 22.

31. George Sullivan, *Journalists at Risk: Reporting America's Wars* (Minneapolis: Twenty-First Century Books, 2006), 33.

32. Mitchel Roth, *Historical Dictionary of War Journalism* (Westport, CT: Greenwood Press, 1997), 352.

33. John Hohenberg, *Foreign Correspondence: The Great Reporters and Their Times* (New York and London: Columbia University Press, 1964), 364.

34. Ben Hibbs, "You Can't Edit a Magazine by Arithmetic," *Journalism Quarterly*, Fall 1950, 369–377, 371.

35. BBC Memo to come from Asa Briggs, *The History of Broadcasting in the United Kingdom*, Vol 3: *War on Words*. 1970, 1.

36. Mitchel Roth, *Historical Dictionary of War Journalism* (Westport, CT: Greenwood Press, 1997), 353.

37. Lawrence E. Davies, "Reporters Killed in War Honored" *New York Times*, August 25, 1945, 24.

38. Ann Elizabeth Pfau and David Hochfelder, " 'Her Voice a Bullet': Imaginary Propaganda and the Legendary Broadcasters of World War II" in *Sound in the Age of Mechanical Reproduction*. David Suisman and Susan Strasser, eds, Philadelphia: University of Pennsylvania Press, 2009, 48–46.

39. Ibid., 61–62.

40. Ibid.

41. John Hohenberg, *Foreign Correspondence: The Great Reporters and Their Times* (New York and London: Columbia University Press, 1964), 384.

42. United Nations Resolution 82 and 83, June 25 and 27, 1950. http://daccess-dds-ny.un.org/doc/RESOLUTION/GEN/NR0/064/95/IMG/NR006495.pdf ?OpenElement (accessed November 4, 2010).

43. Miles Hudson and John Stanier, *War and the Media: A Random Searchlight*, New York: New York University Press, 1998, 94.

44. Ibid., 95.

45. Mitchel Roth, *Historical Dictionary of War Journalism*, Westport, CT: Greenwood Press, 172.

46. Ibid.

47. Hugh Lunn, *Vietnam: A Reporter's War*, New York: Stein and Day, 1986, 7.

48. Mark Atwood Lawrence, "Mission Intolerable: Harrison Salisbury's Trip to Hanoi and the Limits of Dissent against the Vietnam War," *Pacific Historical Review*, Vol. 75, No. 3 Aug., 2006, 429–459.

49. Daniel C. Hallin, *The "Uncensored War": The Media and Vietnam*, Berkeley: University of California Press, 1986, 42.

50. Robin Andersen, *A Century of Media, A Century of War*, New York: Peter Lang, 2007, 49.

51. Barbara Tuchman, *The March of Folly*, London: Cardinal, 1990, 415.

52. Miles Judson and John Stanier, *War and the Media: A Random Searchlight*, New York: New York University Press, 1998, 111.

53. Michelle Ferrari, comp., with commentary by James Tobin, *"Reporting America at War: An Oral History*, New York: Hyperion, 2003, 26.

54. Ibid.

55. Robin Andersen, *A Century of Media, A Century of War*, New York: Peter Lang, 2007, xxii.

56. Ibid.

57. Daniel C. Hallin, *The "Uncensored War": The Media and Vietnam*, Berkeley: University of California Press, 1986, 3.

58. Andersen, 54.

59. Douglas Kellner, "From Vietnam to the Gulf: Postmodern Wars?" in *The Vietnam War and Postmodernity*, ed. Michael Biddy, Amherst: University of Massachusetts Press, 1999, 200.

60. Mitchel Roth, *Historical Dictionary of War Journalism*, Westport, CT: Greenwood Press, 1997, 326.

61. Knightly, 479.

62. A. Trevor Thrall, *War in the Media Age*, Cresskill, NJ: Hampton Press, 2000, 110.

63. Ibid.

64. Steven Hurst, *The Foreign Policy of the Bush Administration, In Search of a New World Order*, London: Cassell, 1999, 50.

65. Edward Herman and Noam Chomsky, *Manufacturing Consent: The Political Economy of the Mass Media*, New York: Pantheon, 1988, 1.

66. Noam Chomsky, *Deterring Democracy*, London: Vintage, 1992, 59.

67. Noam Chomsky, *For Reasons of State*, New York: Vintage, 1973, 18.

68. Ekaterina Balabanova, *Media, Wars and Politics: Comparing the Incomparable in Western and Eastern Europe*, England: Ashgate, 2007.

69. Mary Kaldor, 31.

70. Committee to Protect Journalists, http://www.cpj.org/killed/europe/bos nia/ (accessed November 8, 2010).

71. Kemal Kurspahić quoted in Nancy J. Woodhull and Robert W. Snyder, eds., *Journalists in Peril*, New Brunswick and London: Transaction Publishers, 1998, 151.

72. Kemal Kurspahić in *Journalist in Peril*, 150.

73. Tim Lambon quoted in Howard Tumber and Frank Webster, *Journalists Under Fire: Information War and Journalistic Practices*, London: Sage Publications, 2006, 130.

74. Paul L. Moorcraft and Philip M. Taylor "Shooting the Messenger: *The Political Impact of War Reporting*. Washington, DC: Potomac Books, Inc., 2008.

75. Quoted in Stephen Hess and Marvin Kalb, eds, *The Media and the War on Terrorism*, Washington, DC: Brookings Institution Press, 2003, 8.

76. Quoted in Paul L. Moorcraft and Philip M. Taylor *Shooting the Messenger: The Political Impact of War Reporting*. Washington, DC: Potomac Books, Inc., 2008, 157.

77. Ibid.

78. Ibid., 158.

79. Committee to Protect Journalists, Iraq Report: Killed by U.S. Forces, http://cpj.org/reports/2006/01/js-killed-by-us-13sept05.ph (accessed November 10, 2010).

80. Ibid.

81. Author interview with Gretchen Peters, November 3, 2010.

82. Committee to Protect Journalists website http://cpj.org/killed/ (accessed March 14, 2011).

83. Ibid.

84. International News Safety Institute, "Killing the Messenger," *International News Safety Institute*, March 2007 (accessed April 14, 2009), www.news safety.com/stories/insi/KillingtheMessenger.pdf. 8.

85. Ibid., 46.

86. Michael Ware, "The Reporter's Privilege," cited in *Homefront Confidential*, 12 August 2002, http://www.rcforg/homefrontconfidential/privilege .html (accessed November 10, 2010).

87. Philip Bennett, "Too Far from the Story?" The *Washington Post*, 2004 (accessed February 20, 2009).

88. Mary Kaldor, *New and Old Wars: Organized Violence in a Global Era*, Stanford: Stanford University Press, 1999. pages 1–30.

89. Howard Tumber and Frank Webster, *Journalists Under Fire: Information War and Journalistic Practices*, London: Sage Publications, 2006, 1.

90. Ibid., 5–6.

91. Joseph Nye, Jr. "The American National Interests and Global Public Goods," *International Affairs*, 78, 2 2002, 233–244, 236.

92. Ibid.

93. Ibid, 233, 244, and 238.

94. Committee to Protect Journalists http://www.cpj.org/killed/ (accessed November 8, 2010).

95. See footnote 2 in Introduction.

96. International News Safety Institute, *Killing the Messenger*, International News Safety Institute, March 2007 (accessed April 14, 2009), www.newssafety .com/stories/insi/KillingtheMessenger.pdf.

97. Ibid.

98. International News Safety Institute, *Journalists and Media Workers Killed in 2008*, International News Safety Institute, 2009 (accessed April 14, 2009). http://www.newssafety.com/index.php?option=com_content&view=arti cle&id=5177&Itemid=100190.

99. International News Safety Institute. http://www.newssafety.org/ index.php?option=com_content&view=article&id=11043&Itemid=100536 (accessed February 21, 2010).

100. International News Safety Institute. www.newssafety.org (First page) (accessed January 8, 2011).

101. International News Safety Institute, "Killing the Messenger." http://www .newssafety.org/images/pdf/KillingtheMessenger.pdf (accessed November 10, 2010).

102. Committee to Protect Journalists, *Attacks on the Press*, New York: CPJ, 2010.

103. INSI, "Peacetime deadliest for journalists in 2009, INSI research shows. http://www.newssafety.org/index.php?option=com_content&view=article&id =19700:qpeacetimeq-deadliest-for-journalists-in-2009-insi-research-shows &catid=314:press-room-news-release&Itemid=100077 (accessed November 8, 2010).

104. Committee to Protect Journalists, *Attacks on the Press in 2009*. New York: Committee to Protect Journalists, 10.

105. Ibid., 11.

106. Piers Robinson, *The CNN Effect: The myth of news, foreign policy and intervention*, Routledge: London, 2003, 1.

107. Christiane Amanpour, "Television's role in foreign policy." *Quill;* April 1996, Vol. 84 Issue 3, 16–18.

108. Lawrence S. Eagleburger, Claus Kleber, Stephen Livingston and Judy Woodruff, "The CNN Effect" in Stephen Hess and Marvin Kalb, eds., *The Media and the War on Terrorism*, Washington, DC: Brookings Institution Press, 2003, 63–83.

109. Ibid., 65.

110. Sarah Blake, "Women War Correspondents," *The Telegraph*, July 12, 2010, http://www.telegraph.co.uk/culture/7872900/Women-war-correspondents.html (accessed November 20, 2010).

111. Joyce Hoffmann, *On Their Own: Women Journalists and the American Experience in Vietnam*, Cambridge, MA: De Capo Press, 2008.

112. Shelia Gibbons, "Female Correspondents Changing War Coverage," *We-News*, October 16, 2002. http://www.womensenews.org/story/uncovering-gender/021016/female-correspondents-changing-war-coverage (accessed November 20, 2010).

113. Milly Buonanno, "Women War Correspondents: Does Gender Make a Difference on the Front Line?" Paper presented at the annual meeting of the International Communication Association, Marriott, Chicago, IL, May 20, 2009, Accessed through EPSCO Host, November 21, 2010. Also see Gerry J. Gillmore, "Women Journalists Came of Age Covering World War II" U.S. Department of Defense News Release, http://www.defense.gov/news/newsarticle.aspx?id=45716 (accessed November 29, 2010).

114. Quoted in Sherry Ricchiardi, "Women on War" *American Journalism Review*, March 1994, Vol. 16 Issue 2: 16, 7, 4, 19.

115. Quoted in Sherry Ricchiardi, "Women on War" *American Journalism Review*, March 1994, Vol. 16 Issue 2, 16, 7, 4, 21.

116. Christiane Amanpour, "On the Frontlines" *The Quill*, October/November, 2005 Supplement, Vol. 93, 40–44, 42.

117. Council of Europe, "Conflict Prevention and Resolution: the Role of Women" http://assembly.coe.int/Documents/WorkingDocs/doc04/EDOC10117.htm (accessed November 20, 2010).

118. Quoted in Sherry Ricchiardi, "Women on War" *American Journalism Review*, March 1994, Vol. 16 Issue 2:16, 7, 4, 18.

119. International News Safety Institute, "Women Reporting War: A Survey by the International News Safety Institute." May 7, 2010. http:www.newssafety.com/stories/insi/wrw.htm (accessed November 15, 2010).

120. Ibid.

121. Quoted in Stephen Hess and Marvin Kalb, *The Media and the War on Terrorism*, Washington, DC: Brookings Institution Press, 2003, 85.

122. The *New York Times* (no author), "Non-British Reporters Kept from Falklands," Section A 10 column 2 Foreign Desk, July 1, 1982.

123. Ibid.

124. A. Trevor Thrall, *War in the Media Age*, Cresskill, NJ: Hampton Press, 2000, 90.

125. Michael C. Emery, *On the Front Lines: Following America's Foreign Correspondents across the Twentieth Century*. Washington, DC: The American University Press, 1995, 269.

126. A. Trevor Thrall, *War in the Media Age*, Cresskill, NJ: Hampton Press, 2000, 143.

127. Quoted in Frank Aukofer and William Lawrence, *America's Team: the Odd Couple: A Report on the Relationship between the Media and the Military*. New York: The Freedom Forum, 1995, 193.

128. Ibid., 194.

129. George Sullivan, *Journalists at risk: Reporting America's wars*. Minneapolis: Twenty-First Century Books, 2006, 76.

130. Everette Dennis, David Stebenne, John Pavlik, Mark Thalhimer, Craig LaMay, Dirk Smillie, Martha FitzSimon, Shirley Gazsi, Seth Rachlin. *The Media at War: The Press and the Persian Gulf Conflict*, 1991, 28.

131. Robin Andersen, *A Century of Media, A Century of War*. New York: Peter Lang, 2007, 228.

132. Mission: Iraq, Media embed ground rules. http:www.militarycity.com/iraq/1631270.html (accessed August 20, 2010).

133. Ibid., 2.

134. Ibid.

135. Douglas Kellner, "Spectacle and Media Propaganda in the War on Iraq: A critique of U.S. broadcasting Networks" in Yahya R. Kamalipour, and Nancy Snow, *War, Media, and Propaganda: A Global Perspective*, Lanham Maryland: Rowman & Littlefield Publishers, 2004, 72, 69–77.

136. Author interview with Robert Nicklesberg, August 12, 2010.

137. International News Safety Institute, "Killing the Messenger," *International News Safety Institute*, March 2007 (accessed April 14, 2009), www.newssafety.com/stories/insi/KillingtheMessenger.pdf. 90.

138. Ibid.

139. Quoted in Robin Andersen, *A Century of Media, A Century of War*. New York: Peter Lang, 2007, 229.

140. Quoted in Robin Andersen, *A Century of Media, A Century of War*. New York: Peter Lang, 2007, 229.

141. Ibid.

142. Reporters sans Frontières, "CNN Crew's Bodyguard Fires Back with Automatic Weapon when Crew Comes Under Fire. News Organization's Use of Firearm Sets Dangerous Precedent," April 13, 2003 (accessed April 14, 2009), http://www.rsf.org/article.php3?id_article=6078.

143. Ben Saul, "The International Protection of Journalists in Armed Conflict and Other Violent Situations," *Australian Journal of Human Rights*, 110, 2008 (accessed April 10, 2009). http://www.austlii.edu.au/au/journals/AJHR/2008/5.pdf.

144. Andrew M. Lindner, "Among the Troops: Seeing the Iraq War through Three Journalistic Vantage Points," *Social Problems*, Vol 56, No. 1: 21–48, 44.

145. Marshall McLuhan, quoted in the *Montreal Gazette*, May 16, 1975.

146. Irving Fang, *A History of Mass Communications: Six Information Revolutions.* Boston: Focal Press 1997: xxxi.

147. Quoted in Johanna Newman, *Lights, Camera, War: Is media technology driving international politics?* New York: St. Martin's Press, 1996: 194.

148. Ibid.

Chapter 2: Measures of Civility: Legal Protections Developed for Journalists Reporting From Danger Zones

1. Geneva Conventions, http://www.redcross.lv/en/conventions.htm (accessed October 11, 2010).

2. International Committee of the Red Cross. "The Geneva Conventions." http://tiny.cc/6ht2a (accessed October 14, 2010).

3. International Humanitarian Law, http://tiny.cc/cr6gq (accessed October 12, 2010).

4. Hans Peter Gasser, 1983. "The Protection of Journalists Engaged in Dangerous Professional Missions," *International Review of the Red Cross*, No 232, 3–18, February 28, 1983 (accessed April 13, 2009), http://tiny.cc/gepvo.

5. Plenipotentiaries of the governments, "Application of the Convention to Certain Categories of Civilians," *ICRC*, 1929, http://tiny.cc/92iks (accessed February 12, 2009).

6. Hans Peter Gasser, "The Protection of Journalists Engaged in Dangerous Professional Missions."

7. Hans Peter Gasser, "The Protection of Journalists Engaged in Dangerous Professional Missions," *International Review of the Red Cross* 232. http://tiny.cc/66lix (accessed October 14, 2010).

8. Ibid.

9. Claude Pilloud, "Protection of Journalists on Dangerous Missions in Armed Conflict Zones" as cited in Hans Peter Gasser, "The Protection of Journalists Engaged in Dangerous Professional Missions."

10. ICRC website, http://tiny.cc/pg7fy (accessed on October 13, 2010).

11. Ibid.

12. Ibid.

13. International Committee of the Red Cross. "Geneva Conventions 1977 Additional Protocols." http://tiny.cc/pkway (accessed October 2010).

14. Ibid.

15. "Many Voices, One World: Toward a New More Just and More Efficient World Information and Communication Order," The MacBride Commission Report, Paris: UNESCO, 1980.

16. Ibid., 234.

17. Principle of distinction is defined within Article 48 of Additional Protocol 1, and states, "the Parties to the conflict shall at all times distinguish

between the civilian population and combatants." Article 48 was adopted by consensus.

18. 1977 Protocol I, Arts 57–58, http://tiny.cc/sbfj1 (accessed October 14, 2010).

19. 1977 Protocol 1, Art 51 (7), http://tiny.cc/t1cxo (accessed October 14, 2010).

20. Ben Saul, "The International Protection of Journalists in Armed Conflict and Other Violent Situations," *Australian Journal of Human Rights*, 109, 2008, http://tiny.cc/oh1ww (accessed April 10, 2009).

21. International Criminal Court, http://tiny.cc/4e5xn (accessed October 13, 2010).

22. Robin Geiss, "How Does International Humanitarian Law Protect Journalists in Armed Conflict Situations?" ICRC Website, 27-07-2010 Interview, http://tiny.cc/x34oh (accessed October 13, 2010).

23. Ibid.

24. Tayo Odunlami, "Journalists Agree That Laws Do Not Protect War Reporters." *The News (Lagos)*. March 13, 2000.

25. Ibid.

26. United Nations Treaty Reference Guide, 2008, "Declaration." http://untreaty.un.org/English/guide.asp.

27. Jeroen Schokkenbroek. Declaration and Recommendation on the Protection of Journalists in Situations of Conflict and Tension, Council of Europe, 1996. http://tiny.cc/ygcxs (accessed March 21, 2011).

28. Ibid.

29. Organization for Security and Cooperation in Europe (OSCE) "Berlin Declaration Journalists in Danger–How We Can Help." http://www.osce.org/fom/40377 (accessed October 14, 2010).

30. Ibid.

31. Reporters sans Frontières. "Declaration on the Safety of Journalists and Media Personnel in Situations Involving Armed Conflict." http://www.rsf.org/IMG/pdf/guide_gb.pdf (accessed October 2010).

32. UNESCO World Press Freedom Day 2007, http://tiny.cc/eypgl (accessed November 15, 2010).

33. United Nations Educational Scientific and Cultural Organization (2007). "Media Professionals from around the World Adopt Medellin Declaration on Safety of Journalists and Combating Impunity." http://tiny.cc/6cdm1 (accessed October 2010).

34. Ibid.

35. Findlaw for Legal Professionals (2008). "Resolution." http://tiny.cc/c8wjt (accessed October 2010).

36. International Federation of Journalists and International Freedom of Expression Exchange. "IFJ Calls on United Nations to Provide Protection for Journalists in Iraq." http://tiny.cc/asyz8 (accessed January 13, 2011).

37. International Federation of Journalists and International News Safety Institute. 2005. "Text for Suggested Resolution of Security Council as Presented to Kofi Annan at World Electronic Media Forum." http://tiny.cc/enji2 (accessed March 28, 2011).

38. "United Nations Security Council SC2989." http://tiny.cc/v21zc (accessed October 13, 2010).

39. Ibid.

40. International News Safety Institute, 2007. "Killing the Messenger: Report of the Global inquiry by the International News Safety Institute into the Protection of Journalists." www.newssafety.com/stories/insi/killingthemessenger.pdf (accessed October 2010).

41. Reporters sans frontières, 2006. "UN Security Council Passes a Resolution on Journalists' Protection." http://tiny.cc/s210i (accessed October 2010).

42. Council of Europe 1535, 2007 "Threats to the Lives and Freedom of Expression of Journalists," Council of Europe Resolution 1535 (accessed October 2009).

43. Ibid. (Council of Europe 1535, 2007:1 "Threats to the Lives and Freedom of Expression of Journalists," Council of Europe Resolution 1535).

44. Resolution A/HRC/RES/13/24. http://tiny.cc/bqsb6 (accessed October 2010).

45. Ibid.

46. United Nations News Service, "Human Rights Council Holds Panel Discussion on the Protection of Journalists in Armed Conflict," June 4, 2010, http://tiny.cc/mapua (accessed October 13, 2010).

47. Ibid.

48. Ibid.

49. Ibid.

50. Ibid.

51. Ibid.

52. Ibid.

53. Robin Geiss, "How Does International Humanitarian Law Protect Journalists in Armed-Conflict Situations?" Interview with Robin Geiss, ICRC legal advisor. July 27, 2010 (accessed September 2010). http://tiny.cc/istwd.

54. "Pledges and Follow-up to the 30th International Conference of the Red Cross and Red Crescent." http://tiny.cc/uto3k (accessed October 13, 2010).

55. " How Does International Humanitarian Law Protect Journalists in Armed-Conflict Situations?" Interview with Robin Geiss, ICRC legal advisor. July 27, 2010. http://tiny.cc/istwd (accessed September 21, 2010).

56. Press Emblem Campaign, Convention. http://tiny.cc/4vcu8 (accessed October 13, 2010).

57. Ibid.

58. Ibid.

59. Ibid.

60. Quoted in Ben Hartman, "Obama to Sign Press Freedom Law Named after Daniel Pearl" *Jerusalem Post*, May 16, 2010, 4 (accessed through Lexis/Nexis, November 15, 2010).

61. Quoted in Ben Hartman, "Obama to Sign Press Freedom Law Named after Daniel Pearl" *Jerusalem Post*, May 16, 2010, 4 (accessed through Lexis/Nexis, November 15, 2010).

62. Quoted in Africa News, *L'Express* (Port Louis), "Daniel Pearl Freedom of the Press Act," June 18, 2010. (accessed through Lexis/Nexis, November 15, 2010).

63. Jane Perlez, "Pakistani Journalist Speaks Out After an Attack" *The New York Times*, September 24, 2010. http://www.nytimes.com/2010/09/25/world/asia/25cheema.html (accessed December 9, 2010).

64. Ibid.

65. Mary Kaldor, *New and Old Wars. Organized Violence in a Global Era*, 2nd ed. Palo Alto, CA: Stanford University Press, 2007.

66. Mary Kaldor, *New and Old Wars: Organized Violence in a Global Era*. Palo Alto: CA: Stanford University Press, 1999, 8.

67. Ibid.

68. Volker Epping and Gottfried Wilhelm Leibniz, International Humanitarian Law Facing New Challenges. "Confronting New Challenges, Knut Ipsen and International Humanitarian Law," 2007. By Volker Epping, Gottfried Wilhelm Leibniz, University of Hannover, 5.

69. Jakob Kellenberger, "Strengthening Legal Protection for Victims of Armed Conflicts. The ICRC study on the current state of international humanitarian law. Address by Dr. Jakob Kellenberger, President of the International Committee of the Red Cross, September 21, 2010, 1–3. http://tiny.cc/10qjx (accessed October 2010).

70. Ibid.

71. Ibid.

72. Ibid.

73. Ibid.

74. Maria Trombly, *Reference Guide to the Geneva Conventions*, 2003, http://spj.org/gc.asp (accessed October 14, 2010).

Chapter 3: From "Name and Shame" to Media Literacy: Nonstate Strategies and Tactics to Protect Journalists

1. Committee to Protect Journalists, http://www.cpj.org/about/ (accessed August 14, 2010).

2. Ibid., 3.

3. Committee to Protect Journalists, 2005, "Who Kills Journalists and Why?": Report by the Committee to Protect Journalists to the Committee of Inquiry,

http://cpj.org/2005/05/who-kills-journalists-and-why-report-by-the-commit.php (accessed April 14, 2008).

4. Quoted in Committee to Protect Journalists, *Attacks on the Press in 2009*, New York: CPJ, 2010, 9.

5. Ibid.

6. Committee to Protect Journalists, "How to help," http://cpj.org/blog/2009/12/how-to-help-journalists-in-prison.php (accessed December 9, 2010).

7. Reporters sans Frontières, http://en.rsf.org/introduction-24-04-2009, 32617.html (accessed August 14, 2010).

8. Reporters sans Frontières, http://www.rsf.org/IMG/pdf/guide_gb.pdf (accessed August, 14, 2010).

9. Reporters sans Frontières, "Reporters without Borders Provides Funding for Journalists and Media in Danger," July 13, 2010. http://en.rsf.org/reporters-without-borders-provides-13-07-2009,27495.html (accessed December 9, 2010).

10. Reporters sans Frontières, "Supporting Media and Journalists Hit by Flooding," September 3, 2010. http://en.rsf.org/pakistan-supporting-media-and-journalists-03-09-2010,38273.html (accessed December 9, 2010).

11. The International News Safety Institute, http://www.newssafety.org/index.php?option=com_content&view=article&id=133&Itemid=100060 (accessed August 14, 2010).

12. Ibid.

13. International News Safety Institute, March 2007. "Killing the Messenger: Report of the Global Inquiry by the International News Safety Institute into the Protection of Journalists," International News Safety Institute. http://www.newssafety.org/images/pdf/KillingtheMessenger.pdf.

14. Ibid., 7.

15. Ibid., 42.

16. Ibid., 52.

17. International News Safety Institute, "INSI Provides Training to Sri Lankan Journalists." http://www.newssafety.org/index.php?option=com_content&view=article&id=19715:insi-provides-training-to-sri-lankan-journalists-&catid=314:press-room-news-release&Itemid=100077 (accessed December 9, 2010).

18. Rodney Pinder, "Why INSI?" (accessed September 15, 2010). http://www.newssafety.org/index.php?option=com_content&view=article&id=134&Itemid=100061.

19. http://www.i-m-s.dk/page/introduction-ims.

20. http://www. mediacovenant.org.

21. http://www.ifj.org/en.

22. http://www.freemedia.at/about-us/ipi-profile/.

23. Ibid.

24. http://www.freemedia.at/about-us/ipi-profile/.

25. International Media Support, "Taking stock of media partnerships," October 2, 2009. http://www.i-m-s.dk/?q=article/taking-stock-joint-international-media-partnerships (accessed November 22, 2010).

26. International Media Support, http://www.i-m-s.dk/files/publications/1557%20Partnership.web_final.pdf, 9.

27. International Media Support, Minutes from the International Partnerships' Meeting, January 26, 2010. Prepared by IMS, Given to authors by IMS. November 22, 2010, 7.

28. Ibid., 8.

29. Ibid., 5.

30. Mariane Pearl, *A Mighty Heart: The Inside Story of the Al Qaeda Kidnapping of Danny Pearl*, New York: Scribner, 2003.

31. Chris Cramer, "What Price Freedom? Global Reporting Trends and Journalistic Integrity." *Pacific Journalism Review*, 12(1) 2010, 15.

32. Ibid.

33. Ibid., 15.

34. The Freedom Forum, European Centre, *Setting the Standard: A Commitment to Frontline Journalism; An Obligation to Frontline Journalism*, September 20, 2000, 3. http://www.freedomforum.org/publications/international/europe/settingthestandard/setting_the_standard.pdf (accessed November 23, 2010).

35. Quoted in *Setting the Standard: A Commitment to Frontline Journalism: An Obligation to Frontline Journalism*. http://www.freedomforum.org/publications/international/europe/settingthestandard/setting_the_standard.pdf. Page 3 (accessed November 10, 2010).

36. http://www.ifj.org/en/pages/about-ifj, 40.

37. Aidan White, International News Safety Fund Report, 2008 (accessed March 20, 2011). http://www.ifj.org/assets/docs/051/212/eb26233-18d15d4.pdf, 35.

38. Ibid.

39. George Sullivan, *Journalists at Risk: Reporting America's Wars*. Minneapolis: Twenty-First Century Books, 2006, 91.

40. U.K. Ministry of Defense, "The Greenbook: MoD Working Arrangements with the Media for Use throughout the Full Spectrum of Military Operations," www.mod.uk/NR/rdonlyres/F83E9C03-FD20-4635-8FFF-715F6 4795763-0-GreenBook.pdf [Online] (accessed on March 21, 2008), 6.

41. Ibid., i.

42. Ibid., 3.

43. Press Emblem Campaign http://www.pressemblem.ch/ (accessed November 10, 2010).

44. INSI, News Release, "The Broadcast News Security Group Opposed the PRESS Protection Emblem." 2 July 27, 2008. http://www.newssafety.org/index.php?option=com_content&view=article&id=6701:the-broadcast-news

-security-group-opposed-to-a-press-protection-emblem&catid=515:global
-inquiry&Itemid=100080.

45. Author interview with Frank Smyth, 2006.

46. Press Emblem Campaign. http://www.pressemblem.ch/4597.html
(accessed August, 15, 2008).

47. Author interview with Blaise Lempen, 2006.

48. Author interview with Blaise Lempen, 2006.

49. Author interview with Knut Dörmann, 2006.

50. Ibid.

51. Ibid.

52. Author interview with Rodney Pinder, 2006.

53. Author interview with Frank Smyth, 2006.

54. Author interview with Blaise Lempen, 2006.

55. Author interview with Thorne Anderson, 2006.

56. Author interview with Rodney Pinder, 2006.

57. Author interview with Jef Julliard, 2006.

58. Author interview with Thorne Anderson, 2006.

59. Author interview with Blaise Lempen, 2006.

60. Ibid.

61. Author interview with Knut Dörmann, 2006.

62. Quoted in : Robert Karniol, "On Alert When Covering Conflicts," *The
Straits Times* (Singapore), October 9, 2010 (accessed through Lexis/Nexis,
November 26, 2010).

63. Ibid.

64. Author interview with Robert Klamser, September 28, 2010.

65. Ibid.

66. Ibid.

67. Author interview with Sarah Ward-Lilley, October 26, 2010.

68. Author interview with John Daniszewski, November 1, 2010.

69. Ibid.

70. Ibid.

71. Vivek Prakash, "Training for the Unforeseen" May 8, 2008, http://blogs
.reuters.com/photo/2008/05/08/11373/ (accessed November 23, 2010).

72. Ibid.

73. Ian Starrett, "Pioneering Cameraman's Legacy Continues to Live On."
The Belfast News Letter, October 29, 2003 (accessed through Lexis/Nexis
November 26, 2010).

74. Author interview with Tina Carr, November 23, 2010.

75. Author interview with Andrew Feinstein, October 6, 2010.

76. Ibid.

77. Ibid.

78. Ibid.

79. The Dart Center Mission Statement. http://dartcenter.org/mission (accessed October 15, 2010). Reprinted with permission.

80. Author interview with Bruce Shapiro, September 27, 2010.

81. Author interview with Bruce Shapiro, September 27, 2010.

82. Robert A. Hackett and William K. Carroll, *Remaking Media: The Struggle to Democratize Public Communication*. New York: Routledge, 2006., 30.

83. Ibid., 31.

84. Ibid.

85. Robert A. Hackett, "Journalism versus Peace? Notes on a Problematic Relationship" *Global Media Journal* [Mediterranean Edition] 2(1), Spring 2007, 47–53, 48.

86. Committee to Protect Journalists, Annual Report 2009–2010, 1. http://cpj.org/about/CPJ.Annual.Report.2010.pdf (accessed October 17, 2010).

87. Stuart Allan and Barbie Zelizer, eds. *Reporting War: Journalism in Wartime*. London: Routledge, 2004, 201.

88. Gaye Tuchman, "Objectivity as Strategic Ritual: An Examination of Newsmen's Notions of Objectivity" *The American Journal of Sociology*, Vol. 77, No. 4 (Jan., 1972), 660–79 (accessed through J-Stor, November 26, 2010).

89. Philip Seib, *The Global Journalist: News and Conscience in a World of Conflict*, Lanham, MD: Bowman & Littlefield Publishers, 2002, 8.

90. Quoted in Philip Seib, The *Global Journalist: News and Conscience in a World of Conflict*, Lanham, MD: Bowman & Littlefield Publishers, 2002, 29.

91. Ross Howard, *Conflict Sensitive Journalism*, International Media Support, 2003, 6. http://www.i-m-s.dk/files/publications/IMS_CSJ_Handbook.pdf (accessed October 24, 2010).

92. Shabelle Media Network, *Africa News*, June 14, 2007, "Djibouti; Training On Conflict Sensitive Journalism for Somali Journalists Ends in Djibouti" (accessed through Lexis/Nexis, October 24, 2010).

93. Ibid.

94. Ibid.

95. AllAfrica Global Media, *The Informer*, May 4, 2010, "INWENT Trains 15 West African Journalists On "Conflict Sensitive" (accessed through Lexis/Nexis October 24, 2010).

96. Ibid.

97. Jake Lynch and Annabel McGoldrick, *Peace Journalism*, Gloucestershire, UK: Hawthorn House, 2005, xviii.

98. Ibid.

99. Ibid.

100. Carl Schmitt, *The Concept of the Political*, New Brunswick; NJ: Rutgers, 1928/1976.

101. Annabel McGoldrick, "Psychological Effects of War Journalism and Peace Journalism," 111–128. in Susan Tente Ross and Majid Tehranian, eds. *Peace Journalism in Times of War: Peace and Policy*, Vol. 13, New Brunswick: Transaction Publishers, 2009.

102. Lynch and McGoldrick, 6.

103. Ibid.

104. Annabel McGoldrick, "Psychological Effects of War Journalism and Peace Journalism," 111–128 in Susan Tente Ross and Majid Tehranian, eds. *Peace Journalism in Times of War: Peace and Policy*, Vol. 13, New Brunswick: Transaction Publishers, 2009, 123.

105. Organization for Security and Cooperation in Europe, 2000, 'OSCE to Continue Focus on Freedom of the Media,' http://www.osce.org/item/14.htmo?print=1 (accessed August 25, 2006).

Chapter 4: Don't Shoot the Messenger: Journalists Who Risk Everything to Tell Stories of Conflict

1. Committee to Protect Journalists, Impunity in Murder Cases, http://cpj.org/killed/2010/ (accessed December 8, 2010).

2. Committee to Protect Journalists, "Getting Away with Murder 2008," April 30, 2008, http://cpj.org/reports/2008/04/getting-away-with-murder.php#countries (accessed December 8, 2010).

3. Ibid.

4. Committee to Protect Journalists, "Iran, China drive prison tally to 14-year high." http://cpj.org/reports/2010/12/cpj-journalist-prison-census-iran-china-highest-14-years.php (accessed December 8, 2010).

5. Ibid.

6. Asra Q. Nomani, *Washington Post*. "Outlook: Not the Daniel Pearl I knew: Liberties taken with 'A Mighty Heart' Go Far Beyond Artistic License," June 25, 2007.

7. Mark Dagostino, Debra Lewis, Pete Norman, Eileen Finan, Dietlind Lerner, Melissa Schorr, Karen Brailsford, David Orr. "Desperate Vigil, *People* Magazine, February 18, 2002, Vol 57, no. 6. http://www.people.com/people/archive/article/0,,20136441,00.html (accessed on November 26, 2010).

8. Evan Thomas; with Rod Nordland, Zahid Hussain and Scott Johnson in Pakistan; Melinda Liu in Beijing; Joshua Hammer in Spin Boldak, Afghanistan; Daniel Klaidman, Tamara Lipper and Colin Soloway in Washington; Andrew Murr in Los Angeles, and Arian Campo-Flores and Gretel C. Kovach in New York, "A Reporter under the Gun," *Newsweek*, February 11, 2002 (accessed through Lexis/Nexis November 26, 2010).

9. Richard Reid was arrested in December for allegedly trying to detonate explosives in his shoes aboard a commercial flight from Paris to Miami.

10. Committee to Protect Journalists, "Daniel Pearl: *Wall Street Journal*: Date unknown, in Karachi, Pakistan," 2002. http://cpj.org/killed/2002/daniel-pearl.php (accessed on November 13, 2010).

11. *Wall Street Journal*, "Reporter Daniel Pearl is Dead, Killed by His Captors in Pakistan: Investigators Have Videotape Confirming the Murder of Journal Correspondent," *Wall Street Journal*. February 24, 2002. http://online.wsj.com/public/resources/documents/pearl-022102.htm (accessed November 13, 2010).

12. Public Broadcasting Service, "OnlineNewshour: The Response after the September 11 Terrorist Attacks: Pakistani Judge Convicts Four Men for Pearl Murder," July 15, 2002. http://www.pbs.org/newshour/media/response/pearl.html (accessed November 13, 2010).

13. Huffington Post, "Daniel Pearl's Family Disagrees with NYC Trial for Khalid Sheikh Mohammed. First posted November 14, 2009. Updated on March 18, 2010. http://www.huffingtonpost.com/2009/11/14/danniel-pearls-family-dis_n_358153.html (accessed November 13, 2010).

14. Ibid.

15. Susan Kinzie, "Reporter's Death Inspires a Seminar and a Lawsuit," *Washington Post*. December 18, 2008. http://www.washingtonpost.com/wp-dyn/content/article/2008/12/17/AR2008121701709.html (accessed on November 13, 2010).

16. The Pearl Project at http://pearlproject.georgetown.edu/investigation1.html (accessed November 13, 2010).

17. Asra Q. Nomani, *Washington Post*. "Outlook: Not the Daniel Pearl I knew: Liberties taken with 'A Mighty Heart' Go Far beyond Artistic License," June 25, 2007.

18. Mariane Pearl, at http://marianepearl.com/insearchofhope.php (accessed November 13, 2010).

19. Anna Politkovskaya, *Russia's Secret Heroes, an excerpt from A Small Corner of Hell: Dispatches from Chechnya*. http://www.press.uchicago.edu/Misc/Chicago/674320.html (accessed November 4, 2010).

20. Andrew Meier, "A Death in Moscow," July 1, 2007. *New York Times*. http://www.nytimes.com/2007/07/01/books/review/Meier-t.html (accessed November 6, 2010).

21. *New York Times*, Anna Politkovskaya, June 26, 2009. http://tinyurl.com/29k5ew6 (accessed November 6, 2010).

22. Amy Knight, "Who Killed Anna Politkovskaya?" November 6, 2008. *New York Review of Books*. http://tinyurl.com/6ew7sno (accessed November 4, 2010).

23. Ibid.

24. CPJ, "CPJ condemns slaying of Russian reporter Anna Politkovskaya." October 7, 2006. http://www.cpj.org/2006/10/cpj-condemns-slaying-of-russian-reporter-anna-poli.php (accessed November 4, 2010).

25. Fred Weir, "Slain Russian Journalist Kept Eye on Chechnya," October 10, 2006. *Christian Science Monitor*. http://www.csmonitor.com/2006/1010/p04s02 -woeu.html (accessed November 4, 2010).

26. Amy Knight, "Who killed Anna Politkovskaya?."November 6, 2008. *New York Review of Books*. http://tinyurl.com/6ew7sno (accessed November 4, 2010).

27. Ibid.

28. Ibid.

29. Ibid.

30. Ibid.

31. Ibid.

32. Eric Bergkraut. *Letter to Anna: The Story of Journalist Politkovskaya's Death.*

33. Artyom Liss."Crowds Drawn to Reporter's Funeral." October 10, 2006, http://news.bbc.co.uk/2/hi/6039084.stm (accessed November 4, 2010).

34. C. J. Chivers, "Chill Wind in Moscow. A Journalist's Revelations, in Life and in Death." October 15, 2006. http://www.nytimes.com/2006/10/15/ weekinreview/15chivers.html (accessed November 4, 2010).

35. Artyom Liss,"Crowds Drawn to Reporter's Funeral." October 10, 2006, http://news.bbc.co.uk/2/hi/6039084.stm (accessed November 4, 2010).

36. Ibid.

37. *New York Times*, Anna Politkovskaya. June 26, 2009. http://tinyurl.com/ 29k5ew6 (accessed November 6, 2010).

38. Ibid.

39. Amy Knight, "Who killed Anna Politkovskaya?" November 6, 2008. *New York Review of Books*. http://tinyurl.com/6ew7sno (accessed November 4, 2010).

40. Ibid.

41. *New York Times*, Anna Politkovskaya. June 26, 2009. http://tinyurl.com/ 29k5ew6 (accessed November 6, 2010).

42. Ibid.

43. Ibid.

44. Fred Weir, "Russian Court Orders Retrial Politkovskaya case." *CS Monitor*. June 25, 2009. http://www.csmonitor.com/World/Global-News/2009/0625/russian -court-orders-retrial-politkovskaya-case (accessed November 4, 2010).

45. CPJ, "Circle of Suspects Widens in Politkovskaya Case," October 6, 2010. http://cpj.org/2010/10/circle-of-suspects-widens-in-politkovskaya-case.php (accessed November 6, 2010).

46. Joel Simon, "Circle of Suspects Widens in Politkovskaya case," October 6, 2010. Committee to Protect Journalists. http://cpj.org/2010/10/circle-of-suspets -widens-in-politkovskaya-case.php (accessed November 6, 2010).

47. Joel Simon, "Mission Journal: A Visit to Russia's Supreme Court." October 19, 2010. Committee to Protect Journalists. http://cpj.org/blog/2010/

10/mission-journal-a-visit-to-russias-supreme-court.php (accessed November 6, 2010).

48. Fred Weir, "In shift, Kremlin Reopens Cases of Russian Reporters' Unsolved Murders." *Christian Science Monitor*, September 30, 2010. http://www .csmonitor.com/layout/set/print/content/view/print/329184 (accessed November 4, 2010).

49. Ibid.

50. Ibid.

51. Elizabeth Witchel, "Marking Maguindanao, events for reflection, justice." CPJ Blog. November 22, 2010. http://cpj.org/blog/2010/11/marking-maguinda nao-events-for-reflection-justice.php (accessed April 29, 2011).

52. Aquiles Zonio, "Inquirer man recounts harrowing tales of survival," Inquirer.net. http://technology.inquirer.net/infotech/infotech/view/20091124 -238100/Inquirer-man-recounts-harrowing-tales-of-survival (accessed November 9, 2010).

53. Carlos H. Conde, "First Charges Filed in Philippine Massacre, Against Mayor," *New York Times*, Dec. 2, 2009, Section A; Column 0; Foreign Desk; 10 (accessed through Lexis/Nexis November 9, 2010).

54. BBC Monitoring Asia Pacific–Political, International journalists to monitor progress of Philippine massacre case, Supplied by BBC Worldwide Monitoring November 29, 2009 (accessed through Lexis/Nexis November 10, 2010).

55. Ibid.

56. Ibid.

57. Ibid.

58. Shawn W. Crispin, "Impunity on Trial in the Philippines, Committee to Protect Journalists," November 10, 2010. http://cpj.org/reports/2010/11/ impunity-on-trial-in-the-philippines.php#more.

59. Report of the Humanitarian and Fact-Finding Mission to Maguindanao. 25-30 November 2009, http://www.ifj.org/assets/docs/038/182/deeff26-cbf56b6 .pdf (accessed November 9, 2010).

60. Ibid., 10.

61. Andreo C. Calonzo, "Official media death count in Ampatuan massacre is now 32." http://www.gmanews.tv/story/182091/official-media-death-count-in-ampatuan-massacre-is-now-32, January 21, 2010 (accessed November 10, 2010).

62. Zonia, Ibid.

63. Committee to Protect Journalists, *Africa News*, "Somalia; Two Suspects Arrested in Murder of Journalists," August 14, 2007 (accessed November 10, 2010).

64. Ibid.

65. Canadian Journalists for Free Expression, Africa News, Africa News, "Somalia: Two Journalists With Popular Radio Network Murdered," August 13, 2007 (accessed through Lexis/Nexis, November 10, 2010).

66. Ross Howard, Special to the *Globe and Mail*, August 15, 2007, http://tinyurl.com/630b4mk (accessed April 30, 2011).

67. Ibid.

68. Committee to Protect Journalists, *Africa News*, "Somalia: Two Suspects Arrested in Murder of Journalists," August 14, 2007, http://allafrica.com/stories/200708141041.html (accessed on November 10, 2010).

69. Stephanie McCrummen, "2 Somali Radio Journalists Slain; Station Had Antagonized Both Government and Insurgency," *Washington Post*, August 13, 2007 (accessed through Lexis/Nexis, November 10, 2010).

70. Ross Howard, Special to the *Globe and Mail*, August 15, 2007, http:/tinyurl.com/630b4mk (accessed April 30, 2011).

71. Stephanie Nolan, "Two Arrested in Slaying of Somali Journalists; Officials pledge justice, but the media remain skeptical of the unstable government, pointing to patterns of harassment," *Globe and Mail*, August 13, 2007 (accessed through Lexis/Nexis, November 10, 2010).

72. Ibid.

73. Ibid.

74. Ibid.

75. National Union of Somali Journalists, Universal Periodic Review, http://www.ifex.org/somalia/2010/10/29/universal_periodic_review_report_nusoj_submission.pdf (accessed November 10, 2010).

76. Ibid., 2.

77. Ibid., 3.

78. Mark C. Toner, Acting Department Spokesman, U.S. State Department, "Conviction on Criminal Charges of Journalist Eynullah Fatullayev of Azerbaijan," July 7, 2010, News Release, http://www.state.gov/r/pa/prs/ps/2010/07/144129.htm (accessed November 10, 2010).

79. John Mulholland, Comment: Your letters: The editor on . . . the real front line of journalism, *Observer* (England), June 7, 2009 (accessed through Lexis/Nexis, November 10, 2010).

80. Human Rights Watch, *Azerbaijan: Beaten, Blacklisted, and Behind Bars: The Vanishing Space for Freedom of Expression in Azerbaijan*, 2010, http://www.hrw.org/en/reports/2010/10/26/beaten-blacklisted-and-behind-bars-vanishing-space-freedom-expression-azerbaijan, 22 (accessed November 10, 2010).

81. European Court of Human Rights, Fatullayev v. Azerbaijan, no. 40984/07. http://sim.law.uu.nl/SIM/CaseLaw/hof.nsf/e4ca7ef017f8c045c1256849004787f5/855031a6da8e4242c125770c002c689d?OpenDocument (accessed November 11, 2010).

82. Bjørn Engesland, Secretary-General, Norwegian Helsinki Committee, http://www.nhc.no/php/index.php?module=article&view=1015 (accessed November 10, 2010).

83. Human Rights Watch, 2010, 23.

84. Mark C. Toner, Acting Department Spokesman, U.S. State Department, "Conviction on Criminal Charges of Journalist Eynullah Fatullayev of Azerbaijan´ July 7, 2010, News Release, http://www.state.gov/r/pa/prs/ps/2010/07/144129.htm (accessed November 10, 2010).

85. Ibid.

86. Abarez.com, "Staff, Journalists in Azerbaijan Silenced with Violence, Prosecution, Says Human Rights Watch," October 28, 2010.http://asbarez.com /87697/journalists-in-azerbaijan-face-violence-and-prosecution-human-rights -report-says/ (accessed November 11, 2010).

87. Ibid.

88. Ibid.

89. U.S. Embassy, "President Obama Meets President Aliyev in New York," http://azerbaijan.usembassy.gov/embassy_highlights_archive.html (accessed November 12, 2010).

90. Lada Yevgrashina, "Azerbaijan Frees Second Critical Blogger," Reuters, November 19, 2010 (accessed April 29, 2011). http://www.reuters.com/article/ 2010/11/19/us-azerbaijan-blogger-idUSTRE6AH20J20I01119.

91. IFEX, "Another reporter assassinated in Durango despite authorities' knowledge of threats against him," November 3, 2009. http://www.ifex.org/ mexico/2009/11/03/antuna_garcia_threatened/ (accessed November 6, 2010).

92. Ibid.

93. Ibid.

94. Jason Beaubien, National Public Radio, "Mexico's Drug Cartels Use Force to Silence Media,"August 3, 2010, http://www.npr.org/templates/story/ story.php?storyId=128929784 (accessed November 12, 2010).

95. IFEX, "More journalists receive death threats following reporter's assassination in Durango." June 1, 2009. http://www.ifex.org/mexico/2009/06/01/ antuna_garcia_death_threat/ (accessed November 6, 2010).

96. Committee to Protect Journalists. "Silence or Death in Mexico's Press: Crime, Violence and Corruption Are Destroying the Country's Journalism. A special report of the Committee to Protect Journalists," 11. Issued September 2010. http://cpj.org/reports/cpj_mexico_english.pdf (accessed November 12, 2010).

97. Ibid.

98. Ibid., p. 3.

99. Jason Beaubien, National Public Radio, "Mexico's Drug Cartels Use Force to Silence Media," August 3, 2010, http://www.npr.org/templates/story/ story.php?storyId=128929784 (accessed November 12, 2010).

100. Quoted in Beaubien, 2010.

101. Beaubien, 2010.

102. Committee to Protect Journalists. "Silence or Death in Mexico's Press: Crime, Violence and Corruption Are Destroying the Country's Journalism. A special report of the Committee to Protect Journalists," 3. Issued September 2010.

103. Amnesty International http://www.amnestyusa.org/individuals-at-risk/priority-cases/china-shi-tao/page.do?id=1101243 (accessed November 12, 2010).

104. Ibid.

105. Ibid.

106. "Shi Tao's Application for Appeal" Human Rights In China, http://www.hrichina.org/public/highlight/hric/appealapp.html (accessed November 14, 2010).

107. Ibid.

108. Quoted in Peter S. Goodman, "Yahoo Says It Gave China Internet Data Journalist Jailed by Tracing E-mail" Washington Post Foreign Service, September 11, 2005, http://www.washingtonpost.com/wp-dyn/content/article/2005/09/10/AR2005091001222.html (accessed November 14, 2010).

109. Quoted in Robert Marquand, "Yahoo!, Chinese police, and a Jailed Journalist," *Christian Science Monitor*, September 9, 2005. http://www.csmonitor.com/2005/0909/p01s03-woap.html (accessed November 14, 2010).

110. Rebecca MacKinnon, "Shi Tao, Yahoo!, and the lessons for corporate social responsibility," http://rconversation.blogs.com/YahooShiTaoLessons.pdf (accessed November 14, 2010).

111. Testimony by U.S. Rep. Tom Lantos, "The Internet in China: A Tool for Freedom or Suppression?" Joint Hearing before the Subcommittee on Africa, Global Human Rights and International Operations and the Subcommittee on Asia and the Pacific of the Committee on International Relations, House of Representatives, 109th Congress, Second Session February 15, 2006; Transcript at: http://commdocs.house.gov/committees/intlrel/hfa26075.000/hfa26075_of.htm (accessed November 14, 2010).

112. Tracey Barnett (opinion) "On the Wrong Side of the Great Wall of China," *New Zealand Herald*, November 27, 2007 (accessed through Lexis/Nexis, November 14, 2010).

113. Catherine Rampell, "Yahoo Settles with Chinese Families: Firm Gave Officials Dissidents' E-Mails," *Washington Post*, November 14, 2007, http://www.washingtonpost.com/wp-dyn/content/article/2007/11/13/AR2007111300885.html (accessed November 14, 2010).

114. David Barboza and Brad Stone, "A Nation that Trips up Many, " *New York Times*, Section B; Column 0; Business/Financial Desk; Pg. 1, January 16, 2010 (accessed through Lexis/Nexis, November 14, 2010).

115. International Federation of Journalists, Africa News, "Uganda; Cyclists Beat Radio Journalist to Death" September 14, 2020 (accessed through Lexis/Nexis, November 12, 2010).

116. Quoted in IFJ, *Africa News*, September 14, 2010.

117. Henry Mukasa and Steven Candia, "Another Radio Journalist Killed" *New Vision*, Kampala, September 15, 2010 (accessed through Lexis/Nexis, November 12, 2010).

118. UN News Service (New York), *Africa News*, September 15, 2010, "Uganda; Unesco Chief Calls On Ugandan Authorities to Punish Journalist's Killers (accessed through Lexis/Nexis, November 12, 2010).

119. Norman Katende, "Police Urged to Quickly Probe Death of Journalists," New Vision (Kampala), October 21, 2010 (accessed through Lexis/Nexis, November 12, 2010).

120. Angelo Izama, "Who Gave Mob the Club to Clobber Kiggundu to Death? [opinion]", September 27, 2010, *The Monitor* (Kampala) (accessed through Lexis/Nexis, November 12, 2010).

121. David Rohde,"Held by the Taliban—A Times Reporter's Account. A Five-Part Series by David Rohde. "7 Months, 10 Days in Captivity." October 18, 2009. http://www.nytimes.com/2009/10/18/world/asia/18hostage.html (accessed November 6, 2010).

122. Ibid.

123. Matthew Cole, "The David Rohde Puzzle." *New York Magazine*. June 22, 2009 . http://nymag.com/news/media/57635/ (accessed November 7, 2010).

124. David Rohde, "Held by the Taliban—A Times Reporter's Account. A Five-Part Series by David Rohde. "7 Months, 10 Days in Captivity. October 18, 2009. http://www.nytimes.com/2009/10/18/world/asia/18hostage.html (accessed November 6, 2010).

125. Ibid.

126. Ibid.

127. *New York Times*. "Times Reporter Escapes Taliban after 7 Months," June 21, 2009. http://www.nytimes.com/2009/06/21/world/asia/21taliban.html (accessed November 6, 2010).

128. Ibid.

129. Ibid.

130. Jason Straziuso, "David Rohde, New York Times Reporter Held By Taliban, Escapes." June 20, 2009. http://www.huffingtonpost.com/2009/06/20/david-rohde-new-york-time_n_218400.html (accessed November 7, 2010).

131. David Rohde, "Held by the Taliban—A Times Reporter's Account. A Five-Part Series by David Rohde. "7 Months, 10 Days in Captivity," October 18, 2009. http://www.nytimes.com/2009/10/18/world/asia/18hostage.html (accessed November 6, 2010).

132. Ibid.

133. Ibid.

134. Quoted in Howard Kurtz, "Media Stayed Silent on Kidnapping: News Organizations Agreed to Protect Reporter's Safety" *Washington Post*, June 21, 2009, http://www.washingtonpost.com/wp-dyn/content/article/2009/06/20/AR2009062001745.html (accessed November 14, 2010).

135. Ibid.

136. Quoted in Kurtz.

137. Quoted in Kurtz.

138. Stephen Farrell, "The Reporter's Account: 4 Days With the Taliban." The *New York Times*, September 9, 2009, Last accessed March 20, 2011 at http://atwar.blogs.nytimes.com/2009/09/09/the-reporters-account-4-days-with-the-taliban/.

139. Ibid.

140. Eric Schmitt, "As Menace to Hostages Grew, British Commandos Moved In," *New York Times*, September 10, 2009, Accessed through Lexis/Nexis, November 17, 2010.

141. Ibid.

142. Tom A. Peter, "Afghan Group Condemns 'Double Standard' in Commando Strike," *Christian Science Monitor*, September 10, 2009 (accessed through Lexis/Nexis, November 17, 2010).

143. Gordon Rayner, Andrew Pierce, and Ben Farmer, Para 'died as he lived, leading from the front'; "Gordon Brown ignites political row over soldier's death in rescue mission" *The Telegraph*, September 9, 2010 (accessed through Lexis/Nexis, November 17, 2010).

144. Quoted in Kim Sengupta IN KABUL and Nigel Morris, Why did you kill my son?; Controversy grows over British commando raid to free journalist Father of Afghan interpreter killed in operation demands answers Gordon Brown distances himself from decision to mount assault Backlash against Afghan rescue operation grows, *Independent*, September 11, 2009 (accessed through Lexis/Nexis, November 17, 2010).

145. *Arman-e Melli* (private Afghan newspaper), "Afghan reporter Sultan Mohammad Munadi was killed by British forces," September 12, 2009. Supplied by BBC Worldwide Monitoring, September 14, 2009 (accessed through Lexis/Nexis, November 17, 2010).

146. David Rohde, "Sultan Munadi: A Gentle Stalwart," September 9, 2009, *New York Times*, http://www.nytimes.com/2009/09/10/world/asia/10munadi.html?_r=1&ref=asia (accessed November 17, 2010).

147. Ibid.

148. Ibid.

149. Jane Armstrong "A passion for life and for getting the story right; Reporter remembered as uncompromising," *Globe and Mail*, January 12, 2010 (accessed through Lexis/Nexis, November 17, 2010).

150. Matthew Fisher, "Vehicle flipped in IED blast that killed 5; Tunnel Under Road" CanWest News Service, January 5, 2010 (accessed through Lexis/Nexis November 17, 2010).

151. Quoted in Petti Fong, "Calgary Mourns War-Zone Journalist" *Toronto Star*, January 1, 2010 (accessed through Lexis/Nexis, November 17, 2010).

152. Patrick White and Anna Mehler Paperny, An award-winning journalist and bride-to-be who loved the work and knew the risks; MICHELLE LANG,

34, *Globe and Mail*, December 31, 2009 (accessed through Lexis/Nexis, November 17, 2010).

153. Ibid.

154. Christie Blatchford, The honour in bearing witness to war; Like the soldiers she covered, Michelle Lang of the *Calgary Herald* was a volunteer, doing her job and doing it well, *Globe and Mail*, January 1, 2010 (accessed through Lexis/Nexis, November 17, 2010).

155. Michelle Lang, Top general optimistic despite 'rough' year; Canada in Afghanistan. Natynczyk to stick with strategies, *Montreal Gazette*, December 27, 2009 (accessed through Lexis/Nexis, November 17, 2010).

156. Quoted in *Calgary Herald*, CanWest News Service, Fellowship honours journalist; In memory of Michelle Lang. To be awarded to Canadian grads with passion for reporting, current events, January 16, 2010 (accessed through Lexis/Nexis, November 17, 2010).

157. Elaine Monaghan, Nicholas Blanford, and David Charter, "Arab fury over al-Jazeera death" *Times* (London) April 9, 2003 (accessed through Lexis/Nexis November 18, 2010).

158. Lisa Abend and Geoff Pingree, "Spain Opens Case against US Soldiers," *Christian Science Monitor*, January 25, 2007 (accessed through Lexis/Nexis, November 18, 2010).

159. Peter Wilson, "Shooting the Messenger," *Australian*, May 10, 2004. (accessed through Lexis/Nexis, November 18, 2010).

160. Ibid.

161. Ibid.

162. Quoted in Emma Daly and Jim Rutenberg, "AFTEREFFECTS: THE PRESS; In Letter, Powell Defends Shelling of Journalists' Hotel," *New York Times*, April 25, 2003 (accessed through Lexis/Nexis, November 18, 2010).

163. Quoted in Elaine Monaghan, Nicholas Blanford, and David Charter, "Arab Fury over al-Jazeera Death" *The Times* (London) April 9, 2003 (accessed through Lexis/Nexis, November 18, 2010).

164. Walter Rogers, "Caveats for Journalists in Combat Zones," *Christian Science Monitor*, August 7, 2009 (accessed through Lexis/Nexis, November 18, 2010).

165. Quoted in Shiv Malik, "BROADCAST AND BE DAMNED; THE NEW EDITOR OF AL-JAZEERA IS UNAPOLOGETIC ABOUT HIS CHANNEL'S," *Independent* (London), January 24, 2005 (accessed through Lexis/Nexis, November 18, 2010).

166. Emma Daly and Jim Rutenberg, "AFTEREFFECTS: THE PRESS; In Letter, Powell Defends Shelling of Journalists' Hotel," *New York Times*, April 25, 2003 (accessed through Lexis/Nexis, November 18, 2010).

167. *Herald Sun* (Australia), "Arrest Order for US Soldiers," July 31, 2010 (accessed through Lexis/Nexis, November 18, 2010).

168. Spanish News, "Supreme Court Orders Jose Couso's Case Reopened," http://www.typicallyspanish.com/news/publish/article_26835.shtml (accessed November 18, 2010).

169. Alan Johnston, "My Kidnap Ordeal," BBC News. http://news.bbc.co.uk/2/hi/programmes/from_our_own_correspondent/7048652.stm (accessed November 18, 2010).

170. Alan Taylor, "Alan Johnston Picking up the Pieces; Four Months On: The First Print Interview" *Sunday Herald*, November 25, 2007 (accessed through Lexis/Nexis, November 18, 2010).

171. Alan Johnston, "My Kidnap Ordeal," BBC News. http://news.bbc.co.uk/2/hi/programmes/from_our_own_correspondent/7048652.stm (accessed November 18, 2010).

172. Ibid.

173. Quoted in David Pratt, "Alan Johnston told the world of the terrible suffering of Palestinians in the Gaza Strip. So why have they held him hostage for 62 days?" *Sunday Herald*, May 13, 2007 (accessed through Lexis/Nexis, November 18, 2010).

174. Ibid.

175. Iqbal Tamimi, "Arab Women: Who Cares about Them? International News Safety Institute, May 20, 2007, http://www.newssafety.org/index.php?option=com_content&view=article&id=4633:arab-women-war-reporters-who-cares-about-them&catid=238:women-reporting-war&Itemid=100081 (accessed November 21, 2010).

176. May Ying Welch, "Atwar Bahjat: A Believing Iraqi" *Counter Currents Al Jazeera*, March 2, 2006, http://www.countercurrents.org/iraq-welsh020306.htm (accessed November 21, 2010).

177. Quoted in Welch, Al Jazeera: A believing Iraqi, *Counter Currents Al Jazeera*, March 2, 2006, http://www.countercurrents.org/iraq-welsh020306.htm (accessed November 21, 2010).

178. Ibid.

179. Quoted in Committee to Protect Journalists, Atwar Bahjat Tribute, March 1, 2006. http://cpj.org/awards/2006/bahjat-article.php (accessed on December 8, 2010).

180. Quoted in Welch, Al Jazeera: A believing Iraqi, *Counter Currents Al Jazeera*, March 2, 2006, http://www.countercurrents.org/iraq-welsh020306.htm (accessed November 21, 2010).

181. "On the Ground" *New York Times* blog, http://kristof.blogs.nytimes.com/2010/10/23/thinking-of-joao-silva-in-afghanistan/ (accessed November 21, 2010).

182. Ibid.

183. Nicholas Fearn, Book Review: *Until They Snapped*; *The Bang-Bang Club*, By Greg Marinovich and Joao Silva, *Independent*, September 17, 2000 (accessed through Lexis/Nexis, November 21, 2010).

184. Quoted in Michael Kamber, "Joao Silva: Acting despite fear," *New York Times* blog, http://lens.blogs.nytimes.com/2010/10/26/joao-silva-acting -despite-fear/ (accessed November 21, 2010).

185. Ibid.

186. Greg Marinovich, "Compassionate, Calm and Fearless in the Line of Fire," *Cape Times* (South Africa) (accessed through Lexis/Nexis, November 21, 2010).

187. Emma Daly, Obituary Kurt Schork, *Independent* (London), May 26, 2000 (accessed through Lexis/Nexis, November 21, 2010).

188. Quoted in Reuters, "Writer Who Covered the Siege in Sarajevo Quit Regular Job," *Globe and Mail*, May 26, 2000 (accessed through Lexis/Nexis, November 21, 2010).

189. Quoted in Reuters, "Writer Who Covered the Siege in Sarajevo Quit Regular Job," *Globe and Mail*, May 26, 2000 (accessed though Lexis/Nexis, November 21, 2010).

190. Ibid.

191. Janine di Giovanni, "A Man Who Seemed to be Immortal" *Times of London*, May 26, 2000 (accessed through Lexis/Nexis, November 21, 2010).

192. Kurt Schork Memorial Fund, http://www.ksmfund.org/ksmfinfo.html (accessed November 21, 2010).

193. The Dawn.com, Editorial, http://news.dawn.com/wps/wcm/connect/ dawn-content-library/dawn/the-newspaper/editorial/attack-on-journalist-790 (accessed December 8, 2010).

194. Quoted in Jane Perlez, "After Pakistani Journalist Speaks Out About an Attack, Eyes Turn to the Military," *New York Times*, September 25, 2010 (accessed through Lexis/Nexis, December 8, 2010).

195. Ibid.

196. Ibid.

197. Wangui Maina, "Umar Cheema encourages Journalists to fight for a cause," *Missourian*. April 21, 2011, http://www.columbiamissourian.com/ stories/2011/04/21/umar-cheema/ (accessed April 30, 2011).

198. Ibid.

199. Luz Rimban and Sheila S. Coronel, "Farewell, Erin Brockovich," The Philippine Center for Investigative Journalism, http://pcij.org/stories/2005/ marlene.html (accessed December 8, 2010).

200. Kaveri Roy. "Philippines: That one murder that saw rare conviction of the killers." Newswatch.in. November 17, 2007, http://www.newswatch.in/ features/131 (accessed November 11, 2010).

201. Committee to Protect Journalists. "Marlene Garcia-Esperat." Midland News and DXKR. March 24, 2005, http://cpj.org/killed/2005/marlene -garcia-esperat.php.

202. Gerry Cabayag, Randy Grecia, Estanislao Bismanos, and Rowie Barua were arrested by police. Madeline Earp and Mayuri Mukherjee, "In Garcia-Esperat

murder, a twisting path of justice." Last accessed November 11, 2010 at http://cpj.org/blog/2010/03/philippine-impunity-in-garcia-esperat-murder.php.

Addendum

1. Committee to Protect Journalists. "Across Middle East, enormous challenges." http://www.cpj.org/mideast/ (accessed March 27, 2011).

2. "In Tunisia, one journalist still jailed, another killed." Committee to Protect Journalists. January 18, 2011. http://www.cpj.org/2011/01/in-tunisia-one-journalist-still-jailed-another-kil.php (accessed March 6, 2011).

3. Ibid.

4. "As Mubarak leaves, the press is freed." Committee to Protect Journalists. February 11, 2011. http://www.cpj.org/mideast/egypt/ (accessed March 6, 2011).

5. "Mubarak intensifies press attacks with assaults, detentions." Committee to Protect Journalists. February 3, 2011. http://www.cpj.org/2011/02/mubarak-intensifies-press-attacks-with-assaults-de.php (accessed March 6, 2011).

6. Ibid.

7. Government obstruction, intimidation continues in Cairo. February 9, 2011. http://www.cpj.org/2011/02/government-obstruction-intimidation-continues-in-c.php (accessed March 6, 2011).

8. Nil Rosen, an experienced journalist and a former fellow at New York University's Center on Law and Security commented that Logan's sexual assault was an attempt to "outdo" Anderson. Another commentator said that the attack on Logan was self-inflicted and that she should have known better than to go to an Islamic country.

9. "Attacks on media continue across Middle East." Committee to Protect Journalists. February 16, 2011. http://www.cpj.org/2011/02/attacks-on-media-continue-across-middle-east.php (accessed March 6, 2011).

10. "Journalists under attack in Libya: The Tally." Committee to Protect Journalists. March 23, 2011 (accessed March 27, 2011).

11. "Bahrain expels CNN reporter, detains WSJ correspondent," Committee to Protect Journalists. March 17, 2011 (accessed March 27, 2011) at www.cpj.org/2011/03/bahrain-expels-cnn-reporter-harasses-journal-corre.php.

12. Committee to Protect Journalists, "Journalists targeted in Bahrain, Yemen, and Libya," Committee to Protect Journalists, February 18, 2011, http://www.cpj.org/2011/02/journalists-targeted-in-bahrain-yemem-and-libya.php (accessed May 15, 2011).

13. Iraq cracks down on media; violations in Yemen, Libya." Committee to Protect Journalists. February 25, 2011. http://www.cpj.org/2011/02/iraq-cracks-down-on-media-violations-ongoing-in-ye.php (accessed March 21, 2011).

14. "In Yemen, a journalist fatally shot, another injured." Committee to Protect Journalists. March 18, 2011 (accessed March 19, 2011) at www.cpj.org/2011/03/in-yemen-a-journalist-fatally-shot-another-injured.php.

15. "Attacks on media continue across Middle East." Committee to Protect Journalists. February 16, 2011. http://www.cpj.org/2011/02/attacks-on-media-continue-across-middle-east.php (accessed March 6, 2011).

16. Committee to Protect Journalists. "Al-Jazeera suspends Syria bureau; attacks on Lebanon crew." April 27, 2011 (accessed April 29, 2011). http://www.cpj.org/2011/04/al-jazeera-suspends-syria-bureau-attacks-on-Lebano.php.

17. Committee to Protect Journalists. "Journalist arrested; Syria crackdown continues." April 14, 2011 (accessed April 29, 2011). http://www.cpj.org/2011/04/journalist-arrested-syria-crackdown-continues.php.

Chapter 5: Are We Doing Enough? What Stakeholders Suggest Should Be Done to Protect Journalists and Media Workers

1. Author interview with Phillip Knightley, October 28, 2010.

2. Author interview with Mogens Schmidt, September 30, 2010.

3. Author interview with Bruce Shapiro, September 27, 2010.

4. Author interview with Daniela Arbex, November 23, 2010.

5. Author interview with Hollman Morris, November 3, 2010.

6. Committee to Protect Journalists, "607 Journalists Murdered Since 1992" http://www.cpj.org/killed/murdered.php (accessed December 4, 2010).

7. Author interview with Tina Carr, November 23, 2010.

8. E-mail to author from Omid Memarian, December 4, 2010.

9. Author interview with John Owen, November 11, 2010.

10. Author interview with Dolia Estévez, November 17, 2010.

11. Author interview with Daniela Arbex, November 23, 2010.

12. Author interview with Charles Odongtho, October 27, 2010.

13. E-mail to author from Judith Matloff, October 4, 2010.

14. Author interview with Holly Picket, October 20, 2010.

15. Author interview with Tina Carr, November 23, 2010.

16. Author interview with Chris Cramer, August 24, 2010.

17. Author interview with Heather Forbes, October 10, 2010.

18. Author interview with Kim Barker, November 5, 2010.

19. Author interview with Cali Bagby, November 21, 2010.

20. Author interview with Gretchen Peters, November 3, 2010.

21. INSI, "Women Reporting War: A Survey by the International News Safety Institute," May 7, 2010. http://www.newssafety.com/stories/insi/wrw.htm (accessed March 21, 2011).

22. Ibid.

23. Author interview with Gretchen Peters, November 3, 2010.

24. Author interview with Kim Barker, November 5, 2010.

25. Author interview with Anne Nivat, November 27, 2010.

26. Author interview with Caroline Vuillemin, November 23, 2010.

27. E-mail to author from Evelyn Abbo, December 5, 2010.

28. Author interview with Juliana Ruhfus, November 19, 2010.

29. Interview with Tala Dowlatshahi, November 29, 2010.

30. E-mail to author from Hedayat Abdel Nabi, November 28, 2010.

31. Author interview with Ross Howard, November 9, 2010.

32. Author interview with John Owen, November 21, 2010.

33. Author interview with Binod Bhattarai, November 25, 2010.

34. Author interview with David Rohde, November 13, 2010.

35. Author interview with Caroline Vuillemin, November 23, 2010.

36. Author interview with Juliana Ruhfus, November 19, 2010.

37. E-mail to author from Hugh Lunn, September 7, 2010.

38. Author interview with Terry Anderson, October 7, 2010.

39. Author interview with Kim Barker, November 5, 2010.

40. Author interview with John Daniszewski, November 1, 2010.

41. Author interview with Joel Simon, November 8, 2010.

42. Author interview with Gretchen Peters, November 3, 2010.

43. Author interview with Ross Howard, November 9, 2010.

44. Author interview with Bruce Shapiro, September 27, 2010.

45. Author interview with Terry Anderson, October 7, 2010.

46. Author interview with Ross Howard, November 9, 2010.

47. Author interview with Dolia Estévez, November 17, 2010.

48. E-mail to author from Emin Huseynov, November 16, 2010.

49. Frank Smyth, "Murdering with Impunity: The Rise in Terror Tactics Against News Reporters," *Harvard International Review*, http://hir.harvard.edu/pressing-change/murdering-with-impunity (accessed November 20, 2010.

50. E-mail from Dan Morrison, November 25, 2010.

51. Author interview with Tala Dowlatshahi, November 29, 2010.

52. Author interview with Jesper Højberg, October 4, 2010.

53. Author interview with Joel Simon, November 8, 2010.

54. Author interview with Carlos Fernando Chamorro, October 25, 2010.

55. Author interview with Daniela Arbex, November 23, 2010.

56. Author interview with Mogens Schmidt, September 30, 2010.

57. E-mail to author from Palestinian photojournalist (anonymous), October 17, 2010.

58. Author interview with Charles Odongtho, October 27, 2010.

59. Author interview with Rodney Pinder, October 14, 2010.

60. E-mail to author from Emin Huseynov, November 16, 2010.

61. Author interview with John Owen, November 21, 2010.

62. Author interview with Caroline Vuillemin, November 23, 2010.

63. Author interview with Jesper Højberg, September 29, 2010.

64. Author interview with Tala Dowlatshahi, November 29, 2010.

65. Author interview with Joel Simon, November 8, 2010.

66. Mustafa Qadri, "In South Asia, Independent Journalism Is a Real Risk" The *Guardian*, November 28, 2010. http://www.guardian.co.uk/commentisfree/libertycentral/2010/nov/28/south-asia-independent-journalism-risk (accessed December 3, 2010).

67. *New York Times* Editorial, "Who Attacked Umar Cheema," September 28, 2010 (accessed December 2, 2010).

68. Email to author from Umar Cheema, November 29, 2010.

69. Author interview with Shaun Filer, November 5, 2010.

70. Author interview with Robert Klamser, September 28, 2010.

71. Author interview with Ross Howard, November 9, 2010.

72. Author interview with Tina Carr, November 23, 2010.

73. Author interview with Heather Forbes, October 10, 2010.

74. Author interview with Daniela Arbex, November 24, 2010.

75. Author interview with Holly Picket, October 20, 2010.

76. Email to author from Evelyn Abbo, December 5, 2010.

77. Email to author from Omid Memarian, December 1, 2010.

78. Author interview with Palestinian journalist (anonymous), November 16, 2010.

79. Author interview with Binod Bhattarai, November 25, 2010.

80. Email to author from John Matuvo, December 4, 2010.

81. Author interview with Michelle Betz, November 23, 2010.

82. Author interview with Charles Odongtho, Ocotber 27, 2010.

83. Author interview with Martin Wanjala Ocholi, October 18, 2010.

84. Author interview with Ross Howard, November 9, 2010.

85. Author interview with Rodney Pinder, October 14, 2010.

86. Author interview with Shaun Filer, November 5, 2010.

87. Author interview with Susan Bennett, October 6, 2010.

88. Author interview with Joel Simon, November 8, 2010.

89. Email sent to author from John Matovu, December 4, 2010.

90. Author interview with Blaise Lempen, October 5, 2010.

91. Author interview with Mogens Schmidt, September 30, 2010.

92. Author interview with Hedayat Abdel Nabi, September 29, 2010.

93. Author interview with Ronald Koven, November 19, 2010.

94. Author interview with Dawit Kebede, December 2, 2010.

95. Author interview with Phillip Knightley, October 28, 2010.

96. Author interview with Holly Picket, October 20, 2010.

97. Author interview with David Rohde, November 13, 2010.

98. Author interview with Robert Nickelsberg, August 11, 2010.

99. Author interview with Robert Woodruff, November 11, 2010.

100. Author interview with Anne Nivat, November 27, 2010.

101. Author interview with Caroline Vuillemin, November 23, 2010.

102. Author interview with Charles Odongtho, October 27, 2010.

103. Author interview with Carlos Fernando Chamorro, October 25, 2010.

104. Author interview with Daniela Arbex, November 24, 2010.

105. Author interview with Jesper Højberg, October 4, 2010.

106. Author interview with Anne Nivat, November 27, 2010.

107. Author interview with Tala Dowlatshahi, November 29, 2010.

108. Author interview with David Rohde, November 13, 2010.

109. Email sent to author from Emin Huseynov, November 16, 2010.

110. Author interview with John Owen, November 21, 2010.

111. Author interview with Gretchen Peters, November 3, 2010.

Selected Bibliography

We list here only the writings that have been of use in the making of this book. This bibliography is by no means a complete record of all the works and sources we have consulted. It indicates the substance and range of reading upon which we have formed our ideas, and we intend for it to serve as a convenience for those who wish to pursue the subject of media protection in conflict and risk environments.

Allan, Stuart, and Barbie Zelizer, eds. *Reporting War: Journalism in Wartime*. London: Routledge, 2004.

Altschull, J. Herbert. *Agents of Power: The Media and Public Policy*. 2nd Edition. New York: Longman, 1995.

Andersen, Robin. *A Century of Media, A Century of War*. New York: Peter Lang, 2007.

Balabanova, Ekaterina. *Media, Wars and Politics: Comparing the Incomparable in Western and Eastern Europe*. England: Ashgate Publishing, 2007.

Chomsky, Noam. *Deterring Democracy*. London: Vintage, 1992.

Cramer, Chris. "What Price Freedom? Global reporting trends and journalistic integrity." *Pacific Journalism Review*, 12(1) 2010.

Emerson, Thomas I. *The System of Freedom of Expression*. New York: Random House, 1970.

Epping, Volker, and Gottfried Wilhelm Leibniz, eds. *International Humanitarian Law Facing New Challenges: Symposium in Honour of Knut Ipsen*. Germany: University of Hannover, 2007.

Ferrari, Michelle. Compiled by with commentary by James Tobin. *Reporting America at War: An Oral History*. New York: Hyperion, 2003.

Hackett, Robert A., and William K. Carroll. *Remaking Media: The Struggle to Democratize Public Communication*. New York: Routledge, 2006.

Hallin, Daniel C. *The "Uncensored War": The Media and Vietnam*. Berkeley: University of California Press, 1986.

Herman, Edward, and Noam Chomsky. *Manufacturing Consent: The Political Economy of the Mass Media*. New York: Pantheon, 1988.

Hess, Stephen, and Kalb, Marvin Kalb, eds. *The Media and the War on Terrorism.* Washington, DC: Brookings Institution Press, 2003.

Hohenberg, John. *Foreign Correspondence: The Great Reporters and Their Times.* Columbia University Press, 1964.

Hudson, Miles, and John Stanier. *War and the Media: a Random Searchlight.* New York University Press, 1998.

Huntington, Samuel B. *The Third Wave: Democratization in the late Twentieth Century.* Norman: University of Oklahoma Press, 1993.

Hurst, Steven. *The Foreign Policy of the Bush Administration, In Search of a New World Order.* London: Cassell, 1999.

Kaldor, Mary. *New and Old Wars: Organized Violence in a Global Era.* Second edition. Polity Press: Malden, MA, 2004.

Knightley, Phillip. *The First Casualty: The War Correspondent as Hero and Myth-Maker from the Crimea to Iraq.* Baltimore: The Johns Hopkins University Press, 2004.

Lasswell, Harold D. *Progaganda Technique in the World War.* New York: MIT Press, 1971.

Lunn, Hugh. *Vietnam: A Reporter's War.* New York: Stein and Day, 1986.

Moorcraft, Paul L., and Philip M. Taylor. *Shooting the Messenger: The Political Impact of War Reporting.* Washington, DC: Potomac Books, Inc., 2008.

Pearl, Mariane. *A Mighty Heart: The Inside story of the Al Qaeda Kidnapping of Danny Pearl.* New York: Scribner, 2003.

Roth, Mitchel P. *Historical Dictionary of War Journalism.* Westport, CT: Greenwood Press, 1997.

Sullivan, George. *Journalists at Risk: Reporting America's Wars.* Minneapolis: Twenty-First Century Books, 2006.

Thrall, Trevor. *War in the Media Age.* Cresskill, NJ: Hampton Press, 2000.

Tumber, Howard, and Frank Webster. *Journalists Under Fire: Information War and Journalistic Practices.* London: Sage Publications, 2006.

Index

About the Authors

JOANNE M. LISOSKY is a professor of journalism and communication at Pacific Lutheran University in Tacoma, Washington. She received her PhD from the University of Washington where her dissertation focused on international media policies. She served as an academic consultant for UNESCO in Nairobi in 2002 where she coauthored a paper on journalism education in Africa. She received a Fulbright Senior Specialist Fellowship to teach journalism at Makerere University in Uganda in 2003. During the summers of 2004 and 2006, she worked as a freelance journalist at the UN in Geneva. In early 2011, she taught Internet journalism and new media courses at Baku Slavic University and media theory courses at ANS-TV Academy in Azerbaijan as a Fulbright Scholar. She has written articles on press freedom and international media education.

JENNIFER R. HENRICHSEN is a project assistant for the Democracy Coalition Project and Open Society Foundations in Washington, DC, where she assists with research and advocacy relating to the advancement of democracy and human rights internationally. She has a Master of Advanced Studies in International and European Security from the University of Geneva's European Institute and the Geneva Center for Security Policy. In 2008, she was awarded a Fulbright scholarship to Switzerland, where she researched the legal and practical implications of journalists in international armed conflict. Prior to this, she worked as a freelance journalist at the UN in Geneva and carried out grant research on the protection of journalists in conflict situations. She graduated with a Bachelor of Arts in political science and communication from Pacific Lutheran University in 2007.